THE PROTEST AND THE silence

Charles M Wood

THE PROTEST AND THE silence

Suffering,
Death,
and Biblical
Theology

G. Tom Milazzo

FORTRESS PRESS   **MINNEAPOLIS**

THE PROTEST AND THE SILENCE
Suffering, Death, and Biblical Theology

Scripture quotations unless otherwise noted are from the Revised Standard Version of the Bible, copyright © 1946, 1952, and 1971 by the Division of Christian Education of the National Council of Churches.

"Time does not bring relief" by Edna St. Vincent Millay is from *Collected Poems* (Harper & Row), copyright © 1917, 1945 by Edna St. Vincent Millay.

Excerpt from *The Rebel* by Albert Camus (New York: Random House, 1956).

Cover design: Spangler Design Team

Library of Congress Cataloging-in-Publication Data

Milazzo, G. Tom, 1951–
    The protest and the silence : suffering, death, and biblical
theology / G. Tom Milazzo.
      p. cm.
    Includes bibliographical references and indexes.
    ISBN 0-8006-2526-9
    1. Suffering—Religious aspects. 2. Death—Religious aspects.
3. Theodicy. 4. Bible—Theology. 5. Hidden God. I. Title.
BL65.S85L39 1992
231'.8—dc20   92-7935
                                     CIP

The paper used in this publication meets the minimum requirements of American National Standard for Information Sciences—Permanence of Paper for Printed Library Materials, ANSI Z329.48-1984. ∞™

Manufactured in the U.S.A.   AF 1-2526

96   95   94   93   92   1   2   3   4   5   6   7   8   9   10

For My Father,
Pasquale Milazzo
December 28, 1918–June 4, 1986

יזכור אלהים נשמת אבי מידי שהלך לעולמו
אנא תהי נפשו צחרה בצחר ההיים
ותהי מנוהתו כבוד

O God, remember the breath of my father, my teacher
who has died, who has passed to his eternity. . . .
Let his breath be bound to the living,
and his resting place be glory.

CONTENTS

PREFACE

*Time does not bring relief; you all have lied
Who told me time would ease me of my pain!
I miss him in the weeping of the rain;
I want him at the shrinking of the tide;
The old snows melt from every mountain-side,
And last year's leaves are smoke in every lane;
But last year's bitter longing must remain
Heaped on my heart, and my old thoughts abide.
There are a hundred places where I fear
To go,—so with his memory they brim.
And entering with relief some quiet place
Where never fell his foot nor shone his face
I say, "There is no memory of him here!"
And so stand stricken, so remembering him.*

Edna St. Vincent Millay,
Collected Poems

*How I sympathized with Job! I did not deny God's existence,
but I doubted his absolute justice.*

Elie Wiesel,
Night

We have all stood beneath the shadow of death. We
have felt the bitter touch of its hand upon our heart.
We have felt its rank breath upon our necks. And
whether we stood beneath the shadows of the smoke
from the crematoria at Auschwitz, or held a dying
child in our arms, or listened to the last gasp of life
from a parent whose voice we shall never hear again,
or stood by the grave of a loved one, the tragedy is
the same. The emptiness is the same. The senseless-
ness is the same. And so is the prayer. "If you love

us, take away the shadow of death. If you love us, why are we given over to suffer and to die? Why in your presence, my God, is there death?"

But whether it is the road to Golgotha on which we walk, or the road to Babylon, or the road to Auschwitz, or the road that leads to our own death, only silence answers our prayer. In that silence, death casts its shadow over more than just our life. It casts its shadow over our faith as well. Where is God while we suffer and die? What are we to make of God's silence? Does God's silence speak of God's absence? Does God's silence speak of God's impotence? Or does God's silence speak of our murder at the hands of God? Thus is the question of the reality of God inseparable from the question of what it means to be human in a world where all things die. In a world where all things die, if we cling to our faith despite or even because of the silence of God, though we might not deny God's existence, we must doubt that God's justice is absolute. We must doubt the sincerity, the efficacy, even the certainty, of God's love.

Can we love a God that is silent in the presence of our death? Can we trust a God that does nothing to prevent our suffering? Whose justice is neither absolute nor perhaps even just? Perhaps not. Can we believe in a God whose impotence embraces our death? A God that may well be our murderer? How can we find God innocent of our death when all the evidence speaks of God's guilt? If we cannot establish God's innocence, if God will not come out of the darkness and absolve itself of complicity in our death, how can we believe in God? What can it mean to have faith? Perhaps because the shadow of death calls into question not only our humanity but our faith in God as well, we cannot understand what it means to have faith in God apart from our concern for understanding what it means to be human, what it means to live in this world where all that is human decays in the presence of the silence of God.

I encountered the Biblical Theology Movement for the first time as a divinity student at Yale. That encounter proved to be a two-edged sword.[1] On the one hand, the force and strength of the movement's systematic and conceptual schema were appealing—in many respects

1. In terms of my own work, the influence of the movement and its approach to biblical theology has been most profound. I am in debt to the late Hans Frei and to Brevard Childs and George Lindbeck, whose instruction was critical to the development of my own thought. The best history of the movement is perhaps Brevard S. Childs, *Biblical Theology in Crisis* (Philadelphia: Westminster, 1970), pt. 1, pp. 13–90.

both convincing and overpowering. On the other hand, I found it ever more difficult to reconcile the movement's vision of God,[2] human nature, and the world with existence in a world where the ashes of Auschwitz and Dachau are still warm, where the embrace of death seems more powerful than the breath of life, where innocence and guilt seem to have no meaning—indeed, in a world where both the innocent and the guilty die. As long as the shadow of death pressed against the movement's claims about God and the world, about existence and death, the question of the presence and facticity of God could not be silenced—not by the force of reason, the power of faith, or the strength of human desire.

Over the next two years, it became more and more difficult to reconcile the movement's articulation of faith with human existence or indeed with Scripture itself. While attempting to formulate a theology of the Book of Hosea, I found myself unable to resolve the tension in the text between the promise of restoration and the wrath and anger of YHWH—a jealous rage that too often led to the exile of Israel. It was at this point that the limitations of biblical theology seemed most acute, that the human experience of suffering and death appeared to call into question God's concern for human being, and that the distance between the human and the divine seemed greatest.

What kind of a God was this? What kind of God could, with one voice, promise life and, with another, offer death? This first theological encounter with the theodicy question closely paralleled some difficult personal circumstances. My son was hospitalized on a cancer ward

---

2. Hebrew has many words for God—El, Elohim, and even YHWH—each of which is used not as a name but almost as a description or an adjective. El and Elohim are thus best translated by the word "god" (with a lower case *g*). In another sense, El and Elohim can even be translated "the divine one," "the God," perhaps even "the one who is divine." The word "Elohim," though technically plural in form, is used to describe both the gods of other nations and YHWH. Derived from the verb *hayah,* which is similar to the English "to be," YHWH appears to mean "the one that is," or perhaps even "the one that is as it is." In any event, YHWH connotes continued or sustained existence, but it does not "name" God. To say YHWH is to describe God, not to name it. That is, YHWH describes God's activity, not God's ontology. Note also that the word YHWH is third person and can be masculine, feminine, or neuter: "he, she, it is." Such possibilities further extend the ambivalence or sense of mystery that surrounds the person of God. Indeed, in some way YHWH is neither male nor female, though the imagery used in Hebrew Scripture for YHWH is often female as well as male. It is my custom to use the word "god" with reference to the divine being or presence. Use of the lower case *g* is consistent with the descriptive nature of the words "YHWH," "El," and "Elohim" in Hebrew Scripture. Use of the lower case, as well as the third person neuter pronoun, retains the rich ambiguity and descriptive texture of the Hebrew. In this book, however, I follow convention and use the more traditional upper case G.

for children; I witnessed the suffering of other children, including the death of Holly, a little girl who had brain cancer; I was faced with the painful deaths of James Sands and Joseph Lovito; and in June 1986, I experienced the agony of my father's suffering unto death. All these events pressed this disparity to its limits. In my encounter with suffering and death, the implicit separation between existential circumstance and theological reflection, between systematic reflection and human existence, between exegesis and experience, no longer seemed tenable.

The categories that the movement brought to the discussion of this problem no longer seemed adequate. Their inadequacy seemed to be rooted in the movement's attempt to explicate human existence by means of a systematic analysis of human existence in categories drawn from Christian faith. That is to say, the theological concepts and structures offered by the movement were called into question by the very real presence of suffering and death and by the darkness that veils the face of God. The discussion of suffering and death as a theological problem, then, raised the issue of how biblical theology might best be done. It also raised the issue of what the relationship between theological reflection and Scripture might be. This much seemed clear—existence was to be the basis for understanding faith, not faith the ground for understanding existence.

In light of these considerations, our interest here is threefold: systematic, exegetical, and "existential."[3] Can theological reflection reconcile human suffering and faith in God? In faith, what can be said about suffering? What is the relationship between faith and existence? Can faith be maintained in the presence of suffering and death? How is it possible to speak of the unity of Scripture after the demise of the Biblical Theology Movement? These questions, it will be argued, are really one and the same concern, which finds its best articulation in a single question: Why in the presence of God is there death? In reflection upon suffering and death as a theological problem, I hope that a proposal may emerge for doing biblical theology that is consonant with its origins and yet is better able to deal with the theological issues raised by the experience of suffering and death in Hebrew Scripture. The focus throughout remains on the problem of suffering and death in Hebrew Scripture and how that perspective shapes the contours of the possibility of faith. The inquiry, I trust, will give rise to the method.

---

3. I use "existential" here in its inclusive, less technical sense, as referring simply to human existence in a broad sense, not to a specific philosophical system.

ABBREVIATIONS

BA	*Biblical Archaeologist*
BJRL	*Bulletin of the John Rylands University Library*
BTB	*Biblical Theology Bulletin*
CBQ	*Catholic Biblical Quarterly*
ChrC	*Christian Century*
ChrSc	*Christian Scholar*
CJT	*Canadian Journal of Theology*
IDBS	*Interpreter's Dictionary of the Bible*, supp. vol.
Int	*Interpretation*
JBL	*Journal of Biblical Literature*
JR	*Journal of Religion*
JTC	*Journal for Theology and the Church*
NTS	*New Testament Studies*
RB	*Revue biblique*
RelL	*Religion in Life*
RevExp	*Review and Expositor*
SBLDS	SBL Dissertation Series
StudBT	*Studia Biblica et Theologica*
TToday	*Theology Today*
VT	*Vetus Testamentum*
VTSup	Vetus Testamentum Supplement
ZAW	*Zeitschrift für die alttestamentliche Wissenschaft*
ZTK	*Zeitschrift für Theologie und Kirche*

THE PROTEST AND THE silence

one | THE RISE AND FALL OF BIBLICAL THEOLOGY

The relevance of biblical interpretation can be found only in a relevant interpretation.

H. H. Rowley,
"The Relevance of Biblical Interpretation"

Man is no longer felt to be set within an ultimate order or context, from which he draws not only his being, but the meaning, standards and values of his life; he is alone and alien in the flux of reality and quite autonomous with regard to meaning and value . . . all the gods are dead—that is, all those structures of coherence, order, and value.

Langdon Gilkey,
"Secularism's Impact on Contemporary Theology"

THE RISE OF THE MOVEMENT

As early as 1936, C. H. Dodd argued that the goal of biblical studies was interpretation. Interpretation unfolded within the context of proclamation and response.[1] Within this context an understanding of the gospel was finally secured and bore fruit within the life of the community. Interpretation, proclamation, and communal and personal response all marked what Rowley termed "relevant interpretation."[2] The search for the meaning of Scripture within the context of

1. C. H. Dodd, *The Present Task in New Testament Studies* (London: Cambridge Univ. Press, 1936), 40; see also P. S. Minear, "Wanted: A Biblical Theology," *T Today* 1 (1944–45): 48. The question of what is or is not biblical is itself deeply problematic and subject to much debate.

2. H. H. Rowley, "The Relevance of Biblical Interpretation," *Int* 1 (1947): 19.

the life of the community of faith,[3] the conviction that "theological
reflection in itself [was] not enough,"[4] and intense dissatisfaction with
the legacy of nineteenth-century biblical studies[5] all marked the genesis
of what we have come to know as the Biblical Theology Movement.

The Roots of the Movement

The movement arose in the early 1940s, but its roots may well be
traced back to the mid-nineteenth century, to the work of Wellhausen,
the History of Religions School, and earlier to the likes of de Wette,
George, Vatke, Graf, and Eduard Reuss.[6] According to Childs, by the
late 1930s and early 1940s, the History of Religions School no longer
exerted a strong influence upon biblical studies.[7] Critics of the school

3. "When the historian has done his work conscientiously and the gap between the
world of the Bible and the world of our day has become a gaping chasm, the church
with full right demands that scholarship go a step farther, bridge this chasm and show
how the word of the Bible in spite of its time-bound quality is still a word of God to
man in the present day" (J. D. Smart, *The Interpretation of Scripture* [Philadelphia:
Westminster, 1961], 38).

4. According to Rowley, the Bible is "a religious book; and religion is more than
theology. . . . [Interpretation] should nurture right relationship to God" ("Relevance,"
16).

5. See, e.g., Rowley, "Relevance," 4–5; Minear, "Biblical Theology," 50–52, esp.
51: "We have engaged in interpreting the Bible by forcing upon it categories alien to
its message. For example, we treat the development of Israel's religion in evolutionary
terms but Israel herself experienced that development in quite different terms: God's
invitation of and fulfillment of his covenant. Our biblical theology has been an historical
reconstruction of the strange ideas of a strange folk; their theology was a continuing
response to God's redemptive activity in weaving the unique web of their destiny." See
also G. E. Wright, "The Problem of Archaizing Ourselves," *Int* 3 [1949], pp. 450–56,
esp. 453–55; Smart, *Interpretation*, 232–304; R. C. Dentan, *Preface to Old Testament
Theology*, rev. ed. (New York: Seabury, 1963), 50–60.

6. See J. Wellhausen, *Prolegomena to the History of Israel* (Gloucester: Peter Smith,
1973; first pub. in 1878 as volume 1 of the two-volume *History of Israel*); W. M. L. de
Wette, *Beiträge zur Einleitung in das Alte Testament*, 2 vols. (1806–7); J. F. L. George,
Die älteren Jüdischen Feste mit einer Kritik der Gesetzgebung des Pentateuch (1835); W. Vatke,
Die biblische Theologie wissenschaftlich dargestellt (1835); and Graf, *Die geschichtlichen Bücher
des Alten Testaments* (1866). According to Robertson Smith, E. Reuss was to become
the pioneer of the historical-critical method. See W. Robertson Smith's preface to Wellhausen's *Prolegomena*, 4.

7. Brevard Childs, *Biblical Theology in Crisis* (Philadelphia: Westminster, 1970), 18–
19, 20, 35, 47–49. Much of the critique that the movement offered of nineteenth-century
liberalism was in essence a critique of the History of Religions School. See Wright,
"Archaizing," 453–54; C. R. North "Pentateuchal Criticism," *The Old Testament and
Modern Study*, ed. H. H. Rowley (London: Oxford University Press, 1961), 58–59;
Dentan, *Preface*, 50–60.

argued that the school's method—a science of history clearly demonstrated in its analysis of the process of development of Israelite
religion—was actually "an invalid application of evolution to history."[8]
Childs implies that in the absence of the school's "science of history,"
proponents of the movement turned instead to archaeology in order
to find an objective, historical explication of the features that made
the Bible unique in its environment.[9] Childs writes, "The Bible reflects
the influence of its environment both in terms of its form and content,
and therefore can not be understood apart from the study of its common Near Eastern background."[10] Furthermore, "in spite of its appropriations the Bible has used these common elements in a way that
is totally distinct and unique from its environment."[11]

In effect, where the History of Religions School had used its historical-critical method to stress the similarities between Israel and
neighboring cultures, the Biblical Theology Movement sought to use
archaeology, first, to situate the Bible within its historical and cultural
context and, then, to demonstrate those elements that seemed unique
to Judaism.[12] The method that had caused Wellhausen to abandon his
faith now became the basis for an affirmation of faith. Furthermore,
the History of Religions School established the context, both theologically and methodologically, and the issues around which later
scholarship took shape, much as the movement has done in this century. Conclusions may have differed on some points, and different
aspects may have been differently stressed. The impact of the school

8. Childs, *Biblical Theology,* 48; Minear, "Biblical Theology," 51.
9. Childs, *Biblical Theology,* 47–49. Archaeology is the focus in the works of Albright,
Wright, and others. See W. F. Albright, *From the Stone Age to Christianity* (Garden City,
N.Y.: Doubleday/Anchor, 1957), 2. A similar opinion was expressed by W. Robertson
Smith in the preface to the first edition of his *Religion of the Semites* (1887; New York:
Meridian Books, 1957), vii. Also see J. L. McKenzie, *The Two-Edged Sword* (1956;
Garden City, N.Y.: Doubleday/Image, 1966), see esp. chaps. 2, 3, 5, 14, pp. 43–82,
95–112, 275–94. Rowley asserts that "the interpreter of the Bible must . . . seek to
apprehend the fact as historical fact, and must have a historical sense, relating the Bible
first of all to its context of history and grasping the whole process through which the
ideas were revealed" ("Relevance," 8–9). Wright takes a similar position: "The Bible
presents few, if any, universally valid truths as abstractions separated from a particular
history. Biblical truth is . . . encased in and transmitted by a particular historical con-
ditioning" ("Archaizing," 450).
10. Childs, *Biblical Theology,* 48; see Rowley, "Relevance," 9; H. H. Rowley, *The
Re-Discovery of the Old Testament* (Philadelphia: Westminster, 1946), 33–82.
11. Childs, *Biblical Theology,* 48; see also G. E. Wright, "How Did Early Israel
Differ from Her Neighbors?" *BA* 6 (1943): 6.
12. Unfortunately, such characterizations were often "wooden" and stereotypical.
See Dentan, *Preface,* 155–56; Wright, "Archaizing," 433.

upon the work of the movement's proponents, however, seems clear: Faith still sought understanding in and through history.

The Movement Itself

Yet, amid the intensity of its search and the passion of its discontent, the Biblical Theology Movement was born, flourished, and died, overcome as much by its own failure as by the ambiguity and the difficulty—if not the impossibility—of its self-appointed task. In its demise, much of the agenda set by the movement remained open and unaddressed. Many of the issues it raised remained both problematic and unresolved. Its desire for relevance and renewal was left unrealized; its quest for unity and identity left unsatisfied. In death, as in its life, the identity of the movement remained as elusive as its search for relevance proved to be.

The identity of the Biblical Theology Movement remains elusive; however, a few things can be said about it with some measure of certainty. First, despite significant contributions by English and European scholars, the movement for the most part was essentially an American phenomenon. Second, while the movement had its supporters among Catholic biblical scholars, the major proponents of the movement were Protestant.[13] Third, the movement had a more or less "definable beginning and an approximate ending."[14] Born in the early 1940s, the Biblical Theology Movement endured no more than two decades.[15] Fourth, the demise of the movement proved to have an impact at least as enduring as the influence the movement exerted upon scholars during its life. While the movement gave credence to the possibility of doing biblical theology,[16] its demise called that possibility into question.

---

13. Any list of proponents would include P. S. Minear, H. H. Rowley, J. D. Smart, G. E. Wright, C. H. Dodd, J. Muilenburg, R. Dentan, H. R. Niebuhr, M. Burrows, B. Anderson, O. Piper, and O. Cullmann (Childs, *Biblical Theology*, 17–31).

14. Childs, *Biblical Theology*, 13.

15. See ibid., 32–33.

16. In fact, even some of the proponents of the movement had serious questions about its ability to attain even the most basic of its self-appointed goals. As early as 1944, just four years after the beginning of the movement, Minear had already expressed concern that the renaissance in biblical theology promised by proponents of the movement might fail to occur. See Minear's critique ("Biblical Theology," 49) of Smart's proclamation of the rebirth of Old Testament theology, "The Death and Rebirth of Old Testament Theology," in *JR* 23 (1943): 1–11, 125–36; later significantly revised and published as *The Interpretation of Scripture* (Philadelphia: Westminster, 1961).

During those two brief decades, as Childs has pointed out, the movement remained little more than a consensus of opinion about the importance of the Bible for theological reflection and for the life of the community of faith. At no time during the movement's twenty years, however, were its major proponents able to come to terms on any one issue.[17] For example, proponents of the movement stressed the systematic and conceptual unity of Scripture as a whole and the importance of that unity for Christian theology. Most proponents characterized that unity by some *Mitte,* or central concept or center point, that brought both Testaments together and thus provided the basis for conceptual and systematic reflection.[18] Continuity and unity within each of the Testaments thus became the basis for establishing the unity of the two Testaments.[19] In response to the earlier History of Religions School, which for the most part stressed the continuity of historical development that led from Judaism to Christianity, the Biblical Theology Movement stressed the continuity of theological reflection within the Testaments, and within Scripture as a whole.

The nature of that center point was never fully explicated and remained subject to much debate.[20] Dentan, for example, held that

17. According to Childs, "To speak of a Biblical Theology Movement is to suggest a unified position regarding the role of the Bible and theology. However, there was never an attempt among its adherents to formulate a 'position.' . . . Little attempt was ever made to bring the different lines into a closely knit theology. . . . However, in spite of the variety . . . the fact remains that there was a remarkable similarity in some major themes that began to be emphasized . . . [which] gave it a coherence because of this broad consensus" (*Biblical Theology,* 32–33).

18. The *Mitte* was typically formulated in terms of a distinctively Christian understanding of Hebrew Scripture. Proponents of the movement understood Hebrew Scripture as the Old Testament, which found its completion in the New Testament. Explication of the unity of Hebrew Scripture thus mirrored its Christian appropriation. F. V. Filson wrote, "It has always been the position of the church that the Old Testament is a witness to Christ and that only as such can it claim a place in Hebrew Scripture" ("The Unity of the Old and the New Testaments," *Int* 5 [1951]: 141). See also H. G. Reventlow, *Hauptprobleme der alttestamentlichen Theologie im 20. Jahrhundert* (Darmstadt: Wissenschaftliche Buchgesellschaft, 1982), 138ff. (translated as *Problems of Old Testament Theology in the Twentieth Century* [Philadelphia: Fortress, 1985], 125ff.); Gerhard Hasel, *Old Testament Theology: Basic Issues in the Current Debate* (Grand Rapids: Eerdmans, 1972), 49–50.

19. "For the Christian, of course, while the unity of the Old Testament seems an obvious and strictly objective fact . . . there is a higher unity which results from the coupling of the Old Testament with the New" (Dentan, *Preface,* 173); see also Rowley, *Re-Discovery,* 285–304.

20. See, for example, R. C. Dentan, "The Unity of the Old Testament," *Int* 5 (1951): 159–60, 173, and *Preface,* 117–18. See also Filson, "Unity," 140–41; Wright, "Archaizing," 453–54; Gerhard Hasel, "The Relationship between the Testaments," in *Old Testament Theology,* 105–27; Rowley, *Re-Discovery,* 285ff.; and Smart, *Interpretation,* 88.

ground was divine activity. God acted in history[21] "to create for himself
a sacred community, a nation that he has hammered upon an anvil of
tragic experience to shape it into an appropriate instrument for ac-
complishing his purpose."[22] Thus was the presence of God manifest
within the horizon of the world and within the events of human history.
For Smart, in contrast, the unifying principle was far less defined.
"The unity of the Bible," he argued, is "the unity of a multitude of
witnesses . . . the same God with the same redemptive purpose for
humanity was at work in each of them. Their oneness is therefore a
oneness in God."[23] Some proponents held that that central concept
was covenant. Others held it was the relationship between the human
and the divine, *Heilsgeschichte,* sin, salvation, or even election.[24] For
others, that unity was not based upon a single concept. Rather, it took
shape around contrasting ideas: law versus gospel, promise versus
fulfillment, and even theocentricity versus christocentricity.[25] Proponents often argued that concepts such as sin, suffering, and death within

21. Rowley, *Re-Discovery,* 93.
22. Dentan, "Unity," 159–60; "What gives vitality to [the message of the prophets]
is the conviction that God once acted in history in an unmistakable manner and created
for himself a peculiar people" (p. 162).
23. Smart, *Interpretation,* 88.
24. Eichrodt, Wright, and others favored the covenant; Vriezen, the human-divine
relation; Rowley, election. "Biblical faith," wrote Will Herberg, "is faith enacted as
history, or it is nothing at all" ("Biblical Faith as *Heilsgeschichte,*" *ChrSc* 39 [1956]: 25;
also see 31). A similar approach was adopted by other proponents of the movement.
Rowley, for example, stressed what he termed the "unity of the Divine revelation given
in the context of history and through the medium of human personality" (*The Unity
of the Bible* [Philadelphia: Westminster, 1955], 17); Childs, *Biblical Theology,* 41; also see
O. Piper, "The Bible as 'Holy History,'" *ChrC* 63 (1946): 362ff.; Oscar Cullmann,
Christ and Time, trans. F. V. Filson (London: SCM, 1951). Of all these concepts, the
concept of *Heilsgeschichte* was perhaps the most important and provided the foundation
for the movement's understanding of Scripture and for its theological reflection.
25. For law vs. gospel, see Filson, "Unity," 141–42. Promise vs. fulfillment was
primarily advanced by Brunner; see also Filson, "Unity," 142–43; Smart, *Interpretation,*
80–83; Brevard S. Childs, "Prophecy and Fulfillment," *Int* 16 (1958): 259–71. The issue
of theocentricity vs. christocentricity was discussed by P. E. Davies ("This whole New
Testament life and literature is the outcome of what God did and continued to do in
Christ" ["Unity and Variety in the New Testament," *Int* 5 (1951): 184]); Filson ("The
theme of unity must deal primarily with the continuous working of God to execute
his holy and gracious purpose, a working which centers in the historical career of Jesus
Christ" ["Unity," 151]); M. Burrows ("True unity and final significance [of the Bible]
are to be found in the general direction and the outcome of the process, culminating
in the supreme and central revelation of God in Christ" [*An Outline of Biblical Theology*
(Philadelphia: Westminster, 1946), 139]); Dentan ("The unity of the Old Testament is
really to be found in Jesus Christ" ["Unity," 173]); and W. Vischer ("Jesus, the end of
the Old Testament, is also its goal" ["Everywhere the Scripture Is about Christ Alone,"
in *The Old Testament and Christian Faith,* ed. B. W. Anderson (New York: Harper and
Row, 1963), 99]).

Hebrew Scripture had complementary concepts in Christian Scripture—sin and judgment, for example, were counterbalanced by grace, death through the sin of Adam by life through the death and resurrection of the Second Adam, the vengeful and angry God by the loving, compassionate God, and even the cross as the sign of our humanity by the cross as the sign of our deliverance and triumph.[26] Yet despite extensive debate and the depth of disagreement, proponents still clung to the belief that Hebrew and Christian Scriptures share a common theological foundation.

This sense of theological continuity and cohesiveness within Judaism, between Judaism and Christianity, and finally within Christianity itself provided the foundation for the interpretation and understanding of the events of human history and the course of human existence. The events of human history had theological significance. The intelligibility of human history and of human existence, proponents implied, rested upon this theological significance and thus upon the possibility that those events were more than just part of the drama of the course of human events—they were part of salvation history. Thus, "history was a medium of revelation. God limited himself by filtering his self-disclosure through finite human personality. . . . God has revealed himself in the real events of human life which are found in the Bible. The theologian who seeks this knowledge of God must therefore study history."[27] Salvation history, as what might be termed the *embodiment* of the divine plan or purpose in the realm of human events, was accessible—perhaps better put, was intelligible—through concepts like sin and grace, revelation and salvation.[28] Without this conceptual framework, the events of human history were arbitrary and meaningless. Thus, for the proponents of the movement, human existence was to be understood and interpreted against the backdrop of this conceptual framework, not the framework concept against the backdrop of human existence.

26. See Dentan, "Unity," 169. For John Dillenberger, "The Cross . . . belongs to the utmost of joy and of suffering. The revelation of God and the life of men in faith coincide at the point of suffering" ("Revelational Discernment and the Problem of the Two Testaments," in *The Old Testament and Christian Faith,* ed. B. W. Anderson [New York: Harper and Row, 1963], 168–69).

27. Childs, *Biblical Theology,* 41–42.

28. Dillenberger offers this analysis: "The categories of promise and fulfillment as well as typological exegesis are related to *Heilsgeschichte,* in which the development of Israel's history is the medium of God's revelation and the movement toward its culmination, Christ" ("Revelational Discernment," 174).

In this sense, it was faith (or more properly, theological reflection) that enlightened, offered insight into, or provided interpretation of the events and problems that seem to dominate human existence. As Dillenberger argued, history was the vehicle of revelation. As the vehicle of revelation, history also was the vehicle of God's self-disclosure. In this sense, Scripture is itself a history of that revelation, the record of that self-disclosure. More, Scripture is the explication of the history of God's offer of itself. The whole of human history, then, was shaped and contoured by "the matrix of God's possibility for man."[29] This understanding of human history as the matrix of the possibility of God's emergence lies at the heart of the concept of *Heilsgeschichte*.[30]

Thus was faith the condition—or even the precondition—for understanding human existence. The events of human history find their intelligibility only within the context of the history of faith, which is in some sense God's offer of itself. Doctrines and dogmatic formulations gleaned from Scripture then become the means whereby that intelligibility, that history of God's offer of itself, is articulated or explicated.[31] Faith does not seek understanding in existence; existence seeks understanding in faith.[32]

THE FALL OF THE MOVEMENT

The movement's search for understanding, however, was short-lived. As we have seen, as early as 1946 there were voices of discontent within the movement. There was no unanimity of opinion, no single method, no one approach to which all opponents could agree. Almost from the beginning, those outside the movement shared neither its vision nor its insight. As Childs points out, by the late 1950s the

29. Dillenberger, "Revelational Discernment," 162.

30. See O. Cullmann, "The Connection of Primal Events and End Events with the New Testament Redemptive History," in *The Old Testament and Christian Faith,* ed. B. W. Anderson (New York: Harper and Row, 1963), 115–16. Insofar as human history is finally subsumed within the rubric of salvation history, the complexity of the matrix of this possibility also lies at the heart of the often rich and tragic tapestry of human history. Thus does human existence find its fullest articulation in terms of this matrix.

31. For example, see Karl Rahner's articulation of what he terms "fundamental theology" or "existential ontology" (*The Foundations of Christian Faith* [New York: Seabury, 1978]); see also Schleiermacher's understanding of sin, grace, and absolute dependence in his *Christian Faith.*

32. See Minear's discussion of "kerygmatic theology" in his "Biblical Theology," 56–57.

movement was already near collapse under the weight of internal and external pressures.[33] Childs offers this analysis:

> It is ironical that many of the issues that the Biblical Theology Movement were most confident to have solved, in actuality were either glossed over or avoided. The decade of the fifties witnessed the return to the theological arena of problems which then increasingly began to cut away at the foundation blocks of the movement. . . . Positions that Biblical theologians had apparently destroyed in their battle with older liberal scholars were revived in a slightly altered form, to be then championed by a younger generation in revolt against the Biblical theologians.[34]

The weight of this challenge and the movement's apparent inability to respond convincingly to this neoliberal critique seriously weakened the credibility of the movement.

Qumran and the "Hebrew Mind"

New challenges to the movement continued to appear in unlikely places. For example, the movement had long stressed the importance of the distinctiveness of the "faith of Israel" and the uniqueness of the Hebrew mind, which was extended to the Bible as well.[35] This distinctiveness "could be scientifically demonstrated . . . objective, historical study could prove the unique features of the Bible."[36] As the History of Religions School had used a "scientific," "objective" analysis to place Hebrew Scripture within the context of the culture and history of the ancient Near East, proponents of the movement used the same method to demonstrate the distinctiveness of the Bible. Where proponents of the History of Religions School had used this analysis to diminish the distinctiveness of the faith of Israel, proponents of the movement attempted to emphasize that faith's distinctiveness.

33. Childs, *Biblical Theology*, 61–87.
34. Ibid., 51.
35. Ibid., 48. According to Rowley, "The most enduring things that Israel attained were not the things she had in common with others, but the differentiae" (*Re-Discovery*, 58). Wright comments, "Even when we have noted all the similarities, the borrowing, and the syncretism, the differences between the literature of Israel and that of Canaan are far more remarkable and significant than the affinities" ("Early Israel," 6).
36. Childs, *Biblical Theology*, 49; see also William A. Irwin, "The Hebrews," in *The Intellectual Adventure of Ancient Man* (Chicago: University of Chicago Press, 1977; 1st ed., 1946), 223–362, as well as the conclusion to that volume by Henri and H. A. Frankfort entitled "The Emancipation of Thought from Myth," esp. 366–69.

Proponents of the movement identified the distinctiveness of the Bible's perspective and proclaimed that revelation reflected a unique Hebrew mentality.[37] Hebrew Scripture was the unique creation of a people who had a unique view of the world and of their relationship to God.[38] This sense of the uniqueness of the mind and faith of Israel was extended in turn to the New Testament;[39] an unbroken path of revelation extended from Abraham through Jesus. Christianity both inherited and fulfilled that revelation with a distinctiveness that equaled that of Judaism.[40]

As early as 1935, however, the idea that there was a distinctive Hebrew mentality began to be called into question.[41] Over the next quarter century, the idea that a special and unique revelation bound Judaism to Christianity became less and less tenable. Even before Barr's final attack, proponents and critics of the movement alike began to doubt the tenability of these theses.[42] Where the study of history and archaeology once was used to establish the distinctiveness both of the Bible and of Israel's salvation history, these disciplines now threatened to overshadow both the Bible and salvation history. The discovery of the Dead Sea Scrolls, for example, challenged the movement's understanding of the uniqueness of the Hebrew mind and of the relationship between Judaism and Christianity.[43] The scrolls enabled scholars to establish "strong lines of religious continuity" between the Dead

---

37. Piper, "Bible as 'Holy History,' " 362; Childs, *Biblical Theology,* 45.

38. See the analysis of Barr's critique of this position later in this chapter.

39. C. H. Dodd, *The Bible Today* (Cambridge: Cambridge University Press, 1962), 1–14, esp. 8–10; Rowley, *Re-Discovery,* 285–88; Smart, *Interpretation,* 81–85; George A. F. Knight, *A Christian Theology of the Old Testament* (Richmond: John Knox, 1959), 7–8; E. Brunner, "The Significance of the Old Testament for Our Faith," in *The Old Testament and Christian Faith,* ed. B. W. Anderson (New York: Harper and Row, 1963), 245–47; Gerhard von Rad, *Old Testament Theology,* 2 vols. (New York: Harper and Row, 1962–65), 2:383–84. Translations of von Rad (*Theologie des Alten Testaments* [2d ed., Munich: K. Verlag, 1958]) are my own from the German. Page numbers for the German edition will be listed in parentheses where appropriate.

40. According to Brunner, "The Old Testament is the beginning of the New. . . . All the ideas I have emphasized as characteristic of the Old Testament, the New Testament . . . has brought to completion and in a certain sense spiritualized. . . . one God, one message, one revelation, one Word, one covenant. If it is now called the new covenant, that is not because it replaces the old but because it intends to fulfill it" ("Significance," 263–64.)

41. Erwin Goodenough, *By Light, Light: The Mystic Gospel of Hellenistic Judaism* (New Haven: Yale University Press, 1935).

42. For example, see Millar Burrows (who supported the movement), "Thy Kingdom Come," *JBL* 74 (1955): 1ff.; L. Knothe (a critic), "Zur Frage des hebräischen Denkens," *ZAW* 70 (1958): 175ff.

43. The Ras Shamra texts also had an impact upon biblical studies, although perhaps

Sea sect and Christianity,[44] which made the movement's understanding of the development of Judaism and Christianity both historically and theologically difficult to maintain. Proponents of the movement were confronted with the possibility that Christianity was not the direct offshoot of "normative" or "mainline" Judaism.[45]

Consequently, the relationship between Judaism and Christianity now seemed less clear and less direct. The claim that Christianity was the completion and sole heir of Judaism could no longer stand unquestioned. In light of Qumran, Christianity appeared to be just one among a number of cults that could trace their point of origin to Judaism in the first century C.E. Even more threatening was the possibility that the point of origin of Christian faith may not have rested in mainline Judaism but in the sectarian community at Qumran, which was already one step away from the faith biblical theologians claimed Christianity had fulfilled.[46] For example, Käsemann wrote, "We find a special nearness to the Qumran community: the Christian community united by Easter in a common hope regards itself as the holy remnant which mediates the continuity of the old covenant with the restored people of the twelve tribes and already represents on earth the new eschatological covenant."[47] The force of such attacks from outside the movement continued to call into question most—if not all—of its fundamental assumptions.[48]

---

not as pronounced or as lasting as that of the Qumran texts. See John Gray, *The Legacy of Canaan: The Ras Shamra Texts and Their Relevance to Old Testament Studies* (Leiden: E. J. Brill, 1957).

44. Childs, *Biblical Theology*, 74. As Childs notes, some scholars at first thought that the discovery of the scrolls might overturn Christian faith.

45. Childs, *Biblical Theology*, 74–75.

46. The Qumran discovery also seemed to dramatize the importance of apocalyptic for understanding the development of Christianity. See Ernst Käsemann, "The Beginnings of Christian Theology," *JTC* 6 (1969): 17–46, and "On the Topic of Primitive Christian Apocalyptic," *JTC* 6 (1969): 99–133; Matthew Black, "The Christological Use of the Old Testament in the New Testament," *NTS* 18 (1971–72): 1–14, and *The Scrolls and Christian Origins: Studies in the Jewish Background of the New Testament* (New York: C. Scribner's Sons, 1961); Joseph Fitzmyer, "The Use of Explicit Old Testament Quotations in Qumran Literature and in the New Testament," *NTS* 7 (1961): 298ff. On Christianity as fulfilling Jewish faith, see David Aune, *Prophecy in Early Christianity and the Ancient Mediterranean World* (Grand Rapids: Eerdmans, 1983), 340–46.

47. Käsemann, "On the Topic," 108. For a critique of Käsemann's views, see Gerhard Ebeling, "The Ground of Christian Theology," *JTC* 6 (1969): 47–68.

48. As a result of the discovery of the Qumran Scrolls, the essentially linear and uniform portrayal of the development of Judaism inherited from the nineteenth century was replaced by a more complex model. Judaism itself appeared to be much less cohesive than proponents of the movement had expected it to be. Proponents of the movement

But the Biblical Theology Movement also faced challenges from within, since there was serious and continued division of opinion over the articulation and definition of key concepts. Any number of important issues remained unresolved and in fact appeared unresolvable. The relationship between theological exegesis and the historical-critical method, the liberal insistence on historicity and objectivity versus the orthodox emphasis on the distinctiveness and uniqueness of Scripture, the relationship between the two Testaments, and the authority of Scripture were all issues that remained unresolved. Failure to settle these important issues plagued the movement from its genesis to its demise. Many of these pressing issues and questions lay at the heart of the critique proponents of the movement had brought against the prior generation of biblical scholars. Now, proponents found themselves unable to address adequately those issues and questions that had been instrumental in the very formation of the movement. The weight of these and other unresolved problems bore heavily on the movement and its proponents.

Unfulfilled Expectations

The movement also lost credibility because it failed to live up to its own expectations. The promised resurgence and rebirth of exegesis did not occur. For the most part, interest in the Bible on the popular level was not rekindled. The movement produced no commentaries that matched the quality of those written by the previous generation. Of all of the works produced by its proponents, the *Interpreter's Bible* was perhaps the greatest disappointment. While many of the introductory articles were "classical expressions of the Biblical Theology Movement," most of the exegetical material stood in relationship not to the movement but to the "critical methodology of the thirties."[49]

Internal Dissent

Almost from its beginning, the movement suffered under the weight of internal dissent.[50] For a time, however, it survived. But with the

---

offered a portrait of Judaism that allowed little divergence or variation. Where the movement had seen but one people participating in one cult and one interpretation of revelation, there now appeared to be many people participating in a multitude of cults sharing a multiplicity of interpretations of revelation. The loss of a sense of the "faith of Israel" seriously undermined the movement. See M. Hengel, *Judaism and Hellenism* (Philadelphia: Fortress, 1981).

49. See Childs, *Biblical Theology*, 54.
50. The main critics were J. Branton and W. L. King. See, for example, J. Branton,

power of the critiques offered by Langdon Gilkey and James Barr,[51] the movement was pressed to its limits and for all intents and purposes came to an end.

Gilkey's critique was simple: "Our central problem has been that, in the shift of cosmology from ancient to modern, fundamental theological concepts have so changed their meaning as almost to have lost all reference. The phrase[s] 'God acts' and 'God speaks,' whatever they may ultimately mean to us, do not signify the wonders and voices of ancient days" (p. 204).[52] In effect, the dawn of modern science, the birth of liberalism, and the rise of the historical-critical method all mark the passing of a specific understanding of the relationship between God and the world. Before the nineteenth century, there was a clear identification between word and event. In a very literal sense, the Bible meant what it said; there was a kind of literal identification between the word of Scripture and the events of history. God acted and revealed itself in historical circumstances. Here the use of language is univocal: words (like "act" and "speak") "were used in the same sense of God as of men" (p. 196).[53]

As a result of the liberal critique of orthodoxy,[54] that univocal relationship between word and event, between Scripture and history, and between language and existence has been lost. Biblical narratives no longer point to events of human history. They no longer offer a history of God's activity. Instead, Hebrew Scripture becomes an expression of a particular understanding of faith. The Bible becomes,

---

"Our Present Situation in Biblical Theology," *RelL* 26 (1956–57): 5ff.; W. L. King, "Some Ambiguities in Biblical Theology," *RelL* 27 (1957–58): 95ff.

51. Gilkey interestingly stresses his adherence to the character of the movement throughout his critique of it. See his "Cosmology, Ontology, and the Travail of Biblical Language," *JR* 41 (1961): 194ff., about which Childs notes: "The article carried a tremendous force. . . . It placed the problem of history within the larger framework of systematic theology, and pursued the theological inconsistencies of various popular positions with a relentless logic" (*Biblical Theology*, 65). Barr's classic work is *The Semantics of Biblical Language* (London: Oxford University Press, 1961).

52. In this section, page references in the text are to Gilkey's article.

53. Gilkey adds, "At the Reformation . . . statements in biblical theology and in systematic theology coalesced because the theologians' understanding of what God did was drawn with no change from the simple narratives of Scripture, and because the verbs of the Bible were thus used univocally throughout" (pp. 198–99).

54. It could be argued that the liberal critique of orthodoxy began long before the nineteenth century. It began with a loosening of the intimacy that characterized the relationship between God and the world, which meant that religious language could no longer be univocal but must be analogical. This separation is reflected in the portrait of the universe offered by Copernicus, Kepler, Bruno, and others. Gilkey is correct, however, in arguing that the impact of that separation was brought against orthodoxy by Schleiermacher in the nineteenth century.

says Gilkey, "a book of the acts Hebrews believed God might have done" (p. 197). This expression of faith rests in a kind of parabolic, analogical use of language. Hebrew Scripture becomes not a recital of the mighty acts of God but a confession of faith. The denial of the mighty acts of God born in liberalism has "shifted our theological language from the univocal to the analogical" (p. 196). Originally, "both the biblical and the orthodox understanding of theological language was univocal. That is, when God was said to have 'acted,' it was believed that he had performed an observable act in space and time so that he functioned as does any secondary cause. . . . In other words, the words 'act' and 'speak' were used in the same sense of God as of men" (p. 195).

According to Gilkey, at the heart of the movement was an attempt to supplant the liberal critique of orthodoxy. That critique had succeeded in drawing a hard and fast distinction between the "objective," historical meaning of events and the theological significance of those events. Liberals did not deny that events could be both theologically and historically significant. They denied the legitimacy of the orthodox assertion that the theological significance of an event and that event's historical significance were one and the same. In their attempt to overturn the liberal critique of orthodoxy, proponents of the movement moved implicitly to erase this distinction between history and faith. That is to say, the birth of neo-orthodoxy and of the Biblical Theology Movement implied—and in some sense required—a return to a univocal use of language.

Gilkey pressed his critique at this point. Proponents of the movement failed to see that despite assertions to the contrary, the distinction between faith and history remained, and as long as that distinction remained, a return to a univocal use of language was not possible.[55] Indeed, as long as the movement remained bound by the distinction between faith and history, its own use of language was itself not univocal but analogical. As a result, proponents of the movement themselves were unable to escape the effects of the liberal critique. They were unable to articulate the significance of the "mighty acts of God" in terms of actual events in human history. Instead, the significance of such acts of God could be understood only in terms of the

55. Gilkey's analysis implies that the movement's failure to recapture a univocal use of language precluded a return to orthodoxy. From the outset, then, neo-orthodoxy stands on shaky ground. The liberal critique of orthodoxy has brought with it a kind of loss of innocence from which there can be no return.

force and power of the response or call to faith that these acts occa-sioned. The significance of the events of history lay not in their his-toricity or facticity but in their relevance for faith (pp. 200–1). Gilkey wrote: "God was not an inference from religious experience but he who acts in special events. And Hebrew religion was not the result of human religious genius or insight into the consistent continuity of God's activity; rather biblical religion was the response of faith to and the recital of the 'mighty acts of God' " (p. 195).

For proponents of the movement, faith was no longer "historical." God was no longer accessible in or revealed itself in history. God no longer acted *in* history. God acted *through* history. "Divine activity was the continual, creative, immanent activity of God, an activity which worked through the natural order and which therefore could be apprehended in general human experiences of dependence, of har-mony, and of value-experiences which in turn issued in developed religious feeling and religious consciousness" (p. 194). Once divine activity is separated from the events of human history, faith is separated from existence. Once faith is separated from existence, faith is separated from history as well. Once faith is separated from history, language about God is then no longer equivocal but becomes analogical. As long as the distinction between faith and history remained, the move-ment remained unable to restore a univocal use and understanding of language.

Consequently, while proponents of the movement appeared to use both biblical and orthodox language to describe the role of divine activity in history, those events were actually understood in analogical, naturalistic, causal terms (pp. 194, 199).[56] As a result, historical events were stripped of the very significance and uniqueness the movement both sought and needed in order to support its systematic structure (p. 199). The movement found itself in a quandary: It could affirm either the theological or the historical significance of events, but not both. Yet it was precisely the claim that the events of human existence were theologically and historically significant that both lay at the heart of the movement and formed the bridge it seemed to offer be-tween nineteenth-century liberal theology and twentieth-century neo-orthodoxy.[57]

56. See Childs, *Biblical Theology,* 65.

57. The metaphor of a bridge must not be pushed too far. As Gilkey notes, neo-orthodoxy and the Biblical Theology Movement were opposed to liberalism on the same grounds (p. 195). It may be better to say that neo-orthodoxy and the movement attempted to offer a response from the orthodox perspective to the development of modern science and the historical-critical method. In this sense, the movement sought to build a bridge over liberalism.

Here, says Gilkey, lies the rub. In the face of nineteenth-century liberalism and its critique of orthodoxy, there is a kind of loss of innocence that precludes a return to biblical faith and to orthodoxy. We no longer perceive the world as we once did. We no longer live in the same world. Unfortunately, says Gilkey, words that were understood univocally, whose theological significance lay in that understanding, are no longer so understood. Thus, we find ourselves with a twofold problem. First, we have not realized that this shift from the univocal to the analogical has taken place. Hence, when we use words that characterize both orthodoxy and biblical faith, we think we are using and understanding those words now as they were used and understood then. Unfortunately, this is not the case: Words that appear to be used equivocally are actually being used analogically.

Second, since the community of faith has not understood that this shift has taken place, the members of that community do not understand that these words are being used analogically and that language about God is itself analogical. "Unless one knows in some sense what the analogy means, how it is being used, and what it points to, the analogy is empty and unintelligible; that is, it becomes equivocal" (p. 196). Language that is equivocal is empty, abstract, and ultimately self-contradictory.

Insofar as language about God is analogical, it has no referent; that is, language about God refers to no object, being, or person within the scope of human experience. Language that has no referent is empty and without meaning (pp. 202–3). If language about God is meaningless and without referent, it is because once language about God becomes analogical and not univocal, God is separated from the world. Once God is separated from the world, the existence of God cannot be ascertained. If God's existence cannot be ascertained and if language about God refers to no being, to no object in space and time, then the existence and facticity of God is itself called into question. For if the word "God" has no referent within the horizon of the phenomenal world, then the existence of God can neither be secured nor proven. Nor for that matter can God's existence be disproven. About God's existence nothing can be said. If nothing can be said about the existence of God, then the facticity of God must remain an open and unresolvable issue. What had begun as a critique of the movement's use of language ended as a critique of language about God and ultimately raised the question of the tenability of faith.

Further Dissent

The question of the relationship between faith and history was also an important part of James Barr's critique of the Biblical Theology Movement. According to Barr, proponents of the movement held that in its essence, the Bible was a set of historical facts interpreted in faith. That faith, Barr wrote, "is based on some things which have taken place in history; even things which are not happenings in history but which are eternal, like the existence of God, are known only in as much as they are implied or revealed by historical events. . . . Primarily, therefore, the Bible is a supreme or unique witness to the saving events. The task [of the interpreter] is not to meditate upon the patterns of the biblical text as it stands; rather, using the biblical text as a source, he presses towards something which lies behind the text."[58]

If Barr is correct, then the Bible is not itself the revelation but is merely the vehicle of revelation, a "*record* of revelatory acts, a testimony to them, a commentary on them . . . a testimony in faith, a record of events as seen through the screen of faith which these same events generated." While the Bible is not a "strict" history of events, it does offer "some kind of analogy between the biblical presentation and the original event" such that the Bible both communicates and makes accessible some aspect of both the original event and its salvific purpose. In effect, events retained and recounted in the Bible are remembered because of their significance. That significance lies not in the events themselves but in the revelation that they occasion.[59]

Barr further argued that because its proponents failed to see that events remembered in Scripture were the occasion for revelation and not the revelation itself, the Biblical Theology Movement did not maintain the balance between the Bible as history and the Bible as the basis for theological reflection. In reality, Barr argued, the movement placed the historicity of events over and above their theological significance.[60] This stress on the historicity of events was actually foreign

58. James Barr, *The Bible in the Modern World* (New York: Harper and Row, 1973), 76.

59. Ibid., 76–77, 79.

60. Gilkey would support Barr's analysis with an accent uniquely his own. According to Gilkey: "The trans-natural reality that neo-orthodoxy proclaimed—the transcendent God, his mighty acts and his Word of revelation—became more and more unreal and incredible to those who learned to speak this language. Younger enthusiasts began to wonder if they were talking about anything they themselves knew about when they spoke of God, of encounter, of the eschatological event and of faith" ("Secularism's Impact on Contemporary Theology," *Christianity and Crisis* 25 [1965]: 65).

to all but a few biblical texts and finally resulted in the distortion of biblical narrative. The Bible is first and foremost a narrative concerned with theological reflection, and not with a history of events.[61] However, the theological significance of those events stands in the shadow of how those events were understood both within the context of the whole of Scripture and as authoritative for the community of faith.

In this respect, the movement's error was twofold. First, proponents of the movement attempted to ground the theological significance of Scripture in the events of human history. The facticity of these events was shaped by Scripture and established through an examination of the text. Scripture was the basis for reconstructing history, and that reconstructed history in turn became the ground for interpreting Scripture. For proponents of the movement, the Bible was history. Second, because the Bible was history, the historicity of biblical events became the ground for theology. In effect, the Bible became normative for theology because in Scripture revelation was bound to history. The Bible was theology. For Barr, the theological reflection and conceptual formulation that the movement sought to discover in biblical texts was unfounded. Such a commitment reflects a distinctively Christian perspective. That is to say, the movement's insistence on the continuity of theological concept and historical event is foreign to the biblical narrative found in Hebrew Scripture. This does not mean, as has often been asserted in the past century, that Hebrew Scripture is void of theological reflection. Nor does it mean that theological reflection is confined to Christian Scripture and its appropriation of Hebrew Scripture. Such is not the case. For Barr, theological reflection is very much a part of Hebrew Scripture.[62] The form and content of the theological reflection offered by Hebrew Scripture, however, seem to be different than that found in Christian Scripture.

These differences are striking. First, Christian Scripture offers a specific interpretation of Hebrew Scripture, and as such is an appropriation of Hebrew reflection. Second, Christian Scripture demonstrates a specific theological commitment to a particular interpretation of Hebrew Scripture. This interpretation construes the theological reflection offered in Hebrew Scripture specifically in light of the proclamation that Jesus was the Christ and Risen Lord. Christian Scripture

---

61. Barr, *Bible,* 89–90. Barr draws an important distinction between the Bible as theology (a position he equates with more traditional Protestantism, where each verse is seen as a theological statement) and the Bible as containing or implying theology.

62. Gilkey, I would say, shares this position.

sees itself and the theological reflection that it offers as in some way completing or fulfilling Hebrew Scripture. The implication is clear—without the New Testament the Old is tragically incomplete. Third, Christian Scripture is presented as the theological and hermeneutical key to Hebrew Scripture. Without Christian Scripture the full scope and depth of the revelation embodied in the Old Testament would not be accessible.

In light of this deliberate construal of Hebrew Scripture, there is a sense in which Christian Scripture stands apart or breaks away from Hebrew Scripture. This construal makes the kind of theological continuity that the movement sought to assert or discover difficult if not impossible to maintain. That is, the notion that Scripture is composed of two testaments is a Christian notion. The idea that Jesus was the Messiah is a distinctively Christian notion, one that shapes Hebrew Scripture in a specific way around a specific theological commitment. These ideas make an implicit claim about the theological unity of Hebrew Scripture and Christian Scripture that is difficult, if not impossible, to maintain from the perspective of Hebrew Scripture.[63] In effect, the possibility of formulating a biblical theology that resonated with the whole of Scripture was eclipsed by the movement's commitment to a theological position that was foreign to Hebrew Scripture.

Barr's critique is intended not to point to the impossibility of formulating a biblical theology but to establish the ground upon which biblical theology is possible. It was the task of Barr's *Semantics of Biblical Language* to establish that ground in the relationship between the use of language and theological reflection in the Bible.[64] Barr's approach was a dramatic departure from the method of the Biblical Theology Movement. For Barr, the key to understanding the theological significance of Scripture was intimately tied to the use, structure, and syntax of language. With Barr there is a return to a sense of the text as in some way normative for and constitutive of the unity of Scripture.

But Barr is careful to point out that that sense of the unity of the Bible lies in what would now be called the "biblical narrative," not

63. This conclusion follows particularly when Hebrew Scripture is accorded its proper theological integrity.

64. It is interesting to compare Barr's approach and analysis in *Semantics* to that in his *Bible*. See esp. chap. 4 ("The Bible as Literature") in the latter work and, in *Semantics*, his analysis of the problem (chap. 1) and exploration of methodological issues (chap. 3).

in a strict semantic analysis of each word.[65] Meaning, says Barr, lies on the level of the narrative, not on the level of the word.[66] This does not mean that the meaning of individual words is not important. The interpretation of the meaning of the text within its narrative context is clearly and closely tied to the syntax and grammar of the structural components of that narrative. Where the Biblical Theology Movement sought to demonstrate the unity of Scripture based upon its analysis of key concepts, which seemed to stand apart from the text, Barr sought to stress the normative nature of the text itself.[67]

Barr's critique of the movement's use of language is coupled with a critique of what he terms the "supposed ethno-psychology of the Hebrews." According to Barr, proponents of the movement argued as though this ethno-psychology were "the key to the linguistic phenomena of Hebrew and at the same time the key to the theological understanding of the Bible." In effect, for proponents of the movement, the key to understanding the Bible lay in understanding the unique Hebrew mind. Barr continues, "It is this starting from the theoretical end, from the assurance of understanding the Hebrew mind, and working from there to its linguistic form, that causes the haphazardness of modern theological treatments of linguistic evidence."[68] The distinctiveness of Hebrew faith and later of Judaism, proponents had argued, was rooted both in the unique events of biblical history and in the unique psychological and intellectual perspective that characterized the mind of the Hebrew. In essence, Barr denied the legitimacy of this contention. In doing so, Barr called into question the movement's attempt to reconstruct the distinctive "ethno-psychology" of the Hebrew mind.

In similar fashion, the movement had argued that language was the mirror of the mind. In this case, the uniqueness of Hebrew as a language

---

65. Cf. Hans Frei, *The Eclipse of Biblical Narrative* (New Haven: Yale University Press, 1974) and *The Identity of Jesus* (Philadelphia: Fortress, 1974). Though Frei refers to the latter as his "brief theological experiment," it is nonetheless perhaps the best example of what Frei understood narrative theology to be. Cf. also Paul Ricoeur, *Essays on Biblical Interpretation* (Philadelphia: Fortress, 1980).

66. Barr, *Semantics*, 274–75, 269.

67. A similar but more pointed critique was made by Bruce Vawter, who commented: "The traditional framework in which inspiration has been considered was erected around the concept that the Bible is a catalogue of doctrines, almost a textbook of revelation . . . whose every phrase was the statement of a dogma" (*Biblical Inspiration* [London: Hutchinson, 1972], 102). See Barr's analysis and summary in *Semantics*, 263–87.

68. Barr, *Semantics*, 23; see also his critique of the linguistic analysis of Hebrew by Boman, who follows Pedersen's work closely (pp. 46–88, 30–31, 41–43).

reflected the uniqueness of the Hebrew mind. Proponents extended this analysis to contrast the Hebrew mind with the Greek.[69] Linguistic differences may well exist,[70] Barr argued, but they are not indications of innate intellectual differences. Such differences do not point to a unique "presuppositional framework" that all biblical authors held in common.[71] Linguistic differences are to be explained not in terms of mental phenomena but in terms of general linguistic theory. With Barr's critique, the mirror between language and mind was broken.

Barr's critique thus called into question the movement's contention that the Old Testament, if not the New as well, was unique in its picture of the world and in its theological content, despite external cultural influences.[72] Also, proponents had argued that the key to determining the core of concepts that gave Hebrew Scripture its uniqueness as well as its order and structure could best be determined via linguistic or historical analysis. Barr's critique, however, invalidated the movement's attempt to establish a close relationship between the mind, language, and the world. For Barr, then, biblical theology was to be done on the level not of the concept or word but of the sentence or narrative.[73] Barr seemed to propose less a biblical theology and more a narrative theology.

THE END OF THE MOVEMENT

Perhaps if this were the extent of the critique offered by its critics, the movement might have survived. It might have found an answer to challenges to its method and assumptions. Yet the demise of the movement was largely the result not of internal dissention but of external pressure. The one, insurmountable challenge that most eroded the credibility of the movement was the challenge of modernity itself, and

69. Dentan, "Unity," 155–57; Brunner, "Significance," 246–47; Smart, *Interpretation,* 178–81.

70. See Wright, "Archaizing," 453. Not all proponents of the movement shared this position. Dentan, for example, maintained that "the unity of the Old Testament is something far deeper and more significant than the mere difference of mentality between the Hebrew and the Greek" ("Unity," 156).

71. Wright, "Archaizing," 453.

72. Again, like Gilkey, Barr points to the inability of the modern mind to penetrate the intention behind and connotation of the usage and meaning of languages we no longer speak ourselves. Gilkey's approach, however, is based not on linguistic analysis (as is Barr's) but upon philosophical grounds. The conclusions, nonetheless, are remarkably similar.

73. Barr, *Semantics,* 270.

it found both concise and powerful statement in the work of Langdon Gilkey.

At the heart of Gilkey's critique of the movement was the assumption that the question of the reality of God was a distinctly modern concern. The question of the reality of God, Gilkey implies, did not—and perhaps could not—arise within the context of either Hebrew or Christian Scripture. Indeed, the whole of Scripture assumes the reality of God. Until the advent of modernity that assumption remained unquestioned and unchallenged. With the coming of age of modernity and the shift from univocal to analogical use of language, that assumption can no longer pass unquestioned. Once the question of the reality of God was raised, however, theological reflection was suspended if not rendered impossible. For Gilkey, therefore, the essential and central question of the modern age was the issue not of the meaning or unity of Scripture but of the reality of God. Once the reality of God is called into question, the issue of theological truth cannot be raised without first addressing the possibility that the word "God" has no existential referent.[74] Since theological reflection proceeds from the presence and reality of God, if this presence and reality cannot be established, then there would be no words to express the futility of theological reflection. The question of the reality of God, Gilkey argued, had to be settled before the Bible could be examined as a source of theological truth.[75]

On the one hand, Gilkey is correct. The reality of God was assumed by the movement. Once the reality of God was called in question, the movement's contentions about Scripture and about the relationship between the human and the divine no longer stood. Yet, on the other

74. Two very distinct directions have been taken after the demise of the movement. On the one hand, there is the kind of exploration of biblical narratives conducted by Frei, Ricoeur, and even David Tracy. Here the Bible is viewed as narrative, the story or explication of a particular experience of God over time, which is the vehicle of theological truth. On the other hand, there is the far less popular canonical method advocated by Childs. (See his *Old Testament Theology in a Canonical Context* [Philadelphia: Fortress, 1986]; see also G. T. Sheppard, "Canon Criticism: The Proposal of Brevard Childs and an Assessment for Evangelical Hermeneutics," *StudBT* 4 [1974]: 3–17. J. A. Sanders proposes a slightly different approach, although he uses the same name. See, for example, his *Torah and Canon* [Philadelphia: Fortress, 1972] and Childs's review in *Int* 27 [1973]: 88–91.) Both directions have their strengths, and both share their predecessor's critical weakness—they proceed from the conviction that the existence of God is a given and is the basis for theological reflection. In fact, this conviction misunderstands both the nature of the biblical experience of God and the nature of theological reflection itself.

75. Gilkey, "Secularism," 66.

hand, Gilkey is wrong with respect to the question itself. The question of the reality of God is not uniquely the child of modernity. The question of the reality of God has burned as long as human existence has been lived before death in the presence of a veiled God. Insofar as death calls all that is human into question, death calls into question the reality of a God that stands so far in the distance that its presence leaves the human condition, the facticity of our death, unchanged. As long as the face of God has been veiled, the facticity of death has overshadowed our existence. As long as death has overshadowed human existence, death itself has overshadowed the possibility that God is there in the darkness.

Thus, as long as human existence takes shape within a world that is bound by our death, on the one hand, and by the presence of a veiled God, on the other, the question of the reality of God remains inseparable from the question of what it means to be human. In the last analysis, then, the question of the reality of God is *not* the end of theological reflection but is in fact its beginning. As we shall see, reflection upon the question of the reality of God has a long history. The question burns in Nietzsche, in Camus, and even, I would argue, in Scripture itself—in the suffering and lamentation psalms, in Job, in many of the apocalyptic texts, and in Qoheleth.

Theological reflection, then, should not—and perhaps cannot—proceed from the reality behind the presence of God, since the question of the reality and existence of God remains open. The reality of God, the face behind the presence, remains veiled in the darkness, in the shadow of the presence. Once we are denied the face of God, God's presence and absence remain problematic. Theological reflection thus seems inescapably bound, not to the existence of God, but to the question that marks the relationship between the human and the divine: Why in the presence of God is there death? Theological reflection, then, proceeds from what is most deeply problematic—the reality of God and the issue of God's involvement in human existence. It is this sense of what is most deeply problematic, this struggle between meaning and absurdity in human existence, that motivates theological reflection.

The alternative, however, is not to return to, or to try to reestablish, a biblical theology that rests upon a sense of the conceptual and theological unity of Scripture. The alternative is to find a way in which the faith of Israel can still be spoken about, both because of and despite the events of the last several decades. It is the purpose of this book to offer a biblical theology that proceeds from the demise of the Biblical Theology Movement. This book will contend that the alternative to the Biblical Theology Movement need not be no theology at all. The demise of the movement and the rise of a more subtle and rich portrait of the faith of Israel need not preclude or exclude the possibility of speaking of the faith of Israel.[76] It will contend that the more complex and certainly richer understanding of the history and development of Judaism does not necessitate the abandonment of any sense of the continuity and unity of the faith of Judaism. The error of the Biblical Theology Movement was its association of theological reflection and continuity with the presence of definable theological concepts.[77]

Faith does not proceed from concepts, but from the encounter between the presence of the divine and the human. As long as this encounter occurs within the realm of human existence, it is necessarily problematic. As von Rad pointed out, for Israel that encounter was defined, shaped, and formed by Israel's relationship with YHWH. From this relationship the whole of the faith of Israel proceeded, not just as a theological concept, but primarily as a lived experience. Faith in YHWH was not extraneous to the way the people of Israel lived and died—it was essential to it. Indeed, this relationship shaped and contoured the fabric of their existence.[78]

That encounter will always be deeply problematic precisely because the divine (perhaps better put, the presence of the divine) seems to recede infinitely into the darkness, perhaps because the presence of the divine is at once elusive, oppressive, overwhelming, and yet ever able to withdraw into the darkness of hiddenness.[79] As Gilkey so rightly pointed out, before we can move to theological reflection, we must

76. The task at hand is to try to find a way in which it is possible to speak of the faith of Israel while still addressing the issues raised by contemporary historical criticism.

77. Both the canonical method and the narrative school follow closely upon the movement's basic assumptions about the structure and unity of Scripture. As a result, they are subject to the same weaknesses and to the same critique.

78. See von Rad, *Old Testament Theology*, 1:355–459, esp. 386–92 (1:385–90); Christoph Barth, *Die Errettung vom Tode in den individuellen Klage- und Dankliedern des Alten Testaments* (Basel: Evangelischer Verlag, 1947), 124–27; Childs, *Canonical Context*, 204–21.

79. See Samuel Terrien, *The Elusive Presence* (New York: Harper and Row, 1983). On oppressiveness, see James L. Crenshaw, *A Whirlpool of Torment: Israelite Traditions of God as an Oppressive Presence* (Philadelphia: Fortress, 1984). On hiddenness, see Samuel Balentine, *The Hidden God* (Oxford: Oxford University Press, 1982). See also the biblical references to the inability of humans to look at the face of God and the imagery we find in prophetic calls.

first come to terms with the issue of the reality of God itself. This, then, is our task: to seek the face of God in the darkness.

The problem is that the reality of God, whatever that reality might be and however God's face might finally appear, remains inaccessible except through the presence of God. Yet, this presence remains deeply problematic. The faces of God, so to speak, are many, and each of the faces in turn offers another side of the presence, another "piece" of the impenetrable reality, another shadow drawn from the face that stands veiled in darkness. Given the many faces of God, we cannot determine which, if any, is *the* face of God. Is the face of God dark or light? Which of the faces of God is most properly or essentially God's? Which are real, and which are an illusion? Is the darkness that veils the face of God indicative of God's absence or hiddenness? Is God really "there" in the darkness?

Insofar as we are human, we find ourselves in a world inhabited by other beings whose faces we can see and whose presence fills and often sustains our lives. To be in relationship with another, with one whose face we can see and whose presence we can touch, is to achieve a kind of intimacy with that other. In that intimacy, each being stands open to the other. Yet for Israel, that other remained veiled. The presence of that other always remained beyond the touch of the human hand. Faith in one who never reveals its face, who always steps back from the outstretched human hand, who seems to prefer silence to words, hiddenness to presence, is nearly impossible. Yet commitment to the relationship with God cannot but lead to the question of God's involvement in human existence, and to the question of the reality of the one whose presence is so eternally elusive.

two | SUFFERING, DEATH, AND THE REALITY OF GOD

Death is a cardinal validating fact of life. It stands sentinel at the end of every corridor of imagination and experience open to us, preventing our escape, turning us back on ourselves. Indifference to death makes mankind's monsters; proper attention to it, its saints. Death gave the world Christianity. If there were no death, it would be necessary for God to invent it for our salvation.

Marvin Barrett,
"Images of Death"

Is Gilkey correct in arguing that the question of the reality of God is uniquely modern? Can it be said that until the critique of Christianity offered by nineteenth-century liberalism, the reality of God had never been an issue? Is any question about the reality of God—which might arise as a result of the Holocaust, the Armenian Massacre, the genocide in Cambodia and East Africa, and the numerous wars we have endured in the last century—without parallel in earlier times? Is Gilkey right in asserting that until the question of the reality of God is in some way settled or resolved, theological reflection is not possible? Perhaps for Gilkey the answer to all of these questions is yes.

In response to the analysis offered by Gilkey and Barr (summarized in chapter 1), I would argue first that the question of the reality of God is neither uniquely modern nor especially new. Questions surrounding the reality, presence, and person of God form the core of the theological reflection of Hebrew Scripture. Second, the error that Gilkey attributes to liberal theology lies not in the liberal critique of Christianity but in the Christian appropriation of Hebrew

Scripture. That is, the starting point for orthodox theological reflection is the unquestioned assumption of the presence, accessibility, and reality of God. This confidence was not shared, I would argue, by Hebrew Scripture, where the reality of God was always deeply problematic, and the question of the accessibility, person, and presence of God central theological concerns. This question does not take shape apart from or independent of human existence but rather within it. It is part of the fabric of human existence.

That encounter is part of the fabric of human existence insofar as God was—and is—encountered in the world in the course of human existence, in the midst of suffering, death, triumph, and tragedy. Furthermore, what defined human being was its relationship to God—to be human was to be in relationship to God; almost implicitly, to be divine was to be in relationship to the human. This encounter was, we shall see, always problematic, always open to interpretation and further explication, in part because the human was always engaged in some measure of self-discovery, and in part because the God that at one moment seemed so radically present to hand[1] seemed at another to be so radically absent and distant. Explication of human existence, therefore, necessarily involved exegesis of the relationship between the divine and the human, which in turn just as necessarily raised the question of who this God was, and why at one moment this God was so radically present and in the next so radically absent.

Hence, the existence of God is most open to question and most problematic at the point where human existence itself is most open to question and most problematic (and where the relationship between the human and the divine is most vulnerable and weak)—in the presence of suffering and death. As we shall see, the awareness of one's own mortality calls into question not only human being but also the reality and the presence of God. Once the reality of God has been called into question, the possibility of establishing a relationship between the human and the divine is also held open to question. Thus, the experience of human pain and suffering is not just part of the contour of human existence. It characterizes the relationship between the human and the divine as well.[2]

---

1. Heidegger uses the phrase "present to hand" to connote a kind of intensity of presence or awareness that causes an object or another being to stand out from and in the world. "Present to hand" is here used in the fullest Heideggerian sense.
2. Walter Brueggemann offers this comment: "Human personhood in the image of . . . God always entails pain-embrace" ("A Shape for Old Testament Theology, II: Embrace of Pain," *CBQ* 47, no. 3 [July 1985]: 414).

Third, if Gilkey's analysis is correct, theological reflection is not possible until the question of the reality and of the experience of the presence of God is settled. Since this question appears to be unanswerable, for all intents and purposes theological reflection is not possible. As we have noted, our alternatives seem limited. We can proclaim the death of God, and thereby reject the possibility of faith in a God whose presence we cannot establish. In part it is an admission that faith in God is empty.[3] If life lived in light of the absence of God proves unbearable, we can continue as though the reality of God were not a problem.[4] Given the absence of proof that God is there in the darkness, we can choose to secure the tenability of faith in word, or in deed, or even in memory.[5] For Gilkey there seems to be no other alternative.

A kind of enduring paralysis remains, for we cannot justify theological reflection and establish the referent for religious language until and unless we first establish the reality of God. We cannot establish God's reality and presence, however, except by theological reflection (at least if we wish to remain within the boundaries of orthodox Christian reflection). This realization more than any other seems to have moved Altizer, Vahanian, and others to formulate what they termed "Christian Atheism." This realization also seems to have motivated Cox's formulation of "Secular Christianity." In both cases, the move is toward a Christianity that neither presupposes nor relies upon the presence of God.

In response to Gilkey's critique, I would argue that the only real alternative to the question of the reality of God need not be no theology at all and need not be the death of God. Indeed, in contrast to both the death of God, which abandons the possibility of faith in the presence

3. This is not, we shall see, what Nietzsche meant when he proclaimed the death of God. See Thomas W. Ogletree, ed., *The Death of God Controversy* (Nashville: Abingdon, 1966), esp. the essay by Thomas J. J. Altizer, "Christian Atheism," 75–108. A somewhat different approach was taken by Gabriel Vahanian. Where Altizer argued that the death of God was a theological fact (and subsequently argued that neo-orthodoxy represented a kind of gnostic response to God's death), Vahanian argued that from the perspective of life in the modern world, faith in God had no meaning; for him, the death of God was a "cultural fact." See Vahanian's *Death of God: The Culture of Our Post-Christian Era* (New York: George Braziller, 1961), 50, 139, 187–88, and also his *Wait without Idols* (New York: George Braziller, 1964), 31–36.

4. In this case the systematic theological reflection we offer would be both empty and vain.

5. This approach is the alternative explored both by the advocates of a canonical method and by those who focus on the structure and shape of biblical narrative.

of the problematic nature of the person of God, and the assertion of God's presence despite all experience to the contrary, which orthodoxy in all of its historical forms seems to offer, there is another alternative—a theology that takes as its starting point the problematic presence of God. I would argue that the theological reflection that one finds in Hebrew Scripture presupposes, or rests upon, not the assumed presence and reality of God, but the often ambiguous, vague, mysterious, inaccessible, elusive, and hidden God, a God whose faces are many and whose "being" is one, a God whose presence, accessibility, and reality are always problematic and open to question.[6]

This point, however, must be conceded. The issue of the presence and reality of God has reemerged in our time with a force not heard for centuries. The reemergence of theodicy as perhaps the central theological problem for modernity has raised the possibility that if there was a God, faith in it would no longer be tenable or justifiable. It remains for us to establish, first, that the theodicy question is not unique to our age; indeed, "the experience of God's hiddenness, just as the experience of his presence, is an integral part of Israelite faith. Both experiences derive from the nature of God himself."[7] Second, this question is not the end of theological reflection but rather is its beginning. Third, the experience of suffering and death, and thus the experience of the absence and hiddenness of God, is the foundation for theological reflection. Fourth, the person, presence, and face of God offer as enduring a dilemma as the experience of mortality itself—an experience that calls into question not only our humanity but also the reality of and faith in God. The question thus becomes, Why in the presence of God is there death?

ELUSIVE PRESENCE

The hiddenness of God has been the subject of two major studies: *The Elusive Presence*, by Samuel Terrien,[8] and *The Hidden God*, by Samuel Balentine. Terrien offers an intricate and detailed examination of what he terms the *Deus Absconditus,* which is, according to Terrien, the

---

6. As we shall see, Terrien argues that the hiddenness of God is inseparable from the presence of God.

7. Samuel Balentine, *The Hidden God* (Oxford: Oxford University Press, 1982), 172.

8. Samuel Terrien, *The Elusive Presence* (New York: Harper and Row, 1983).

hidden God.[9] The difficulty, as far as Terrien is concerned, is that the God that hides itself is actually not hidden—if hidden is taken to mean absent. The presence of God endures, even in God's hiddenness. According to Terrien, "*Deus absconditus,* 'the hidden God,'" may fail to convey the meaning of active and sustained determination which the Hebrew original carries. For the prophet, there is no doubt that the God who hides his face is very much alive. During the eclipse of God, the man of faith formulates a theology of hope. . . . The presence which conceals itself is not an absence."[10] Thus, for Terrien, we should not speak about the hiddenness of God but about a presence that is self-concealing. This presence is elusive, moving first to disclose and then to conceal itself. The moment of disclosure and the moment of concealment often cannot be separated. Furthermore, Terrien argues that the very elusiveness of God serves not to obscure or conceal the person and presence of God but rather as the vehicle of God's self-disclosure. Of the psalmists and their search for God, Terrien writes, "By evading [the pleas of the psalmists] . . . God became more and more manifest to them. . . . It was that very hiding which disclosed to them not only the meaning of their existence but also the intrinsic quality of divinity. The God of the psalmists made them live in this world, and they lived without using him. *It is when man tries to grasp him that God veils himself. The Deus revelatus is the Deus absconditus.*"[11]

The absence or self-concealment of God offers the human the fullest picture of who and what this God is. Biblical faith, then, is by its nature paradoxical: the presence of God, which ought to reveal, conceals; the absence of God, which ought to conceal, reveals. The kind of haunting, elusive, ethereal presence that is God calls us into the darkness that enshrouds its presence. And in that darkness, God opens itself to us. For Terrien, this affirmation of the presence of an absence is an affirmation of the *activity* of God's self-concealment. This affirmation is "a necessary corollary of a belief in God's presence," which

9. It is of interest to note that Terrien begins his book with this quotation from Pascal: "A religion which does not affirm that God is hidden is not true. *Vere tu es Deus absconditus!*"
10. Ibid., 251.
11. Ibid., 325–26 (emphasis added). Terrien, after asserting the mystery of God's presence in absence and the self-concealment of God as the vehicle of its self-disclosure, is quick to support the more traditional approaches to Job and Qoheleth, which see the one as an agnostic and the other as an atheistic response to the hiddenness of God. I would argue that Terrien's own analysis should prevent him from reaching these conclusions (see 361–80).

reflects and maintains the Hebraic understanding of the hiddenness of God as a sign of God's sovereignty and freedom.[12]

HIDDEN GOD

While Balentine finds much to praise in Terrien's work (pp. 174–75),[13] he concludes that on one point at least, Terrien has come up short. Terrien, says Balentine, "has perhaps been too ready to follow the traditional understanding that God's hiding is always and in every case a response to sin" (p. 175).[14] I would take Balentine's critique a step further. Certainly Terrien is correct in asserting that the Hebrew verb *satar*, "to hide," does appear in the hithpa'el, or reflexive, form and in the hiphil, or causative. Terrien is correct in concluding that it is best in light of the grammatical structure of the Hebrew to conclude that God is not hidden—rather, God hides itself; God causes itself to be hidden. While, as the prophets remind Israel, God can hide itself in response to human transgressions, God's hiddenness is not always a response to human transgressions. Accordingly, Balentine argues, "God's hiddenness is not primarily related to his punishment for disobedience. It is not basically a reflection of man's inability to understand or even perceive God's presence in the world. It is manifest in both these ways but is not restricted to them. It is rather an integral part of the nature of God that is not to be explained away by theological exposition of human failures or human limitations. God is hidden, just as he is present" (p. 175).

Neither can it be argued that the experience of God's hiding itself and withdrawing into the darkness necessarily or inevitably lends itself to a further revelation of the divine presence as such. Indeed, if the

---

12. Ibid., 251; Balentine, *Hidden God*, 174. Similar analyses have been offered by others; see, for example, several works by James L. Crenshaw: "In Search of Divine Presence (Some Remarks Preliminary to a Theology of Wisdom)," *RevExp* 74 (1977): 353–69; "The Birth of Skepticism in Ancient Israel," in *The Divine Helmsman: Studies on God's Control of Human Events, Presented to Lou H. Silberman*, ed. Crenshaw and Samuel Sandmel (New York: KTAV, 1980), 1–19; *A Whirlpool of Torment: Israelite Traditions of God as an Oppressive Presence* (Philadelphia: Fortress, 1984), esp. the conclusion; and *Theodicy in the Old Testament* (Philadelphia: Fortress, 1983), esp. the introduction. See also W. Lee Humphreys, *The Tragic Vision and the Hebrew Tradition* (Philadelphia: Fortress, 1985), esp. 79–83, 131–33; and Kornelius Miskotte, *When the Gods Are Silent* (New York: Harper and Row, 1967).

13. In this section, page references in the text are to Balentine, *Hidden God*.

14. Note that in the same passage Balentine is also very critical of Terrien's understanding of the image of God's hiding its face.

absence of God or God's self-concealment were simply a matter of
punishment for transgressions or of the limitations of human understanding, the force of Job's lament, the power of Qoheleth's questions,
and the cry of the psalmists in the presence of suffering and death
would be stilled—if not by the reemergence of God from the darkness,
then by human prayer and supplication.

In either case, the absence of God would always be indicative of
God's willful withdrawal of itself into the darkness in the face of human
frailty, but under no circumstances would God's hiddenness imply or
raise the possibility that God was not in some way "there" in the
darkness. In such a framework, the reality of God, as Gilkey would
put it, would never be open to question. For Terrien, in Hebrew
Scripture, in what has often been referred to as "the faith of Israel,"
the presence and reality of God was never actually an issue. Even in
exile and suffering, confidence in the presence and reality of God
endured. Only in our time was this confidence broken. And with its
passing, the question of the reality of God became very real for us.

In response to Terrien, Balentine has argued, first, that the problem
of God's hiddenness is an essential part of Israel's faith (pp. 171, 173).

Second, while some historical circumstances may have deepened
the awareness of God's hiddenness and the extent to which God could
hide itself, these experiences must be examined not in isolation but in
the larger context of which they are a part (p. 171). Presumably that
context is provided by the whole of the theological reflection that
constitutes what might be termed the faith of Israel.

Third, though expressed in a variety of ways in the various *Gat-
tungen* of Hebrew Scripture, the problem of God's hiddenness finds
expression "in virtually every stratum of the Old Testament" (p. 171).
Balentine writes: "Israel's struggle with God's hiddenness ought not
to be treated as if it were merely a footnote to an otherwise optimistic
and unshakeable faith. . . . Israel was repeatedly plagued by the experience of God's hiddenness. Time and again the disparity between
religious convictions and the realities of actual experience brought the
issue into the forefront of Israel's thought" (pp. 171–72).

Fourth, the dilemma of faith is that the God that is at once near
and present is the very God that at the next moment is distant and
withdrawn. The one is not distinct from the other. Both presence and
hiddenness are aspects of God. The classic interpretation, offered in
prophetic texts and supported by Terrien's analysis, counters this dilemma by attaching the hiddenness of God to human transgression.

However, the classic interpretation breaks down at the point where God's absence appears without warrant, at the point where the innocent, the righteous, the just, all suffer and die despite—or even because of—their innocence, righteousness, and justness. Here God's hiddenness exceeds human comprehensibility (p. 172). In a sense, then, the dilemma is not so much God's hiddenness as it is God's hiddenness in the presence of human suffering. For human suffering intensifies the possibility that God's hiddenness may transcend the moment—God might remain hidden forever (p. 120).

Finally, only when the hiddenness of God is seen as a primary and not a secondary dilemma can the importance of the hiddenness of God for the faith of Israel be seen (p. 172).

Balentine supports his argument through a detailed grammatical analysis of biblical passages where the theme of the hiddenness of God occurs. Balentine notes that there are fifty-five references to God hiding (p. 9). Fourteen references are to God's hiding someone,[15] eight to God's hiding something.[16] The remaining thirty-three are all references to God's hiding itself. Of these, seven are concerned with God's hiding itself,[17] and twenty-six refer in general to God's hiding its face.[18] Five different verbs are used in all these occurrences: satar, haba>, sapan, kahad, and ʿalam.[19]

Only one of these five verbs is found in passages that refer to God's hiding its face: satar. Of all of the occurrences of the root satar with reference to God's hiding itself, one of the most important is found in Isaiah 45:15: "Certainly, you are a God that hides itself." Here the verb is also satar, but the form is the hithpaʿel, or reflexive,[20] and while

15. Ps. 17:8; 27:5 (bis); 31:21 (20bis); 64:3(2); Isa. 49:2 (bis); Jer. 36:26; Job 14:13 (bis); Exod. 23:23; 2 Chron. 32:21; Zech. 11:8 (where the Hebrew and English versifications differ, the English is given in parentheses).

16. Ps. 31:20(19); 119:19; Prov. 2:7; 23:2; 2 Kings 4:27; Job 10:13; 21:19; 24:1.

17. Ps. 10:1; 55:2(1); 89:47(46); Isa. 1:15; (eyes); 45:15; 57:17; Lam. 3:56 (ears).

18. Deut. 31:17-18; 32:20; Ps. 10:11; 13:2(1); 22:25(24); 27:9; 30:8(7); 44:25(24); 51:11(9); 69:18(17); 88:15(14); 102:3(2); 104:29; 143:7; Isa. 8:17; 54:8; 59:2; 64:6(7); Ezek. 39:23, 24, 29; Mic. 3:4; Jer. 33:5; Job 13:24; 34:29. Three of these occurrences, Ps. 10:11, 13:2, 44:25, according to Balentine, suggest that God's hiddenness is a kind of forgetting. In this sense, forgetting is a rejection of Israel by God. See Balentine, Hidden God, 136, 142–47).

19. While all these verbs mean "hide," two have slightly different connotations: haba> also means "withdraw," and ʿalam also means "conceal."

20. This is the only occurrence of satar with reference to God's hiddenness that is in the hithpaʿel; all others are in the hiphil. For a summary of the use and form of the hithpaʿel, see Gesenius, Kautzsch, and Cowley, Hebrew Grammar, 2d ed. (London: Oxford University Press, 1980), sec. 54. An analysis of the hiphil appears in sec. 53.

there is no exact translation that can be offered in English, the emphasis is clearly on the reflexive. YHWH is characterized by Isaiah as a God that conceals itself. God's hiddenness is a consequence of God's own actions. God chooses to be hidden—or more precisely, God chooses to hide itself. In a more literal translation, Isaiah 45:15 could be rendered, "Certainly, you are a God that has hidden itself," or "Certainly, you are a God that has made itself hidden."

All other occurrences of *satar* are in the hiphil, or causative. In these other occurrences, the hiphil stresses God's hiddenness as a consequence of God's own actions. That is, God causes itself to be hidden. Of those thirty-three references to the hiddenness of God, only one verb other than *satar* is used. *Alam* is used only four times and only with reference to God's hiding itself.[21] It is not used with reference to God's hiding its face.

Although the verb *satar* occurs more than any of these other verbs (thirty-eight times, to be exact), the number of its occurrences is less important than its connotation: withdrawal, isolation, willful concealment, covering oneself over, hiding oneself in darkness. The implications are enormous: God is hidden because God has willfully turned away, intentionally concealed itself and turned its back. YHWH has purposefully withdrawn into the darkness, covered its face, and chosen to isolate itself from Israel.[22]

HIDDENNESS AND RECIPROCITY

More important, however, than YHWH's simply hiding itself or deliberately withdrawing into the darkness of concealment is the image of YHWH's hiding its face. Once again let us note that of the thirty-three references to God's hiding itself, twenty-six are references to God's hiding its face. In itself, the image of the face of God is of great importance in Hebrew Scripture. The word for face and presence in Hebrew is the same—*panim*.[23] This noun has as its root the verb *panah*,

---

21. Ps. 10:1; 55:2(1); Isa. 1:15; Lam. 3:56.

22. L. Koehler and W. Baumgartner, *Lexicon in Veteris Testamenti Libros* (Leiden: E. J. Brill, 1958), 668 (hereafter referred to as K-B). The translation "God hides" or "God withdraws its face" is offered for the following references: Deut. 31:17-18; 32:20; Isa. 8:17; 54:8; 57:17; 59:2; 64:6; Jer. 33:5; Ezek. 39:23-29; Mic. 3:4; Ps. 10:11; 13:2; 22:25; 27:9; 30:8; 44:25; 51:11; 69:18; 88:15; 102:3; 104:29; 143:7; Job 13:24; 34:29.

23. F. Brown, S. R. Driver, and C. A. Briggs, *A Hebrew and English Lexicon* (Oxford: Oxford University Press, 1980), 815d–816c (hereafter referred to as BDB); K-B, 766–67: the side turned toward one, the face, the visible side, the self, or the person's presence. Although the grammatical form of the word is plural, the meaning is singular.

which means "to turn," "to turn toward," "to turn and look."[24] To
see a face is literally to turn and look at another, to turn toward the
other. Moreover, this turning-in-order-to-look implies relationship.
For to turn toward the other in order to look upon the face of the
other is at the same time to let oneself be seen. To look upon another
is to be looked upon by another.[25] There is, therefore, a kind of
reciprocity implied in the word *panim*. To desire to look upon another
is to offer oneself to the eyes of the other.

In the case of Israel's relationship to YHWH, much the same reciprocity applies. That is, Israel's experience of being chosen by YHWH
is an experience of being looked upon by God. Being looked at by
another implies that there is an other there looking. This other in turn
can be looked upon. To be chosen, in this sense, is more than being
chosen to be looked upon by God. To be chosen also implicitly means
that one is chosen to look upon the face of God. To look upon the
face of God is to stand there "face to face," as it were, and to see the
other as the other is. To stand there face to face with the other is to
be both in the presence of and present to the other. For Israel, the face
of YHWH was the breath of life, and the presence of YHWH its
sustenance.

But Israel did not experience the reciprocity implied in its having
been chosen by God. The face of God remained elusive. This elusiveness was not a consequence of human transgressions because
YHWH chose to remain veiled in darkness and shrouded in mystery.
Mystery and darkness preclude knowledge and engender uncertainty,
ambiguity, distress—even infidelity. As long as YHWH remains in the
darkness and its face hidden from view, Israel cannot be certain that
anyone is really there, or, if someone is there, who or what that
someone might be.

Consider, for example, Exodus 33:12-23. In an effort to see the
face of YHWH, Moses says, "Show me your glory, I beg you." YHWH
replies: "I will let my splendor pass in front of you, and I will pronounce
the name of YHWH before you; . . . I will show pity to whom I
please. You cannot see my face, for no human being can see my face
and live. . . . Here is a place beside me, and when my glory passes
by, I will put you in a cleft of the rock and shield you with my hand

24. BDB, 815a–c; K-B, 765b–d.
25. In this sense Buber's I-Thou relationship takes as its starting point the Hebrew
concept of face.

as I pass by. Then I will take away my hand and you will see the back of me; but my face is not to be seen."

Here we are brought to what might be the fundamental paradox that underlies the Hebrew Scripture. To be human is to be, to exist, before and in the presence of God, to turn one's face toward God. To be human is to be turned toward God. This turning in order to see the face of God is to allow oneself to be seen by God. Human being is always turned toward God and present to God. The human face is always open, accessible, able to be seen. The presence of the human before the divine is thus always unmediated. Israel is naked before God.[26]

The presence of God, in contrast, is always mediated. Israel never stands directly before God or directly looks upon the face of God. Like Moses, Israel does not see the face of God, only God's glory (Ezek. 1:38). For that matter, only the presence of God is made accessible in God's rage and anger, or through the mediation of Torah or the "word" of YHWH, or even through the intervention and mediation of the prophets (see, e.g., Jer. 1:4; Ezek. 1:3; Hos. 1:1). To this paradox there is still another dimension. However elusive, mysterious, or hidden the face of God might be, both the face and the presence of God are the lifeblood, the sustaining force of Israel. There is no life apart from YHWH. "Turn your face away," wrote the psalmist, "and they suffer; you stop their breath, and they die and revert to dust" (Ps. 104:28-29).[27]

This passion for the presence of God is sustained in Scripture. For example Psalm 80 reads, "The God Sabaoth will restore us; make your face shine, and we will be delivered" (v. 8[7]). There are several interesting points of contrast throughout this psalm. The central point of contrast is the face of YHWH as both the source of life or deliverance and the vehicle of YHWH's vengeance. Note verse 17(16): "What has been cut away[28] is burned with fire by the rebuke of your face." This image of vengeance is contrasted with the image of Israel as the vine of YHWH. Here YHWH, the one who planted the vine, is the one who sustains it. The image of the face of YHWH as the source of the vine's sustenance and life seems clear.[29] A similar contrast can be found in Psalm 102. The connection between God's hiding its face and the

26. The imagery of Gen. 3:8-13 is deliberately alluded to here.
27. See also Exod. 33:18-23; Hos. 5:5; Ps. 13:2(1); 69:17; 88:15(14); 102:2-3(1-2).
28. See K-B, 447b; BDB, 492d.
29. See the refrain quoted above, as well as vv. 4, 15-16, and 20 (3, 14-15, 19).

movement toward death is clear.[30] Here, however, it is not the face of YHWH but the return of YHWH's glory that restores life.[31] The connection between the presence of God and life is made even more explicit in Deuteronomy: "Humans live on all that comes from the mouth of God" (8:3).[32] In the presence of YHWH there is life. In the hiddenness of the face of God, there is death.[33]

Here the paradox reaches a kind of climax. That which defines human being, bestows life, and offers protection from oppression (and which Israel longs for) always remains hidden. Thus to turn toward the face of YHWH is to turn toward the darkness, toward the mystery, toward the elusive presence. That turning toward the darkness in response to the call from God, or in order to call to God, has two dimensions. First, to look into the darkness is to look in order to find the face that will finally end the mystery and the darkness. Second, to look into the darkness is to look in order to see if anyone or anything is really there in the darkness. Yet if God is there, God remains veiled in the darkness.

The very darkness that is intended to protect the human from the overpowering presence of the face of God[34] becomes that which conceals, hides, obscures both the face and faith, both the human and the divine, both the presence and the darkness. The God that calls Israel to faith and that chooses to remain hidden in darkness nonetheless calls Israel to believe and to be faithful, despite the darkness, the shadows, and the concealment.

Yet behind the darkness hides the sustaining presence that gives life and that is turned toward Israel. Behind the presence hides the face that sustains, breathes life, and turns and looks upon Israel from out of the darkness. The face that is concealed within the darkness is nonetheless there. In this way, more than Torah, the word, or the glory and "mighty acts" of God, the presence of YHWH is mediated by the darkness that veils its face. In hearing the call, Israel knows that it has been called by someone, that someone is there in and speaks from the darkness. Someone loves, bestows life, and calls to the heart of Israel. And despite the darkness, someone is there. Here, as Terrien has argued, hiddenness is not absence. It is concealment.

---

30. Contrast vv. 2-3(1-2) and 17-18(16-17).
31. Also see Ps. 13; 88:14-19 (13-18); Hos. 5:15.
32. See also Deut. 32:15-43, esp. v. 39: "It is I who deal death and life." Also see the law of the heart in 30:6-20.
33. See Deut. 31:17-18.
34. Exod. 20:19; 33:19-21; no human could look upon the face of God and live.

THE OTHER SIDE OF DARKNESS

There is, however, another side to this hiddenness, for there are times when the darkness does more than conceal that face upon which no human being can look. At times the darkness points not to the hiddenness of one who is concealed but to the possibility that the one who was once there is no longer there in the darkness. Sometimes the darkness that covers the face of God points to a twofold possibility: Either the one who was once there is now absent and in absence has forsaken or forgotten those to whom it once extended its love and to whom it turned its face, or no one was ever there. Both of these possibilities call faith in God into question.

It is clear that the experience of forsakenness was powerful. This experience, as Balentine notes,[35] was akin to the experience of forgottenness. Three of the passages that refer to God's hiding its face also refer to God's having forgotten Israel.[36] That is, in each of these three passages, there is a parallel drawn between YHWH's hiddenness and Israel's experience of forgottenness. The same verb is used in each of these passages: *shakah,* "to forget," "to cease to care about."[37] As Balentine notes, "God's hiding and his forgetting are two aspects of the same lament."[38] Inasmuch as God's presence sustains life, as though God calls to mind or keeps in mind or keeps in sight those who live,[39] God's hiddenness seems to be accompanied by a kind of forgetting or no longer caring that is accompanied by the experience of abandonment and forsakenness.

The experience of abandonment seems most acute at the point where life itself is most open to question: in the presence of death and suffering. For in the presence of suffering and death the sense that one has been forgotten and abandoned by God, that God has ceased to care and has removed its sustaining presence, is likewise most acute.[40]

---

35. Balentine, *Hidden God,* 136–37.
36. Ps. 10:11; 13:2(1); 44:25(24).
37. K-B, 968d–969b.
38. Balentine, *Hidden God,* 136.
39. The Hebrew verb *zakar* means "call to mind; remember" (K-B, 255d–257a); see Balentine, *Hidden God,* 136–37. Brevard S. Childs, *Memory and Tradition in Israel* (London: SMC, 1962), offers an extensive examination of memory and remembering.
40. Here it is helpful to note the wide semantic range of four Hebrew verbs usually translated by some form of the English "forgotten" or "abandoned": *ma'as,* "reject; despise" (K-B, 490b–d; BDB, 549b–c; see Job 8:20; 10:3; Lam. 5:22; as a passive participle, it may also mean worthless); *rahaq,* "withdraw; be or become distant" (K-B, 887c–888a; BDB, 934d–935b; Job 13:21; 19:13; Ps. 22:12, 20; 38:22-23; 35:22; 71:12;

If the face and presence of YHWH sustain and promote life, then the hiddenness of God abandons the living to death.[41] The trauma of death is not, as we might expect, the expectation that life will cease. Rather, the trauma of death lies in the belief that the dead suffer a kind of eternal forgottenness, an eternal dispersion into the darkness of nothingness filled by the absence of God. Once forgotten, the dead no longer abide in the presence of God; unlike the living, who live in the hope of seeing the face of God, the dead have no hope. There is no hope that they may be saved from the snares of death. The dead have no life and thus no hope. They are forever cut off from the possibility of seeing the face of God. And in death, "that presence is not experienced. The dead have no experience either of God or of anything else. They are shadows gone from the scene where God and man are related."[42]

In death the face of God is totally darkened.[43] Death appears to overtake the living when the face of God becomes hidden and darkened. It is because the face of God has turned away from the living that the just and the unjust alike die. Furthermore, that darkness and hiddenness extend beyond the actual moment of death. Those who are dead are cut off from the possibility of standing in the presence of God. The face that in life turns toward the human, in death seems to turn away forever.

As Balentine notes, the verb *shakah* occurs over one hundred times in Hebrew Scripture. Of these occurrences, God is the subject in seventeen. Most of these occurrences are in the Psalms and in prayers that share themes similar to the Psalms.[44] *Shakah* seems to be used in

88:9, 19; 103:12); *zanah,* "reject; spurn" (K-B, 262a–b; BDB, 276b; Ps. 43:2; 60:3; 77:8; 88:15; Zech. 10:6); and *ʿahab,* "leave, leave behind; loose; forsake" (K-B, 693b–694a; BDB, 736d–737d; Lam. 5:20; Ezra 9:9; Neh. 9:17, 19, 28, 31; 1 Chron. 12:5; 15:2; 24:20; 32:31; Ps. 38:22-23; besides the meanings cited, *ʿahab* also can mean "let go, set free; give up, entrust [in the sense of abandoning one's legal rights to another]").

41. See Lou H. Silberman, "Death in the Hebrew Bible and Apocalyptic Literature," in *Perspectives on Death,* ed. Liston O. Mills (Nashville: Abingdon, 1969), esp. 21ff. "The dead," writes Silberman, "are the echo of life; they are not part of creation but its shadow" (p. 25).

42. Silberman, "Death," 25.

43. Job 7:21 offers an interesting comment on the separation between God and the dead: "It will not be long before I lie in the earth; then you will look for me, but I shall be no more." See also Ps. 13:4–6(3-5). "Come back YHWH, rescue me. Save me if you love me, for in death there is no remembrance of you" (Ps. 6:5-6 [4-5]) indicates that not only were the dead forgotten by God, God was also forgotten by the dead.

44. Balentine, *Hidden God,* 137; see Ps. 9:13(12); 10:11-12; 13:2(1); 42:10(9); 44:25(24); 74:19, 23; 77:10(9); 1 Sam. 1:11; Lam. 2:6; 5:20.

two different contexts. In the prophetic texts, *shakah* is used in the context of the announcement of judgment or promise. In the Psalms, it is used in the context of individual or communal lament.[45] In the psalms of lament, the verb is used in three contexts. The first, according to Balentine, takes the form of a question directed to God. The second Balentine characterizes as a "negative imperative."[46]

Typically, the questions addressed to God in the psalms of lament ask about both the reason why God has abandoned Israel and how long the abandonment will last.[47] The questions go unanswered. What is clear, says Balentine, "is that God's forgetting is perceived as another dimension of his hiddenness, and as such is lamented and protested against in much the same way. . . . God's forgetting, forsaking, hiding are all part of a similar lament in which the suppliant protests against his experience of the aloofness of God."[48] As a negative imperative, *shakah* is a protest against the apparent open-ended abandonment the suppliant suffers.[49]

The third context centers on a kind of assurance that God, despite all evidence to the contrary, has not forgotten the faithful. This form is usually found in the context of a psalm of thanksgiving, in which the community that had been abandoned by God now in return from exile offers its thanksgiving. Such psalms offer the reassurance that the suffering of the community, including its exile and abandonment, has been overcome by a return of the presence of God.

ABANDONMENT

The metaphor of abandonment, then, evokes a myriad of images and feelings: desertion, anger, hate, bitter rejection, loneliness, forgotten-ness, despair, rejection, and forsakenness. Most of all, however, the metaphor of abandonment calls to mind the image of God's turning its face away, of God's pulling the darkness over its face as one would pull a cloak over one's head in order to conceal oneself. The metaphor of abandonment also awakens the image of desolation that often dom-inates the descriptions of Jerusalem after judgment.[50]

45. Balentine, *Hidden God,* 137.
46. A "negative imperative" would take the form "Do not forget. . . ."
47. Ps. 13:2(1); 89:47(46); 94:3; Lam. 5:20; Exod. 33:18-23; Hos. 5:15.
48. Balentine, *Hidden God,* 137.
49. See, for example, Ps. 10:12; 74:19, 23.
50. The most moving descriptions of abandonment can be found throughout Lam-entations and in Ps. 88.

Abandonment by YHWH leads to destruction, death, emptiness, and exile. Moreover, it leads to a destruction of all that is human since, once deprived of the presence of God, human being is deprived both of its humanity and its very breath of life.[51] For to be human is to be in relationship to God, to draw one's sustenance from the presence of God. Furthermore, to be human is to love and be loved by God. Without the love of God, human being is given over to suffering and death. Death is all the more unbearable, not because existence is brought to an end, but because in death there is only forgottenness. In death, the love and face of God are no longer accessible.

Unanswered in the experience of abandonment is the question of God's involvement in human suffering and death. Also unanswered is how long the faithful will have to endure an abandonment that, for all intents and purposes, is unwarranted by human actions.[52] According to Balentine's analysis, in these laments, which ponder the presence of suffering that appears without warrant and cause, the faithful challenge the God whose hiddenness is the source of the current circumstances.[53] The suppliant's questions are answered only by God's continued silence.

WHY?

Several issues need to be addressed here. First, is Balentine's analysis of these laments correct? Are these laments challenges? Second, how is God's silence in the presence of human suffering to be understood? With regard to Balentine's analysis, I would argue, first, that the semantic range of the interrogative *lamah* is much broader than his translation allows. Second, an examination of the broader semantic range of this interrogative offers an insight into aspects—both of the

51. The word *nephesh* is difficult to translate. Usually it is rendered in English by the word "soul." Such a translation, however, interjects explicitly Christian theological categories that cannot be supported within the context of Hebrew Scripture. Here it is translated with the phrase "Breath of Life." Like the Greek *psychē* or the Latin *anima*, *nephesh* is that which distinguishes an animate being from an inanimate object as well as the living from the dead. In death the *nephesh* is disembodied, freed—or condemned—to wander among the shadows in Sheol. It is thus forever cut off from the living and from God and endures a kind of eternal forsakenness and abandonment in forgottenness. See Ps. 88:6, 12(5, 11).

52. See, for example, Ps. 10:1; 44:24(23); 89:47, 50(46, 49); 119:84; Exod. 5:22; 32:11; Num. 11:11, 16. See also Balentine, *Hidden God,* 117. Job is a textbook case of the suffering of the innocent.

53. Balentine, *Hidden God,* 117.

questions addressed to God in these laments and of the involvement of YHWH in human suffering—that are not accessible through Balentine's analysis. Third, at the point where these questions are most acute and God's silence and hiddenness most pronounced, questions about the tenability of faith and the reality of God are themselves most pronounced.

Balentine is certainly correct in translating *lamah* by the English interrogative "why." Balentine, however, seems to miss much of the force of the use of this interrogative in Hebrew Scripture. To ask *lamah* of God is indeed to ask why God has chosen to remain silent. More is at stake, however. To ask God why God is silent is to place the issue of human suffering before and in front of God. To ask God why humans suffer and die is to ask for what reason, for what purpose, to what end, God has chosen to hide itself in darkness. Thus, to ask God why it has chosen to hide itself is also to ask what reason or purpose hiddenness fulfills, or even to what end God has chosen hiddenness. To ask God to disclose the reason God has hidden itself is to ask God to put human suffering into perspective by providing access to the reason for God's hiddenness. In effect, the experience of human suffering becomes tied to the issue of divine responsibility.

Lamah, again as Balentine notes, is a cry of lament. If nothing more, it is a lament in the presence of the incomprehensibility and hiddenness, not only of God's ways, but of God's face and presence as well. *Lamah* is also, in the context of a lament, a protest against God's silence and hiddenness, against what for all intents and purposes seems to be unjust suffering and torment. For the righteous, as paradigmatically for Job, suffering and death would be bearable if only God's reason for subjecting them to their agony were known. Yet it seems that even when revealed, that reason remains incomprehensible.

This is the power of the theophany at the end of Job. Job's questions remain unanswered. Or if they are answered, the answer escapes human reason and comprehension. But Job seems to rest comforted that however incomprehensible God's reason might be, a reason nonetheless exists. In this sense, the presence of God resolves Job's dilemma. But the presence of God leaves unexplained the reason why Job suffered. As long as the problem of the suffering of the innocent remains open, so too does the death question. As long as the death question remains open, it presses against the reality of God.

Furthermore, however much Job is comforted by the presence of God, that presence does not soften the issue of God's involvement in human suffering and death. In the face of suffering that appears to be without reason, the absence of God or God's silence raises the possibility that God's silence and hiddenness are deliberate, that human suffering and death are wrought intentionally by the hand of God. If God cannot provide the reason why humans suffer and die, a reason that would justify the presence of suffering and death, then God would appear to be responsible for human suffering and death.

The God that chooses to be silent in the presence of suffering and death is a God whose face is darkened by our agony and whose hands are covered with our blood. If the face of God is darkened by our suffering, a God whose reason and purpose is unknown to us, the faithful cannot but protest God's injustice, hiddenness, and absence. Yet inasmuch as this lament is a protest against God's silence, it is also a call to God to come out of the darkness that God might absolve itself of complicity in our suffering and tragedy. For only God can absolve itself of complicity in our suffering. Only God can put human suffering into perspective. Only God can provide the context within which our suffering and death are comprehensible—or at least bearable. And only the emergence of God from the darkness can establish once and for all the reality of the one who is hidden.

THE SUSTAINED SILENCE

Yet despite the lament, the call, and even the protest, the silence of God endures. In the endurance of this silence the reality of God becomes an unresolvable problem. Faced with an experience of suffering and death that seems without reason, and given the apparent silence of God, there are three responses that one can have: First, one can say, as we find in Proverbs and elsewhere, that no one is righteous before the law, that no human can love God with purity of heart.[54] Here one can affirm the freedom of God, even though it inevitably costs us our life. Second, one can refuse to accept God's silence as a sign of one's guilt and as a mark of transgressions as yet unknown. That is, one can proclaim one's innocence, although one's suffering points to the contrary. A God who punishes the just as well as the unjust, the righteous and the wicked, the faithful and the unfaithful, is a God in whom it is difficult, if not impossible, to believe. Or, third, one can raise the possibility that the silence of God is indicative not of God's hiddenness but of God's absence.

54. See Job 4:6-7; Prov. 20:9; Ps. 19:13(12).

If one refuses to accept the relationship between one's suffering and guilt, then one can only proclaim one's innocence and protest one's suffering. If God remains silent in the presence of this proclamation and protest, then the question of the reality of God remains open and the mystery of God's silence cannot be resolved. Either God is not there, and God's hiddenness is really absence, or the God who is there is a cruel, angry, brutal God that seems to relish human suffering. Either God is absent, or God is implicated in, if not responsible for, our death. Furthermore, a God whose law cannot be fulfilled and whose presence and law oppress is a God too dark to believe in. Either God is an illusion, or God is our murderer. In either case, both faith in and the existence of God are called into question.

The problem, then, is that only God can resolve the tension between our experience of its hiddenness and its absence, between our suffering and our innocence, between our death and its presence, but for whatever reason, God remains veiled in silence. The reality of God, then, is an issue wherever and whenever humans suffer and die in innocence in the presence of a silent God. Israel's lament and protest against the hiddenness and silence of God calls God to strip away the darkness and end the tragedy of our suffering. Yet so long as the silence endures, we do not know whether the silence is because God is hidden or because there is no God there. So long as God is silent, we do not know whether we suffer by the hand of God or by God's absence. We do not know whether the face of God is darkened by our suffering or enlightened by our lives.

Against the backdrop of human suffering and death and the paradox of presence and hiddenness, the faces of God appear to be many. Which is the God of Israel? The warrior *YHWH Sabaoth*? The angry, bitter, punishing, and vengeful God of the prophets? The lustful, jealous God, who cannot be served?[55] The God whose loving-kindness extends life to the faithful?[56] The God of wisdom and truth? The hidden God?

55. See Josh. 24:19. Here YHWH is characterized as *El qanno'*. *Qanno'* has been variously translated, with the most common English words being "zealous" and "jealous." Of these two alternatives, "jealous" seems closer to the portrayal of YHWH as a God whose passion and love for Israel was often unrequited. That is, however much Israel loved YHWH, that love was not enough. Such an inability to satisfy God's desire seemed to fuel YHWH's rage and jealousy to the point where that jealousy was a lust after Israel's heart. The rage and fury that often seems to have no cause, the suffering of the innocent and the righteous at the hand of God, point to a God whose love has turned to jealousy, and whose jealousy has turned to rage and lust.

56. The Hebrew word used here is *hesed*. This word can not be translated by a simple word in English. It seems to mean something like "loving-kindness," "steadfast love," "compassionate mercy," or perhaps "gentle kindness." See Isa. 54:6-8.

YHWH is all of these. While God is one, the faces of God are many. Amid the multiplicity of faces the presence of God recedes infinitely into the darkness, ever further from the touch of a human hand.[57]

The theological reflection that we find in Hebrew Scripture, then, is marked by an ongoing exegesis of human existence as it is lived in the presence of an ambiguous God. This exegesis takes shape around that existence as it is lived both in the world and in relationship to a God that is at once present and absent, loving and lustful, vengeful and forgiving. To be human, then, is to exist in a world that is bound by the question of the reality of God. On the one hand, the presence of God offers life. On the other hand, the absence of God extends the shadow of death across human existence. The multiplicity of the faces of God shrouds the world in ambiguity. So long as death remains that which marks the human precisely as human, the question of what it means to be human cannot be separated from the question of the reality of God. Conversely, so long as the humanity of our being remains bound to death, the question of the reality of God is inseparable from the question of what it means to be human.

Bound both by the presence of death and by the ambiguity of God, the relationship between the human and the divine is marked by a sense of both radical continuity and equally radical discontinuity. The relationship is marked by a sense of radical continuity insofar as that relationship is, first, the basis for and definitive of the life of the individual and the community and, second, the subject of ongoing explication and articulation. The relationship between the human and the divine is radically continuous insofar as the relationship between Israel as chosen and YHWH as the one who chose has a history. The faith of Israel is the faith of Abraham, Isaac, and Jacob. The history of the faith of Israel is very much the ongoing interpretation and appropriation of that relationship in the lives of those people for whom this relationship is the basis of existence.[58] Beneath this exegesis lies a continuous and consistent movement toward further articulation and

---

57. Understanding that the faces of God are many is the key to understanding the prohibition against making images of God. Certainly monotheism is part of the faith of Israel. But monotheism presupposes that there is one God in whom one believes. The problem in Hebrew Scripture is that the question of who that God is remains open. There is no way to tell which of the many faces is really the face of God—at least not as long as God remains in the darkness.

58. As rabbinic Judaism has both shown and stressed, Scripture and its interpreters form the "complete" Torah—that is, the unity of Scripture is fixed both by written word and by the body of oral interpretations passed from one generation to the next.

explication. Exegesis of the relationship between Israel and YHWH brings light to both dimensions of the relation—the human and the divine—as well as to the nature of the relationship itself. It remains for each generation to appropriate for itself the relationship, the presence, and the absence.

Similarly, that relationship is the point of radical discontinuity, born in our inability to explicate exhaustively the depth, meaning, and nature of that relationship. The discontinuity is between two different and distinct beings, the human and the divine, whose existence and presence give life to the relationship. Discontinuity is born in the fragility of all aspects of the relationship itself, a fragility that is as much a part of the divine as it is a part of the human.

On the one hand, the promise of the relationship between Israel as chosen and YHWH as the one who chose is life, continuity, and endurance, born in the love that moves the heart of God to step out of the darkness and offer itself to the human. Yet the God that reaches out of the darkness withdraws and hides itself in the darkness from which it emerged.[59] Israel lives in the sense of having been chosen by YHWH. Israel's heart has been sought by God. It was not Israel who chose God.[60] Yet those pursued by God turn around and find that there is no God there. The presence that pursues the heart of Israel has no face, no presence, no embrace.

Where there was presence, we find absence.[61] Where there was love, we find jealous rage.[62] Where there was loving-kindness, we find bitter anger.[63] The God that consistently sought the heart of Israel extends and withdraws, reaches out and draws back, emerges and eludes. Furthermore, the God that opens and offers itself to the human, as though lonely and in need of the touch of a human hand, shows itself to be powerful and consuming in its anger and jealous rage, anguished by our distance yet distant and beyond the reach of our anguished

---

59. See Jer. 31:33; 32:38; Deut. 6:7; Ezek. 36:28; 37:27.

60. This motif is seen clearest in the call of Abraham, Moses, and the prophets. It is also echoed in the Apocalypse of Abraham 5:1-17; see also 4 Ezra 1:24-32, where we see juxtaposed v. 25 ("Because you have forsaken me, I also will forsake you") and v. 29 ("you should be my people, and I should be your God").

61. Jer. 39:15-18 is interesting in this regard; see also Isa. 54:7-10.

62. See the "Rebellious Son Speech" in Hos. 11:1-6; see also Josh. 24:19-20.

63. Hos. 6:3b-5a; 13:10-11; 2 Sam. 24:10-17 (note especially the brutality of YHWH's actions); 2 Chron. 32:21-22; Isa. 37:36-37; 2 Macc. 8:19-20; Isa. 6:11-12; 29:1-7 (note here that no mention is made of a transgression that has motivated YHWH's actions—YHWH's anger seems totally capricious); Ezek. 21:10-11; 28:22-23.

lament, fragile in its loneliness and tormented by its need for our love,[64] yet steadfast in its refusal to accept human embrace.

Yet when that human love is refused God, God suffers abandonment. When Israel whores after another God, as in the Book of Hosea, God's suffering becomes an angry rage. YHWH, like Hosea, is the husband whose love is rejected by a wife who cannot give her heart. Hosea's suffering is the suffering of one whose love is unrequited. Hosea's torment comes from this unrequited love. It is a torment shared by YHWH in its pursuit of the heart of Israel. A God that suffers is a fragile God. Yet the God that suffers is also an angry, jealous God, one whose rage unveils overwhelming power and strength. Amid a myriad of faces, we do not know which face is the face of God.

The human, however, finds itself in the midst of a world, having been chosen by a God whose presence extends beyond the world, given over to a fate that can neither be chosen nor refused. Because we are human, we die.[65] That death is as much a part of our humanity as love and sorrow. Death cannot be separated from our being. In the presence of our death, we find ourselves confronted by the limit of our humanity,[66] a limit that marks and demonstrates our fragility.

> For we are cast into the world at a time and in a place we did not choose, and we are destined to leave that world . . . at a time and in a place that is not ours to choose. Gifted with self-awareness and reason, man is aware of his powerlessness, of his ignorance; he is aware of his end: death. Self-awareness, reason, and imagination have disrupted the "harmony" that characterizes animal existence. Their emergence has made

---

64. An interesting study has been done on the suffering of God. While it is flawed in many ways because the approach to Hebrew Scripture is indebted to Christian theological assumptions, primarily those concerning the divinity of Jesus and the role of the ontological deformity of sin, it nonetheless offers deep insight into the issue of the suffering of God. See Terence E. Fretheim, *The Suffering of God* (Philadelphia: Fortress, 1984), esp. 97–101, 149ff.; "It is not enough to say that one believes in God. What is important finally is the kind of God one believes in" (p. 1). The implications of Fretheim's insight seem enormous in light of this paradox.

65. The story of the "Fall" in Genesis has been read by Christians as placing the origin of death in the sin of Adam and Eve. A close reading of the text does not support this argument. The myth of the Fall does not imply or state that death is a consequence of a fall from immortality. The myth simply says that as a result of the Fall, humans know the pain of death. The Fall therefore did not bring about an ontological change in human being but instead brought a change to the relationship between human being and death. As a result of the Fall, we now know we shall die. As a result of the Fall, following Gunkel's analysis of an etiology (see his *Legends of Genesis*), the presence of death becomes a problem, not just for human being, but for the relationship between the human and the divine.

66. Cf. Martin Heidegger, *Being and Time* (New York: Harper and Row, 1962), 279ff.

man an anomaly, the freak of the universe. He is part of nature, subject to her physical laws and unable to change them, yet he transcends nature. He is a being set apart while being a part; he is homeless, yet chained to a home he shares with all creatures. Cast into the world at an accidental place and time he is forced out of it accidentally and against his will. Being aware of himself, he realizes his powerlessness and the limitations of his existence. . . . Man is the only animal who does not feel at home in nature, who can feel evicted from paradise, the only animal for whom his own existence is a problem that he has to solve and from which he cannot escape.[67]

As 4 Ezra notes, we pass from the world like locusts; our life is like a mist (4:22-25). As beings who still possess and taste the breath of life, we are painfully aware of the passage of time and of the apparently inescapable end of our existence—an end we share with all who are human (Eccles. 2:15; 9:2-3), but one that, it seems, we cannot share with God. If there is a consolation for us, at least according to Qoheleth, it is this: "The living know at least that they will die, the dead know nothing; no more reward for them, their memory has passed out of mind. Their loves, their hates, their jealousies, these all have perished, nor will they ever again take part in what is done under the sun" (Eccles. 9:5-6). In the absence of a sense of endurance and permanence, in the hiddenness of the face of God, in the presence of our suffering and death, and in our confrontation with our humanity, a kind of torment strikes our heart that speaks of our loneliness, of our separation from God, of our finitude and our death. At the same time, there is a kind of fragility, brokenness, and instability that marks the relationship between the human and the divine as well. This relationship is fragile because this relationship draws its presence and sustenance from two beings who are themselves marked by an enduring fragility.

On the one hand, the relationship between the human and the divine is fragile because both the human and the divine can withdraw from or abandon the relationship. The longer that relationship endures, the more constant and pressing the fear of estrangement, withdrawal, and abandonment becomes. Indeed, involvement in the relationship, for the divine and the human, seems to raise the specter that the hand that extends into the darkness will find no hand to touch, the heart that reaches into the emptiness will embrace no other heart, and the presence

67. Erich Fromm, *The Anatomy of Human Destructiveness* (New York: Holt, Rinehart and Winston, 1973), 225.

that unveils itself will find itself abandoned. With or without reason or cause, one or the other can abandon the relationship. In anger and rage, God can forsake and abandon the human by hiding its face in darkness.[68] Without apparent reason God can veil its face in darkness. When the face of God is veiled, death always seems to be close at hand.[69] Perhaps never more stark is that face than when God's righteousness overshadows its love for human beings. The righteous God has no compassion. The righteous God's face is darkened by bitterness, vengeance, and jealousy. So dark is God's face that we speak not of its darkness but of human guilt, frailty, and sin. Death, in this context, becomes a kind of final punishment from a God whose rage seems to know no limit, no cause.[70] In turn, the human can spurn YHWH's love and turn to other gods. The human can refuse God's offer of its love. The human can interpret God's hiddenness as absence and refuse to be open to the possibility that God is there.

Yet despite the abandonment of the relationship by the human or the divine, that relationship can be reestablished. Fragile though it may be, once broken by desertion, the relationship can be reborn. Israel can return to YHWH. In returning to YHWH, Israel can extend its love to God and thus can beckon to God to come out of the darkness. Similarly, YHWH can return Israel from exile or can overthrow those who oppress Israel. In restoration, YHWH can emerge from the darkness in order to deliver Israel. Permanence in transience;[71] brokenness in the midst of continuity; restoration in the midst of abandonment.

On the other hand, the relationship between the human and the divine is fragile because there is a point where the relationship can be broken or dissolved without possibility of restoration. That point emerges where the force and sustenance of the relationship between the human and the divine is eclipsed by the shadow of death. That point occurs when, in the presence of suffering and death, in fear and trembling, the human is withdrawn from the presence of the divine

---

68. See Prov. 20:9; Eccles. 7:19-20.

69. Note, for example, the consequences of the withdrawal of YHWH's presence and favor on the fall of such figures as Saul, David, Solomon, Absalom, and Abimelech.

70. Or, if such a cause exists, it is beyond human comprehension. See 2 Sam. 24:10-17.

71. See Peter R. Ackroyd, *Exile and Restoration* (Philadelphia: Westminster, 1968), chaps. 12 and 13, esp. 237–56; also see Hos. 2:16 (14); 5:15—6:1; 9:10; 12:10-11(9-10); 13:4, with exile and deliverance theme; see also Hos. 8:11—9:6; 11:1-6; 13:4-8; Deut. 4:37; 5:6; 6:12-13, 20-22; Jer. 2:6-7; 7:21, 25; 1 Sam. 12:6-8; Mic. 7:15; Josh. 24:2-13; Judg. 11:12-18; Num. 20:14-29; 23:21-22.

and thereby from the relationship—in part because of its concern for
its own mortality, in part because in the presence of suffering and
death the face of God appears to withdraw still further into the darkness, and in part because in death the human is forever separated from
the divine.[72]

Death precludes endurance and relationship. In calling human existence into question, suffering and death also call into question the
possibility of relationship to God. As the human is pressed to the limits
of its existence in the presence of suffering and death, so too is the
relationship. In the presence of the shadow of death, the already-fragile
relationship is shattered. According to von Rad, "Death begins to be
a reality at the point where YHWH forsakes a human being, where
[YHWH] is silent, i.e. at whatever point the relationship of the living
to YHWH wears thin. From there it is only a step till the final cessation
of life. . . . Death radically called human being and all that it lived
for into question."[73]

GOD AND DEATH

Death calls into question, not just all that is human, but the meaning
and value of faith in a God that is sometimes silent while the innocent
suffer and die, and sometimes, as we find for example in Isaiah 29:1-
4, the one by whose hand humans suffer and die. Yet insofar as Israel
was chosen by God and Israel's existence stems from and is sustained
by the presence of YHWH, the experience of estrangement from
YHWH and the experience of suffering and death are one and the
same. Death, as much as life itself, is wrought by the hand of God.
The giver of life and the giver of death are one and the same.[74] "The
characteristics of life as well as death are characteristic of the almighty
God. Consequently God embodies the light in which all the living
flourish. In the same way God also embodies the darkness in which
the living die. God wills what is good, what is right, what is true,

72. Job 7:6-21; Lou Silberman has argued that the problematic nature of death was
not that in death life ceased forever but that in death human existence underwent a
qualitative change: in some way the *nephesh*, the life force, continued after physical
termination and endured a kind of eternal dispersion into nothingness. Death was as
much a process, a movement toward total yet seemingly complete dispersion of the
life force, as was life. Death is existence without life ("Death," 20–26).
73. Gerhard von Rad, *Old Testament Theology*, 2 vols. (New York: Harper and Row,
1962–65), 1:388, 389(1:386).
74. Ibid., 1:387–88.

what is beautiful. God also wills at the same time, in the eyes of human beings, what is evil, what is wrong, what is false, and what is ugly. . . . Good and evil, life and death, heaven and hell, are both aspects of the Godhead."[75] In this way human existence moves between two absolute points: absolute life and absolute death—neither of which are finally attainable, but both of which embody the ambiguity of the presence and face of God. Divine ambiguity marks the limits of our world. To be human is to be in a world that is shaped and formed by the ambiguity of a God that is both present and absent. Thus, death emerges at the point where God's absence is most intense. Life is at its strongest when the human has drawn near God.[76] To be human is to be in the world between God's presence and God's absence, between life and death.

Thus, when human existence is brought to its limit and when the relationship between the human and the divine is most in danger of being irrevocably broken, the question of how and why the one who has chosen Israel to live in its presence could let human beings die is very real. Why in the presence of God is there death? The death question raises the issue of God's culpability and responsibility in human suffering and death.[77] That is, if it is by the presence of God that human life is sustained and by the absence of God that it is eclipsed, then the presence of suffering and death raises the issue of God's involvement in and responsibility for human suffering and death.

The issue of God's involvement in human suffering and death stands open and unanswered. This issue is all the more perplexing because the problem of death is the problem of God. In the presence of suffering and death, we cannot determine if God's hiddenness is intentional or accidental, whether we die by God's deliberate withdrawal or by God's actions, or whether we die because there was never a God there to begin with.

75. Christoph Barth, *Die Errettung vom Tode in den individuellen Klage- und Dankliedern des Alten Testaments* (Basel: Evangelischer Verlag, 1947), 69.

76. Death was more than the physical cessation of life, the absolute point at which life ended. According to von Rad: "For Israel death's domain reached far further into the realm of the living. Weakness, illness, imprisonment, and oppression by enemies are a kind of death. . . . It was YHWH who apportioned death for men" (*Old Testament Theology,* 1:387–88 [1:385–87]).

77. "We can only say God by embodying exile in our voice, only by making openly manifest our exile from eternal silence and presence. . . . God is the name of the source of our estrangement from the source of eternal presence" (Thomas J. J. Altizer, *The Self-Embodiment of God* [New York: Harper and Row, 1977], 31).

Furthermore, we find ourselves caught in a paradox. If God is there in the darkness and its silence is indicative of its refusal to end our suffering, or if perhaps God's silence is indicative of God's inability to change our fate or of God's powerlessness in the presence of death, then, in a very real sense, faith in God is open to question. It is difficult to believe in a God who is responsible for our death. It is just as difficult to believe in a God that is unable to alter the reality and certainty of our death. Yet God's silence in the presence of death also raises the possibility that we are alone in the world and in our suffering. That silence raises the possibility that there is no God there. As long as the possibility that God is not there endures, the question of the reality of God and the tenability of faith endures.

In the presence of death, then, all aspects of the relationship between the human and the divine are called into question. As long as God remains silent, the death question remains without answer. As long as the death question is without answer, the questions of the reality of God and the meaning of human existence remain open and un-answered. As long as the death question endures, our lives are without consolation, our bitterness without resolution. Throughout our search for an answer to the death question, the silence of God is more than conspicuous. It is unnerving, frustrating, embittering. Try as we might, we can not answer the death question. It must be answered for us.

Our search for the answer to the death question is more than a search for the reason for our death. It is a search for the reason for our existence. More than a search for some veiled divine purpose that would make our burden acceptable, our suffering reasonable, it is the search for God itself. Once again we find ourselves caught in a paradox. Only the face of God can bring resolution to the death question, but in the presence of death there is no access to the face of God, and hence the death question can have no resolution. Without resolution, the death question holds open to question both the reality of God and the meaning of human existence. This is the dilemma that dwelt upon the heart and mind and scarred the faith of Israel.

three | SUFFERING AND HIDDENNESS

Apocalyptic Literature and the Search for the Face of God

In classical biblical prophecy the issue had always been the life of the nation. Apocalyptic still deals with a communal context. . . . However, its concern has extended to the life of the individual. By its focus on heavenly, supernatural realities it provides a possibility that the human life can transcend death, . . . by passing to the higher, heavenly sphere. It is this hope for the transcendence of death which is the distinctive character of apocalyptic.

J. J. Collins,
"Apocalyptic Eschatology and the
Transcendence of Death"

The attempt at theodicy formed a continuing accompaniment to the interior of Judaism, casting its shadow across the picture of God, the understanding of history, the life of prayer, and the eschatological hope.

Walther Eichrodt,
Theology of the Old Testament

Three distinct but related responses to the death question in Hebrew Scripture offer insight into the dilemma of the death question. These responses are related because each approach is part of the larger context of the theological reflection that shaped the faith of Israel. The first response is that of the prophets; the second, that of the apocalyptic texts; and the third, that of wisdom literature.[1] Of these, the responses

---

1. Concern for this question indeed appears in all parts of Hebrew Scripture—Genesis, Deuteronomy, Samuel, Kings, as well as the prophets and wisdom and apocalyptic texts.

offered by the apocalyptic texts and wisdom literature will figure prominently in our discussion. Our task here is to explore the context within which the death question takes shape in the faith of Israel.[2]

While the prophetic texts will not be examined in detail here, we can briefly summarize the prophetic response to the experience of suffering and death.

1. The prophet is chosen to be a mediator between God and Israel. This mediation is twofold: before God, the prophet embodies Israel; before Israel, the prophet speaks for God.[3]

2. The prophet is concerned with returning Israel to God.[4]

3. As a result, the prophet calls to a people who has abandoned its relationship to God. Thus, the call of the prophet is a call to a people whose suffering, impending exile, and oppression for the most part is wrought by their own hand.

4. Suffering and death, punishment and exile, are marks of divine retribution. YHWH's pain stems from Israel's transgressions. YHWH's anger and rage has an air of justice about it. Punishment chastens Israel's heart.[5]

---

2. Much of the material that follows was presented to the Pseudepigrapha Group of the Society of Biblical Literature at the Society's national convention in Chicago in 1984 and in Anaheim in 1985. I am indebted to John J. Collins, Paul D. Hanson, and James VanderKam for their assistance, friendship, guidance, patience, and encouragement.

3. Gerhard von Rad, *The Message of the Prophets* (New York: Harper and Row, 1965), 11–14; Abraham Heschel, *The Prophets,* 2 vols. (New York: Harper and Row, 1975), 2:1–26; Heschel comments: "The prophets had no theory or 'idea' of God. What they had was an *understanding,* . . . They did not offer an exposition of the nature of God, but rather an exposition of God's insight into man and His concern for man" (2:1). See also Brevard Childs, *Old Testament Theology in a Canonical Context* (Philadelphia: Fortress, 1986), 127–28, and Num. 12:6-7; Amos 3:7-8; Deut. 18:13-22; Exod. 4:12; 20:18-21.

4. Hos. 14:2ff.(1ff.); Walther Eichrodt, *Theology of the Old Testament,* 2 vols. (Philadelphia: Westminster, 1961–67), 1:457–71 (*Theologie des Alten Testaments* [Stuttgart: E. Klotz Verlag, 1957]), 1:309-19). Eichrodt argues that the point of judgment is not the dissolution of the covenant but the covenant's rejuvenation. Von Rad extends this position to the Deuteronomist. He wrote: "Israel alone through its own guilt had lost God's deliverance. YHWH's judgement in history was justified" (*Old Testament Theology,* 2 vols. [New York: Harper and Row, 1962–65], 1:342. This is my own translation of the German edition (see chap. 2, n.39). See also Hans Walter Wolff, *Hosea* (Philadelphia: Fortress, 1974), 231–40.

5. Heschel, *Prophets,* 2:5–10, 57–86; Deut. 18:13-22; Hos. 8:11-13; 9:3-6; 12:11-12(10-11); 14:2-3 (1-2). Note the use of the wilderness theme in Hebrew Scripture, in Hos. 2:1-3(1-2), 14(13); 9:10; 12:10-11(9-10); 13:4; an exile and deliverance theme appears in Hos. 8:11—9:6; 11:1-6; 12:10-11(9-10); 13:4-8; Deut. 4:37; 5:6; 6:12-13, 20-22; Jer. 2:6-7; 7:21, 25; 1 Sam. 12:6-8; Mic. 7:15; Josh. 24:2-13; Judg. 11:12-18; Num. 20:14-

5. Restoration follows upon the return of Israel's wayward heart.[6] YHWH's actions and anger are just.[7]

The logic of the prophets seems clear: YHWH chose Israel—indeed, YHWH carried Israel out of Egypt and bore Israel through exile in the wilderness. YHWH extended its love to Israel. In turn, Israel turned away from God, or worse yet, Israel whored after other gods. A return to YHWH was synonymous with an end to suffering. The issue of the suffering of the innocent and the righteous does not seem to arise— or if this issue does arise, it is only within the context of Israel's guilt and YHWH's innocence and righteousness. YHWH's motives are rarely questioned; nor, for that matter, is the justice of God's actions.

Yet for whatever reason, this logic seems to have changed during the restoration.[8] In some way, this change seems to lie at the heart of what many scholars have termed the decline of classical prophecy. That decline may well have been rooted in the growing distance between prophetic promise and historical fulfillment. In effect, the restoration was not a restoration. In the last analysis the restoration seems to have been little more than a return from exile. The force and the power of the Davidic monarchy did not return. The remnant that returned remained exiled in its own land, subject to a distant power.[9]

Failed restoration raised the issue of the justice of YHWH's actions and the fullness of YHWH's promises. In the return from exile, the community was confronted with circumstances that left YHWH's promises unfulfilled. If the remnant that returned was righteous, then certainly the failure of restoration could not have been the result of Israel's disobedience. If the failure was not Israel's, was the fault YHWH's? Perhaps. If so, belief in a just God would be difficult to maintain.

29; 23:21-22. Lists of offenses appear in Amos 6:3-7; Hos. 13:1-2; Deut. 5:8-10; 9:10-11; Mic. 6:5-6. See Peter R. Ackroyd, *Exile and Restoration* (Philadelphia: Westminster, 1968), 43–49.

6. Isa. 41:17-20; 61:1-11; 65:17-18.

7. In effect, this conclusion is the point of the wilderness theme—restoration of the remnant or the nation. See Ackroyd, *Exile and Restoration,* 232–56; Childs, *Canonical Context,* 233–34; Hos. 3:1-2; Amos 5:15; Jer. 3:18-19; 23:5-6; Isa. 4:3-4; Mic. 2:12-13; 4:1-2; Ezek. 34:1-2; 37:15-28.

8. Ackroyd, *Exile and Restoration,* 138–217.

9. As Ackroyd has often noted, there is little hard historical information about the events of the Persian period (*Exile and Restoration,* 13–38). Thus, any historical analysis runs the risk of misconstruing events.

This does not mean that the issue of the justice of God's actions and the suffering of the innocent was never an issue before the restoration, for certainly Job and the suffering and lamentation psalms predate the period of the restoration. However, the question of the suffering of the innocent was for the most part absent from prophetic reflection. The case can be made that the disillusionment of Ezra-Nehemiah, which some feel is so important for the rise of apocalypticism in the last three centuries B.C.E., is rooted in the intrusion of the theodicy question into prophetic reflection.

While the theodicy question seems to provide a link between the apocalyptic texts and the body of prophetic literature, the relationship of most of the apocalyptic texts to the rest of the canon of Hebrew Scripture is itself an open issue. Although the exclusion from the canon of such texts as 4 Ezra and the Enoch corpus places them outside the body of canonical reflection, these texts nonetheless play an important, if not crucial, role in our understanding of the death question. In this way, apocalyptic texts provide insight into the shape, structure, and formation of theological reflection in Hebrew Scripture. Nonetheless, the response that they offer to the death question takes shape within and presupposes the contours of canonical Scripture.

THE HISTORY OF INTERPRETATION

The history of the interpretation of the apocalyptic texts in the last 150 years has been long and varied.[10] As Hanson notes, the first comprehensive study was completed by Friedrich Lücke in 1832.[11] Lücke argued that (1) apocalyptic arose in the demise of classical prophecy; (2) the influence of Zoroastrianism and Hellenism on Jewish apocalyptic texts was largely formal and had little impact upon the content of apocalyptic reflection; (3) the rise of apocalyptic could be traced to

---

10. Excellent histories of the study of apocalyptic literature have appeared over the last several decades. Most significant among these is Paul Hanson's "Prolegomena to the Study of Jewish Apocalyptic," in *Magnalia Dei: The Mighty Acts of God*, Festschrift for G. Ernest Wright, ed. F. M. Cross, W. E. Lemke, and P. D. Miller (Garden City, N.Y.: Doubleday, 1976), 389–413. See also J. Barr, "Jewish Apocalyptic in Recent Scholarly Study," *BJRL* 58, no. 1 (1975): 9–35; Klaus Koch, *The Rediscovery of Apocalyptic* (London: SCM Press, 1981); W. G. Kümmel, "Consistent Eschatology," in *The New Testament: The History of the Investigation of Its Problems* (Nashville: Abingdon, 1972), 226–44; and Johann M. Schmidt, *Die jüdische Apokalyptik* (Neukirchen: Neukirchener Verlag, 1969).

11. Hanson, "Prolegomena," 389–90.

the disillusion of the postexilic period, to strife within the community, and to continued foreign oppression; and (4) the central and essential aspect of apocalyptic reflection was its view of history. With some modification, Lücke's position has remained mostly intact.[12]

The Rise of Apocalyptic Literature

Plöger, following Lücke's focus on the postexilic community as the source of apocalyptic literature, argued that there was a marked change in the Israel's eschatology from the time of preexilic prophecy to the time of Ezra-Nehemiah.[13] According to Plöger, this change could be demonstrated by contrasting the preexilic and postexilic articulation of Israel's understanding of itself. That self-portrait rested upon Israel's understanding of its relationship to YHWH. In preexilic times Israel understood itself to be chosen among the nations because Israel experienced itself as chosen by God. What was distinctive about Israel in relationship to other nations was its perceived relationship to YHWH, one that other nations did not enjoy.

In the experience of exile, more than the community's understanding of when or how YHWH would deliver the faithful remnant changed.[14] The community's understanding of its identity and its relation to God also was altered, despite (or perhaps even because of) the very hope by which the community was sustained. With the reemergence of this cherished hope from earlier times amid the growing realization that restoration of the nation might not be a real possibility, those who returned from exile found themselves caught in a difficult situation.

12. Two important works provide a more or less direct link between Lücke and the present generation of scholars: Otto Plöger, *Theocracy and Eschatology* (Richmond: John Knox, 1968), and Th. C. Vriezen, "Prophecy and Eschatology," VTSup 1 (1953), 199–229.

13. Plöger, *Theocracy and Eschatology*, 108–9. Much of the superstructure of Plöger's work is derived from the earlier analysis offered by Volz—a debt Plöger himself is quick to acknowledge (see Plöger, *Die Eschatologie der jüdischen Gemeinde im neutestamentlichen Zeitalter*, 2d ed. [Tübingen: Paul Mohr, 1934]). While I remain critical of Plöger's analysis, his work nevertheless seems to be an important link between Lücke and the nineteenth century and Hanson and others in our own time. Plöger is held in much less esteem by Klaus Koch ("Whereas Plöger's theses hardly came up against any exegetical criticism, [they] were also without influence" [*Rediscovery*, 41]), a point that, in light of Hanson's work, I would much debate.

14. The restoration of the remnant is an important theme. The remnant is the community of the faithful who endure and survive exile and the purgation of suffering. See Isa. 1:10-20; 7:3-4, 14-15; 11:1-9; Mic. 2:12; 5:1-6b; Zech. 3:8ff.; 6:12; Amos 5:15; Zech. 8:6-7, 11-12. See also von Rad, *Old Testament Theology*, 2:21ff., 165–68, 186–87.

The promise—the hope by which the community sustained itself in exile—seemed no nearer realization now, even though the community had returned to Jerusalem. The community was faced with a choice: either abandon the hope for and promise of restoration, or in some way transform that hope and promise so that faith would remain a source of continued support and sustenance for the community.

The rise of apocalyptic is to be found in the transformation of this promise and hope.[15] Thus while prophetic eschatology "embodied the future hope of a nation which was conscious of being separate from the other nations of the world as a result of its relationship to God," apocalyptic eschatology extended that future hope only to the few whose life was tied to the righteous remnant that was to be restored.[16] Where there had been the promise of and hope for the restoration of the nation in history, there was now a growing sense of the restoration of the remnant. Instead of a sense of restoration in history, there was now a sense of restoration beyond or outside history. In place of Israel versus the nations, it was now the righteous remnant versus the damned. Where there was nationalism, there was now sectarianism.[17] According to Plöger, the "transition from the nation of Israel to the community of YHWH, which may be regarded as an act of withdrawal into a specifically religious sphere, bears within itself the seed of sectarian narrowness. . . . This was the beginning of a path that was bound to lead to further divisions and splits as a result of the claim to represent the true Israel.[18]

Note Plöger's use of the term "restoration eschatology" in *Theocracy and Eschatology*. While Plöger never explicitly defines it, his use of this term to describe, or perhaps even to define, the "stage" to which the eschatological reflection of the exilic community belongs, offers an insight into his understanding of the development of apocalyptic eschatology from earlier prophetic formulations. Restoration eschatology seems to be the hope that the community of faith nurtured while

---

15. "The transformation of the nation of Israel into the community of YHWH established the basis which inevitably led to the change of the prophetic eschatology into the apocalyptic view of the future, as soon as the new community, itself pssibly regarded as the fulfillment of an earlier cherished hope in connection *inter alia* with the remnant idea, was confronted with the claims of eschatological faith once again" (Plöger, *Theocracy and Eschatology*, 49).

16. This limitation leads Plöger to argue against Iranian origins for the dualism that characterizes apocalyptic literature (see ibid., 50).

17. Ibid., 109.

18. Ibid., 50.

in exile, a hope that pointed to the restoration of the community as a nation. Restoration of the nation implicitly involved renewal of the cult in Jerusalem. It was the failure of the restoration of the nation that forced the remnant community to redefine both its expectation and its hope. The rise of apocalyptic eschatology, then, seems tied to the community's need for renewed self-definition in the face of failed restoration. The continuation of this restoration eschatology by those who had returned from exile

> signified the consolidation of a condition of suspense and uncertainty, which was unfavourable to any attempt to regulate the situation with definiteness and led instead to a provisional acceptance of whatever happened to be the position, the final solution being left to a future initiative on YHWH's part. The only way to neutralize such influences was not by combating or discrediting living eschatological hopes . . . but by burying them in the foundations of the community which was to be rebuilt . . . which could be understood *inter alia* as the fulfilment of prophetic promises.[19]

For Plöger, apocalyptic eschatology represents the continuation, and in some sense the continued fulfillment, of prophetic eschatology. Where once the exiles had hoped for a return to Jerusalem, the exiles in Jerusalem now hoped for a return to a new Jerusalem, a kingdom of God that stood beyond or in some way outside history. For those exiles who experienced this separation from the postexilic community and from the kingdom of God, only a new social, political, and religious order could stem the frustration and could restore and fulfill the promise of deliverance. But the expectation that this new order would be born in the return from exile was short-lived. Faced with concessions made to dominating foreign powers by the postexilic hierarchy, the community of faith became disillusioned.[20] This disillusion and distrust led to a confrontation with the postexilic theocracy. The righteous rule of YHWH, in some way very real and present to the community, yet in some way still distant and unattainable, was counterbalanced by the illegitimate theocracy to which the community found itself subject.[21] This conflict, which was to continue through

---

19. Ibid., 109.

20. This discouragement seems to underline the material in Ezra-Nehemiah and the conflicts to which the text alludes.

21. The theocracy was illegitimate at least in the eyes of those who returned from exile (ibid., 113). On the intracommunal conflict in Ezekiel, see ibid., 19.

the Maccabean period,[22] was a conflict between very different the-
ocracies, which had at their core very different—perhaps even irrec-
oncilable—eschatologies. In this conflict, apocalyptic reflection was
born.

A final note should be added. While the above analysis tends to
stress the continuity between prophetic and apocalyptic eschatology,
Plöger did not obscure this distinction. In fact, his analysis may be
more rigid than one might suspect. For example, following Volz,
Plöger stressed these differences between the two eschatologies: prophetic eschatology offers a monistic view of the world, apocalyptic
offers a dualistic view of God and the world; the prophetic speaks in
terms of fulfillment, apocalyptic in terms of dissolution and replace-
ment; in prophecy judgment is imminent and repeatable, in apocalyptic, judgment is unique and unrepeatable for all time.[23]

Four Stages of Prophecy

Th. C. Vriezen also offered an extensive analysis of the development
of apocalyptic from prophetic eschatology. Like Plöger, Vriezen's
analysis has also had a strong impact on the shape of current scholarship
on prophetic and apocalyptic texts.[24] Vriezen prefaces his own conclusions about the shape of prophetic eschatology by examining crit-
ically the work of earlier scholars, including Gressmann, Lindblom,
Charles, and Volz, in order to lay the foundation for his own analysis
(pp. 199–220). Much of his analysis both presupposes and proceeds
from the work of these other scholars.

Vriezen's discussion of apocalyptic eschatology is cast within the
scope of his analysis of prophetic literature. He divides the history of

22. Ibid., 1–9.
23. Ibid., 28–30.
24. See Vriezen, "Prophecy and Eschatology." In this section, page references in the
text are to Vriezen's article. At the outset I should note that I find Vriezen's work marred
by certain assumptions about the "Hebrew mind" and language. After an extensive
review of scholarship until about 1950, he does not advance his own opinion until the
final section of the paper. It is here that these assumptions are most obvious and most
damaging to his analysis. See 224 n. 2 for example: "The statistical idea is unknown
in ancient Israel, and so is the all-embracing idea of the world as a whole." Also on
that page, he writes that "Hebrew thought does not know our idea of time and so it
can not divide time, for this way of thinking is not analytical but totalizing." As a
result, Vriezen attributes most abstract ideas found in apocalyptic texts to Hellenistic
influence.

prophecy into four distinct stages: preeschatological, protoeschatological, actual eschatological, and transcendentalizing eschatology. The
first stage, the preeschatological, is the period before classical prophecy.
Here the concerns are primarily political. This stage, Vriezen argues,
cannot really be called eschatological because the expectation that dom-
inates this period is not the renewal of the world. Its concern, rather,
lies with Israel's destiny and the promise of national glory. Prophetic
reflection takes as its starting point, according to Vriezen, the relationship between YHWH and Israel (pp. 222, 228–29). "Eschatology
is not a wish-dream that admits of a psychological explanation, but a
religious certainty which springs immediately from the Israelitic faith
in God as rooted in the history of its salvation. . . . Eschatology is
the form in which the critical realism of faith of the prophets maintained
its confession of YHWH, the Lord of the World" (p. 229). Once freed
from purely political concerns, prophetic reflection becomes concerned with maintaining, supporting, and sustaining this relationship.
For this relationship between Israel as chosen and YHWH as the one
who chose is subject to repeated disruption by Israel's infidelity. The
prophetic task is to pronounce judgment and thus to return Israel's
wayward heart. The return of the wayward heart brings the restoration
of the relationship. Renewal of the relationship "is historical and at
the same time supra-historical, it takes place within the framework of
history but is caused by forces that transcend history, so that what is
coming is a new order of things in which the glory and the Spirit of
God (Is. 11) reveals itself" (p. 222).

Pronouncement of judgment is not a reflection upon the divine but
upon the human. Judgment marks Israel's refusal to heed YHWH's
call. Israel is punished with a "particular severity" (p. 221) because it
has been chosen by YHWH, but YHWH's judgment has ramifications
for all the world. YHWH judges Israel in order to fashion or shape a
new Israel and a new world. Israel is not judged for the sake of
judgment. Judgment is the means to re-creation and restoration. This
concern for impending judgment and subsequent restoration is the
hallmark of classical or preexilic prophecy (p. 223; see Isa. 11:9).

This concern for future restoration also marks the awakening of
eschatological concerns. Included in this second period are the prophecies of the first Isaiah, Jeremiah, Hosea, and Amos (pp. 203ff.). Vriezen calls this period protoeschatological.

The transition from expectation of judgment to expectation of salvation dominates the third period.[25] "Looking back on Israelitic
prophetism . . . [there are] two culminating-points: Isaiah (surrounded
by Amos, Hosea and Micah) and Deutero-Isaiah, the one at the entrance to the dark tunnel through which Israel must pass, the other
at the end" (p. 220). Zechariah, Haggai, and Deutero-Isaiah belong
to this period. In the prophecies of Deutero-Isaiah, the cry of judgment
is overshadowed by the proclamation that the time of deliverance was
at hand (p. 223). With deliverance comes the dawn of the new age
and subsequently the transformation of the world. This twofold expectation—of deliverance and transformation of the world—dominated the first few centuries after the exile (p. 223). Pronouncements
of judgment are now of secondary importance because "the kingdom
of God is not only seen coming in *visions* but it is *experienced* as coming"
(p. 227). This awareness of the immanence of restoration Vriezen terms
actual (or actualizing) eschatology (p. 227).

For Vriezen, the prophecies of Deutero-Isaiah mark a turning point
in the history of prophetic activity.[26] With the transition from pronouncement of judgment to pronouncement of the immediacy of
restoration, there is a shift from eschatology in a broad sense to eschatology in a narrow sense (p. 223). The former addresses the issue
of the shape of the judgment that is intended to bring about a new
world and a new age. Both that new world and that new age are to
be the result of the transformation of this world through the mighty
acts of God in general and through the judgment of Israel in particular.

Eschatology in the narrow sense points to a new world and a new
age that extend beyond the realm of the historical, beyond the world
in which there is suffering and death and that borders on hopelessness.
The birth of this new world parallels the initial creation of the world
by God. This new world is a world freed from the deformity that
plagues the present world. Entrance into that new world is to be

25. Vriezen traces the origin of the Zion theology in this period to the claim that
Jerusalem stood at the center of the universe.

26. The idea that there is a history to prophetic activity is debatable. Most biblical
scholars seem to presuppose that a history of the development can be constructed (if
not reconstructed) from the prophetic texts. That such a construction may be possible
in the Isaianic texts, all of which are presented to us in the canon as one document,
seems defensible. That a construction of the history of prophecy is possible, given the
diversity of time, point of origin, etc., of the canonical prophetic texts, seems less
defensible. Such a construction proceeds on much the same premises as the Biblical
Theology Movement's analysis of the conceptual structure of Scripture as a whole; as
such, it is subject to the same critique.

extended only to the righteous, to the remnant that has survived judgment.

But that new world was never born. The fourth and final stage begins here, with the growing sense of disillusion and frustration that accompanies the absence of the expected deliverance and transformation. At this point eschatology becomes transcendental.[27] Transcendental eschatology marks the emergence of apocalyptic. The rise of apocalyptic brings with it a dualism of two worlds—the one below, which is destined to pass away, and the one above, which is destined to replace it. One world is to be destroyed, the other is to endure forever (p. 223). Where God and the world once stood together, they now stand apart. Where God was once present to the world, God is now present only to the faithful (pp. 223, 225–28).

If Vriezen is correct, the whole of the movement from exile to restoration has at its heart YHWH's call to Israel to be its people. YHWH's call restricts, overshadows, or even precludes the human exercise of freedom. God's call cannot be refused. The call of a reluctant Jeremiah (Jer. 1:5-6) or Elijah's repeated attempt to avoid the death that certainly would be his if he heeded the word of God (1 Kings 18–20) points to the force and power of God's call. In the story of the call of Ezekiel, the prophet is said to have eaten the scroll that contained a pronouncement of judgment, as though the word of God, the mission of God, is forced upon him (Ezek. 2:8—3:3). If human beings have no freedom to accept or to refuse the call of God, or at least have no freedom to refuse God's call without the threat of judgment, then the theodicy question would also seem to involve the question of the meaning of human freedom. The ability to say yes or no to any state of affairs, even to God, is an essential aspect of that freedom.[28]

27. "The apocalyptic movement may be briefly described as the late Jewish attempt to revive older biblical doctrines of history. . . . Prophecy became eschatology. . . . The main impulse of the apocalyptic is the Old Testament understanding of the history of salvation. . . . Prophecy was transformed. . . . With the fall of the kingdom, classical prophecy ceased. Haggai and Zechariah are the only apparent exceptions. . . . Prophecy and kingship in fact expired together" (F. M. Cross, "New Directions in the Study of Apocalyptic," *JTC* 6 [1969]: 157–61). Vriezen's analysis seems clear, especially in light of the concluding summary Cross offers on 165. Cross's analysis is distinctive, however, in stressing the role of the mythic, especially those elements arising from Canaanite mythology. The introduction of the importance of myth to a rather linear understanding of the development of apocalyptic from prophecy set the stage, as we shall see, for Hanson's work on apocalyptic.

28. It could be argued, however, as would be possible within the guise of classical Greek philosophy, that freedom is not freedom from restraints—that is, freedom to say

More is at issue here than human freedom, however. YHWH chose
Israel as the object of YHWH's love. YHWH called Israel to return
that love—to live in that love or to die in its absence.[29] Human love,
however, cannot be demanded—no matter what punishment is in-
flicted in its absence. The heart must be won through love, not through
judgment. The human heart can only be given freely, and no one—
YHWH included—can override that freedom. YHWH's call to Israel
in judgment calls the human freedom to love into question, for it calls
human beings to give what cannot be given upon demand—the human
heart. Theodicy becomes a problem at the point where the human
freedom to love is eclipsed by the force of God's demand for human
love. Deliverance, therefore, is as much a demonstration of God's love
as it is an attempt by God to secure our love through our suffering.

Apocalyptic Reflection

In contemporary scholarship, the sustaining influence of Lücke, Vriezen, and Plöger is most apparent in the work of Paul D. Hanson.[30]
That sustaining influence is most evident in the following summaries
that Hanson offers:

> The "taproot" of apocalyptic lies in prophecy . . . [and] the "new"
> influences giving rise to Jewish apocalyptic literature are to be traced

---

yes or no without limit—but rather freedom within limits. The Greek words *nomos*
("law, order") and *polis* ("ring wall") were the basis for that experience of freedom and
for the Greek understanding of the city. See Hannah Arendt, *The Human Condition*
(Garden City, N.Y.: Doubleday, 1959), 317–18 n. 63, 318 n. 65. Law that was the fabric
of the *polis* formed the *peras*, or limit, within which human being took shape and form,
not in the absence of order, but through its presence. Action without order was chaos.
See John C. Gunnell, *Political Philosophy and Time* (Middletown, Conn.: Wesleyan
University Press, 1968), chap. 5, "The Idea of the Political: Plato," esp. 209; Erich
Fromm, *Escape from Freedom* (New York: Avon, 1972), 17–55. This understanding of
freedom may have been dominant within Greek culture, but it does not follow that
such was the case in the ancient Near East.
   29. See, for example, the so-called law of the heart in Deut. 10:12ff., 30:6ff.
   30. Any examination of the history of scholarship on the nature and origin of
apocalyptic would be amiss if it ignored the importance of the contributions made by
H. H. Rowley (see his *Relevance of Apocalyptic* [London: Lutterworth, 1950]) and S.
Mowinckel (*He That Cometh* [New York: Abingdon, 1954]), whose work rekindled
interest in apocalyptic literature. They were followed by D. S. Russell (*The Method and
Message of Jewish Apocalyptic* [Philadelphia: Westminster, 1964]), Klaus Koch (*Rediscovery)*, and others. Any such examination, however, just as clearly establishes the continuity of thought and analysis in the tradition that stretches from Lücke to Hanson, a
tradition that has dominated and shaped current scholarship.

first to the recrudescence of old mythic material long at home on Israelite soil, and *second,* to the trying circumstances rending the Jewish community in the post-exilic period. . . . For it is there that one can detect prophetic eschatology being transformed into apocalyptic.[31]

The rise of apocalyptic is neither sudden nor anomalous, but follows the pattern of an unbroken development . . . which is perfectly comprehensible against the environment of the post-exilic Jewish community.[32]

Like Vriezen and Plöger before him, Hanson places the origin of apocalyptic in the decline of prophecy. Like Cross, Hanson acknowledges the importance of mythic elements long a part of the fabric of Judaism.[33] Thus, Hanson is critical of those who place the origin of apocalyptic in foreign influences on Judaism—most notably Zoroastrianism and Hellenism.[34] The important link that Hanson establishes

31. Paul D. Hanson, "Old Testament Apocalyptic Reexamined," *Int* 25 (1971): 456–57. It is important to note that Hanson begins by taking issue with Schmidt (*Jüdische Apokalyptik*) and others who press for an understanding of Daniel as the paradigmatic apocalyptic text. According to Hanson, this position leads to a misinterpretation of the origin of apocalyptic and its relation to prophecy, and to the mistaken stress on the influence of foreign religious elements on the rise of apocalyptic (p. 456).

32. Paul Hanson "Jewish Apocalyptic against Its Near Eastern Environment," *RB* 78 (1971): 32.

33. Paul D. Hanson, *The Dawn of Apocalyptic* (Philadelphia: Fortress, 1979), 24–27, 292–337, 369–80; see also his "Jewish Apocalyptic," 40–41.

34. Hanson feels that this misguided approach has dominated scholarship, at least in this century. (I question, however, whether those who took this position constitute the "main line" analysis.) Hanson criticizes, among others, von Rad, who stresses the influence of wisdom literature on the development of apocalyptic, and Schmidt, both of whom tend to place the origin of apocalyptic late and to see it deriving from foreign influences. See Hanson's "Old Testament Apocalyptic," 456; *Dawn,* 5–9; and "Jewish Apocalyptic," 31–33. Hanson places Plöger in this category, as well as W. R. Murdock, "History and Revelation in Jewish Apocalypticism," *Int* 21 (1967): 165ff.; Martin Buber, *Kampf um Israel* (Berlin: Schocken Verlag, 1933); and Helmer Ringgren, *Israelite Religion* (Philadelphia: Fortress Press, 1966, 1980). Translation of *Israelitische Religion* (1963) by D. Green.

As we shall see in the next chapter, von Rad's attempt to emphasize the dominance of the influence of wisdom upon apocalyptic was short-lived. It also met with extensive and rather hostile critique by biblical scholars, although many scholars, Cross and Hanson among them, see the rise of wisdom literature in general (and specifically Job) as a turning point in the development of the faith of Israel. According to Cross, "Job brings the ancient religion of Israel to an end" ("New Directions," 162); "Job was a major force in the evolution of Israel's religion" (p. 163). See Hanson's "Jewish Apocalyptic," 34, 47–48, and *Dawn,* 8–9, 380. Also see Michael Stone, "Lists of Revealed Things in the Apocalyptic Literature," in *Magnalia Dei: The Mighty Acts of God,* Festschrift for G. Ernest Wright, ed. F. M. Cross, W. E. Lemke, and P. D. Miller (Garden City, N.Y.: Doubleday, 1976), 414–52, esp. 436–38; Stone, "Apocalyptic Literature," in *Jewish Writings of the Second Temple Period,* sec. 2 of the Compendium Rerum Iudai-

between the tradition that saw apocalyptic as the last phase in the development of prophetic tradition, represented by Vriezen and Plöger, and the position represented by Cross, which stressed the significance of the reappropriation in apocalyptic literature of older mythic patterns that were already a part of the fabric of Judaism, allows Hanson to offer a subtle and rich portrait of the origin and development of apocalyptic.

Hanson stresses the continuity between prophecy and apocalyptic, between the earlier mythic elements of Judaism and their later appropriations, between prophet and seer. At the same time, however, Hanson is able to stress the distinctive and unique reshaping the faith of Israel receives by the hand of the apocalyptic seer. For Hanson, those moments of radical continuity and discontinuity, of restoration and reappropriation, are aspects of one and the same phenomenon—apocalyptic reflection. Indeed, Hanson argues that while Israelite faith emerged from the mythico-poetic world of Canaanite mythology, largely through the efforts of the prophets who are responsible for "historicizing Israel's religion, for translating cosmic vision into history. . . . Prophets were the ones who forged the visionary and realistic aspects of the religious experience into one tension-filled whole, thereby making Yahwism an ethical religion of the highest order."[35]

The concern for the resolution of the events of human history, which apocalyptic inherits from prophecy, and the resurgence and reappropriation of the visionary elements of preprophetic times mark and shape apocalyptic reflection. The balanced tension between history and vision forged by the prophet,[36] which saw the mythic in service to the events of history, now became redefined, reshaped, reappropriated. The seer "was called by Yahweh to straddle two worlds, to view the deliberations and events of the cosmic realm, but then immediately to integrate that vision into the events of the politico-historical order." In this reappropriation, history would be in service

---

carum ad Novum Testamentum, ed. Michael Stone (Assen: Van Gorcum Press, 1984), 383–441, esp. 388–89; Gerhard von Rad, *Theologie des Alten Testaments* (Munich: Kaiser Verlag, 1969), 2:316–31, and *Wisdom in Israel* (Nashville: Abingdon, 1972), 109, 115–24, 304–7.

35. Hanson, "Jewish Apocalyptic," 46.

36. "The prophets were inheritors of [the] historical view of divine activity which view they tempered with a continued attention to the cosmic perspective. . . . [Their] determination to maintain the balance between reality and vision explains the significance of the prophet's self-consciousness as a messenger" (Hanson, "Old Testament Apocalyptic," 459).

of vision.[37] The events of human history, the ongoing experience of
exile and failed restoration, the separation of promise and fulfillment,
and the progressive dissolution of the delicate balance forged by the
prophets saw the formation of a new relationship between history and
myth. In the apocalyptic reformation of history, the visionary would
be torn from its moorings in history.[38]

The turning point for this reformation of history, according to
Hanson, is to be found in 2 (or Deutero-) Isaiah.[39] Insofar as 2 Isaiah
stands within what might be termed the Isaianic tradition,[40] there is
both a dependence upon the older Isaianic traditions and a reformulation of that material to explicate Israel's relationship to YHWH and
to reveal YHWH's involvement in new historical circumstances. This
reshaping of earlier material points to the origin of apocalyptic in the
demise of prophecy.

While the earlier Isaianic material precisely balanced vision and
reality,[41] 2 Isaiah sought to reestablish the sense of YHWH's involvement in and control over the events of history. Second Isaiah's reformulation can be viewed from two perspectives. On the one hand, that
reformulation can be seen as a response to the "systematic application
of the principle of promise and fulfillment" to the history of Israel
offered by the Deuteronomic historian. On the other hand, it could
be viewed as an attempt to surmount the kind of skepticism one finds
in Job and Qoheleth. The older visionary material, specifically the
Divine Warrior material, provided 2 Isaiah with a means to both ends.[42]

Furthermore, where there was, in Isaiah of Jerusalem, a kind of
historical continuity between promise and fulfillment, between Israel's

37. Hanson would stress history's service to myth. I regard the difference between
myth and history to be largely semantic. In one sense, however, the word "myth" is
not comprehensive enough, given the scope of Hanson's argument. For Hanson, vision
is couched in terms of the mythic elements Judaism appropriated from its neighbors.
Mythic language is also the vehicle through which the vision of the seer is articulated.

38. "Unsullied by the bitter disappointments of this world, mythic motifs began to
serve less the function of giving cosmic significance to YHWH's historical acts than of
offering a means of escape from the growing contradiction between glorious promise
and harsh reality" (Hanson, Dawn, 27).

39. Hanson, "Old Testament Apocalyptic," 461, 468–69; Dawn, 24–27, 122–34;
"Jewish Apocalyptic," 46–51.

40. The whole question of the relationship of 2 and 3 Isaiah to the Isaianic material
in chapters 1–39 is still open. Here we may note simply that the following chapters are
appended to the "original" material apparently as a further explication or appropriation
of what precedes.

41. Hanson, "Jewish Apocalyptic," 45.

42. See Hanson, "Jewish Apocalyptic," 49; Dawn, 124–27, 314–15; and "Old Testament Apocalyptic," 467.

betrayal of the covenant and YHWH's announcement of judgment and the pronouncement of deliverance, between the experience of exile and the hope for restoration, there is in 2 Isaiah a division of history into two periods. The first period includes the events of history from creation to the exile. This is the period of history before God's intervention.

The second period is the consequence of the intervention of YHWH in history. God intervened for the restoration of Israel as a "historical entity . . . in its historical land of Palestine." Yet while this intervention is "anchored tightly to the realm of plain history,"[43] YHWH no longer sustains and maintains the community of faith through the events of human history in quite the same way as YHWH had for Isaiah of Jerusalem. Rather, for 2 Isaiah, the hope for deliverance in history was sustained by the vision of YHWH's ultimate triumph over the cosmic forces of evil. What transpired in human history had its counterpart in the cosmic struggle between good and evil. "To an increasing extent," Hanson wrote, "salvation is portrayed not in the terms of political events, but in the idiom of the cosmic victory of the Divine Warrior." In 3 Isaiah, this deliverance comes not to the whole of the community, but to the faithful alone.[44]

Moreover, where for Isaiah of Jerusalem restoration and deliverance were events that held significance for the community of faith alone, 2 Isaiah asserts the significance of these events for the whole of creation. Here the events of human history provide the context for divine intervention for all creation. These events are not simply ends in themselves, but means to an end. These events have a significance far greater than any one moment by itself. This transformation of events from ends to means carried with it the assurance of deliverance, and sustained the confidence in the triumph of YHWH, which would transform the world once and for all.[45]

While 2 Isaiah pressed the tension between vision and history to its breaking point, he nonetheless remained well within the realm of classical prophecy. In fact, "Second Isaiah would have been Israel's first apocalyptic seer if at the same time he had not maintained the other side of the dialectic of prophecy, the integration of the cosmic vision into the realities of this world."[46] Yet, if the genius of 2 Isaiah

43. Hanson, "Jewish Apocalyptic," 49.
44. Hanson, *Dawn*, 315.
45. See Isa. 49:1ff.; 51:9-11.
46. Hanson, "Old Testament Apocalyptic," 467. Hanson claims that apocalyptic actually finds its first expression in Ezekiel 40–48, Ezekiel's reflections on the destruction of the Temple ("Jewish Apocalyptic," 46; "Old Testament Apocalyptic," 468).

was his ability to remain within the bounds of classical prophecy while introducing or reviving earlier mythic patterns, it was a genius that was not sustained by his disciples.[47] Either his disciples lacked his theological skills, or different historical circumstances strained and finally broke the balance he sought to maintain.[48] With those disciples the transition to apocalyptic is made,[49] and it seems to be made over the issue of God's involvement in history. For the disciples of 2 Isaiah, while faith in deliverance remained, its possibility in history was denied.

Third Isaiah was one of those disciples. While 3 Isaiah still seems to share the perspective of 2 Isaiah, there are some clear points of contrast. First, while both 2 and 3 Isaiah share the confidence that deliverance will come, 3 Isaiah finds himself confronted with a dilemma: The deliverance that seemed so near for 2 Isaiah has been "delayed." His task is to sustain the conviction that deliverance will come, despite both the delay in its realization and historical conditions that seem to preclude the possibility of deliverance. Second, 3 Isaiah announced a future, impending judgment that was to precede the long-awaited restoration. In a sense the expectation of impending restoration was replaced by the awareness (or by the acceptance) of the necessity of further judgment. For 2 Isaiah, on the other hand, the time of judgment had passed. Israel was to be restored through YHWH's forgiveness. Third, where 2 Isaiah had extended the promise of restoration and deliverance to the whole of Israel, 3 Isaiah offers that promise only to part of the nation.[50]

For Hanson, then, 3 Isaiah marks a clear turning point in the development of apocalyptic. Coupled with the continued, prolonged experience of disillusionment in the absence of the expected deliverance, strife within the community itself further alienated the visionary from the historical. By the time Zechariah 14 was written,[51] the separation between vision and history was more or less complete.[52] Apoc-

47. Hanson, "Jewish Apocalyptic," 50.
48. Both are perhaps defensible hypotheses. It also seems just as possible that, as 2 Isaiah had in some sense "explicated" and appropriated the work of Isaiah of Jerusalem before him, so his disciples did the same with his work.
49. How far Hanson wants to press this claim is unclear. In "Old Testament Apocalyptic," for example, he asserts that apocalyptic is born after 3 Isaiah (p. 468). In "Jewish Apocalyptic," however, he seems more inclined to trace that birth to the half century after 2 Isaiah, that is, to the time of 3 Isaiah (p. 50).
50. Hanson, Dawn, 61. Hanson includes Isa. 60–62 in the material that belongs to 2 Isaiah.
51. Ibid., 369–88.
52. Ibid., 280–85.

alyptic reflection was stripped of its concern for the historical and was consumed in its passion for understanding the cosmic struggle between good and evil. With the death of prophecy,[53] the balance between history and vision was itself broken.[54]

Within the community itself, conflict was stirred by the rise of the Zadokite priesthood and embodied in the debate surrounding their claim to legitimacy, the continued presence of foreign rule, and the absence of a sustained prophetic voice.[55] The issue became the discernment of YHWH's intervention in history for the deliverance of the oppressed faithful. The nation made great by the mighty acts of God became the remnant that was delivered by its faith. Offered to the faithful was an often-vivid portrayal of YHWH's sovereignty, which transcended the realm of historical events. Israel's significance as a people was no longer tied to its future as a nation, but to its future as YHWH's chosen, as YHWH's people, as a community of faith. These circumstances led to schism, to sectarianism, and finally to the flowering of apocalyptic.

The seeds of this transformation, which begins the final phase in the development of apocalyptic, are to be found in Zechariah 14. In 2 Zechariah the themes that so often shape apocalyptic texts are found. First, the "dualism and division of history into eras" is most evident. Second, the cataclysm and horror of the present are seen as a sign of the transition from the old, evil era to the new world, where YHWH's final triumph and the restoration of the faithful will be assured. Third, the description of the events that point to the coming final struggle are vivid. Fourth, there is no attempt to link "eschatological events to events and persons of plain history . . . the vision remains suspended in the cosmic realm of the Divine Warrior."[56] Fifth, the struggle between the visionary and hierocratic, which Hanson terms "the matrix for the development of apocalyptic," seems to be quite strong.[57]

---

53. Hanson argues that prophecy was born with the monarchy and perished with it ("Jewish Apocalyptic," 45–46). With the rise of the monarchy, prophetic eschatology reflected the expectations of a growing and developing nation. Here prophetic pronouncement "interprets for the king and the people how the plans of the divine council will be effected within the context of their nation's history and the history of the world" (*Dawn*, 11).

54. Hanson, *Dawn*, 240–68.

55. Here Hanson seems to follow Cross in linking the rise and fall of prophecy to the monarchy. According to Cross, "Prophecy and kingship in fact expired together" ("New Directions," 161).

56. Hanson, "Jewish Apocalyptic," 56.

57. Hanson, "Dawn," 399.

If Zechariah 14 begins the transition to apocalyptic, Daniel 7 represents its peak.[58] For it is here that the "connections with politico-historical realities have been lost: Neither the human community, nor any other human agent, takes part in the conflict which would be won 'by no human hand' (8:25). . . . Events on earth merely reflect phases in the cosmic drama, involving struggles between the patron princes. The world view is the mythopoeic one which forms the basis of a myth like the *Enuma elish*."[59] Also, in Daniel 7 the sense of isolation or alienation from the world and the accompanying call to abandon a world consumed in darkness are at or near their peak.[60] For Daniel, the events of human history have no significance in or of themselves. Events are significant only insofar as they are part of the movement toward YHWH's final triumph. The events of history reveal the signs of the times, which are made accessible and rendered intelligible to the faithful through the interpretation of the seer.

As such, these signs are vehicles for discerning the mystery of the meaning of human existence and the meaning of the history of the world. That is to say, meaning lies not in the historical significance of events but in their cosmic significance. In this concern for discerning the visionary, the integration of history and myth that so dominates the work of Isaiah of Jerusalem is lost. Where the significance of the cosmic struggle between good and evil once lay in the light it cast upon the events of history, the events of human history now find their significance in the light they shed upon the cosmic struggle between good and evil. History has been eclipsed by myth, and the prophet supplanted by the seer.

CRITICAL ASSESSMENT

Hanson's position is open to question and challenge at several points. First, this approach assumes that there is a clear and discernible line of development from prophetic to apocalyptic eschatology. Essentially, this approach assumes that this process of development can be substantiated through an examination of biblical texts. The assumption

58. " 'Apocalyptic' belongs to the eschatological tradition originating in the classical prophets and culminating in works such as Daniel 7–12, Revelation, and 4 Ezra" (Hanson, *Dawn*, 10).

59. Hanson, "Old Testament Apocalyptic," 476.

60. See Hanson's article in *IDBS*, 30, for his analysis of the relationship between apocalyptic and the experience of alienation.

is that simple ideas give rise to more complex and abstract ones, that concern for the historical precedes concern for the transcendent, that there is an identifiable process of historical development in Hebrew Scripture that mirrors and parallels its theological development. As such, ideas like resurrection of the dead or immortality of the soul of the individual are seen as necessarily late developments. These ideas may be seen as the result of the transformation of the idea of corporate deliverance, of restoration of the nation after judgment, which, in the absence of realization, became detached from historical circumstance and ever more abstract.

This approach has two consequences. First, once outlined, this process of development becomes the basis for determining what is or is not consonant with an orthodox expression of faith. What is normative is defined by the process of development, and what is normative in this sense, precludes and excludes by necessity certain expressions of faith. Insofar as this approach most often seems to define prophecy as representative of mainline (or normative) Judaism, wisdom and apocalyptic reflection are seen as secondary expressions of faith that to a greater or lesser extent depart from orthodoxy. The portrait of orthodoxy that emerges is very narrow and exclusive, rather than broad and inclusive.

We have no grounds upon which to substantiate such a portrait of orthodoxy—except perhaps through an analysis that first establishes the conditions for determining what may or may not have been an orthodox expression of faith. The tradition that stretches from Lücke to Hanson attempts to place the rise of apocalyptic reflection within such a reconstruction. At best such a reconstruction is arbitrary and narrowly construes the breadth and depth of Hebrew Scripture. Furthermore, the presence of such a broad range of texts in Hebrew Scripture—including wisdom and apocalyptic—calls into question a narrow portrayal of orthodoxy and suggests that "mainline" Judaism, if such a term is even applicable, was much more diverse and rich in its texture than Hanson's analysis might otherwise indicate.

The second point is closely related to the first. Hanson relies heavily on the text of Ezra-Nehemiah to establish a kind of hermeneutical circle between text and history. First, he analyzes these texts in order to determine the historical circumstances within which these texts arose. Once he has completed this reconstruction, he then uses this reconstruction to inform and enlighten the texts themselves. An important assumption is made here, namely, that text and event are mutually enlightening. The events of history, within which the texts themselves arose, can be recovered from these very texts. Once recovered, the historical context can and does offer deeper insight into the origin and meaning of the text. Once established, the historical stages of development become the basis for determining the date of and historical circumstances behind those texts. At best this reasoning is circular. The relationship between text and history is not a closed hermeneutical circle. Closure of this hermeneutical circle presumes a relationship between text and history that cannot be established.

Furthermore, as scholars who have studied Josephus, Herodotus, Thucydides, Xenophon, or even Virgil have learned, in the ancient world, recounting history was not distinct from interpreting it. That is, the accounts of history the ancients offered were *apologia,* in the broad sense of that word. Events were retold and reinterpreted with a particular end in mind and from a particular perspective. Much the same can be said about the books in Hebrew Scripture. These texts proceed from a more or less distinctive theological perspective that colors and shapes the interpretation of historical circumstances these texts offer. Often, those events are accessible only through allusion, or through the author's interpretation of those events. In effect, our only access to the events behind the text is through their significance for salvation history.

This does not mean that ancient historiography was any less historical. It simply means that discovering the historical context—that is, the historical events behind these texts—imposes an idea of history upon those texts that is foreign to them. Furthermore, since those events were not themselves the subject of these texts, it is difficult if not impossible to recover them from the texts alone. Hanson, Plöger, and Vriezen all assume that the historical context is accessible in and through the text. It need not be. In fact, I would argue, the historical context within which these texts emerged is for the most part inaccessible. Moreover, where it is accessible, it is accessible only implicitly. In short, it is not possible to move from text to context with any degree of certainty. Reconstruction asks more of these texts than they, or any text, can give.

Second, such a method assumes that historical development is linear. In effect, the relationship between apocalyptic and prophetic eschatology, between apocalyptic and "normative" Judaism, is linear.[61]

___

61. That there was a "normative" Judaism at any period has been called into question,

Apocalyptic is the final stage in a long historical process. Clearly, Hanson, Vriezen, Plöger, and others all see apocalyptic as a late development, and even as an aberration—that is, as an expression of faith that falls outside normative Judaism. If not an aberration, then it is an increasingly sectarian phenomenon that eventually falls outside mainline Judaism. I would argue, first, that apocalyptic need be neither late nor an aberration; second, that apocalyptic reflection is an essential part of the ongoing reflection that characterizes the faith of Israel;[62] and third, that apocalyptic reflection has, at its core, concerns and problems that are at the heart of Judaism itself.[63] With respect to the first point, Christopher Rowland has argued that "the attempt to understand the divine will in the midst of the power-politics of the ancient world had a long pedigree in Judaism. . . . Thus it is hardly surprising that at a later stage of her history the distinctive beliefs about God and history should have demanded an understanding of the Jewish nation's role in history, the relationship of the divine promises to the circumstances of the present, and the conviction that there was a divine dimension to human existence, however obscure it might seem in the present."[64] If Rowland is correct, apocalyptic does not represent the intensification of the mythical or visionary in an ever-increasing abandonment of or separation from the historical. Apocalyptic begins with, or is rooted in, the conviction that there is a divine dimension to human existence and to the events of history—a conviction that has a long history in the faith of Israel. Apocalyptic is the search for and the articulation of the divine dimension in human existence. Insofar as apocalyptic explicates the divine dimension in human

---

for example, in Martin Hengel, *Judaism and Hellenism* (Philadelphia: Fortress, 1981), esp. 1:32–57. In one sense Hengel's analysis offers a portrait of Judaism that allows for a broader understanding of Judaism. In another sense, his analysis still mirrors and embodies more traditional assumptions—and stereotypes—about various aspects of Judaism. "At that late period there was an alliance between oriental Jewish wisdom and Greek popular philosophy. Common to both was their rational, empirical character, their universalist tendency, their interest in the divine ordering of the cosmos" (p. 311); "A second fruit of the controversy with Hellenism was *hope for the future*, which among the simple populace usually took the form of an imminent eschatological expectation. This was hope, for the whole people, of the rule of God or the messianic kingdom, and for the individual, of resurrection or immortality" (p. 312).

62. This point has been argued to some extent in John Collins, "Apocalyptic Eschatology and the Transcendence of Death," *CBQ* 36 (1979): 21–43; and Christopher Rowland, *The Open Heaven* (New York: Crossroad, 1982).

63. The following material has been adapted from a paper entitled "Apocalypticism and Death," presented in 1984 to the national convention of the Society of Biblical Literature, Chicago.

64. Rowland, *Open Heaven*, 9.

existence, that articulation extends to the events of human history as well. Apocalyptic thought begins at the crossroads of historical event and theological reflection.

Thus, apocalyptic reflection does not necessarily involve an abdication of concern for history. It does not necessarily offer a view of a cosmic struggle between good and evil that is set over against historical reality. Apocalyptic reflection is not necessarily born in a growing pessimism about the possibility of deliverance. Dualism of this world and the next, a doctrine of two ages, concern for the end time, are neither exclusive nor necessary characterizations of apocalyptic texts. Rather, essential to apocalyptic literature is the interpretation it offers, albeit from a theological perspective, of historical events that form the life of the community. This interpretation is couched in the form of a revelation that is intended to explicate the deeper meaning of those events. Apocalyptic provides meaning, an interpretation of human events that places them within the larger context of divine revelation.

Proceeding from a similar perspective, John Collins has argued, against the analyses offered by Hanson, Mowinckel, and others, that "despite the fact that the term *eschatology* is normally used to describe it, the future hope of late postexilic and intertestamental Judaism cannot be defined with reference to 'the end' of something. . . . If the apocalyptic books were written, as is widely believed, to give hope to the faithful in times of oppression, it would be indeed extraordinary if they were primarily concerned with 'the end' and not with what lies beyond it."[65] If Collins is correct, apocalyptic revelation is shaped not by its concern for the end time but by its concern for the application of existing theological categories and concepts to the present historical circumstances. Most often, this revelation or reflection is cast in terms that include or support the hope that the world has not been abandoned by God, despite what appears to be historical evidence to the contrary. This hope carries with it the assurance and promise that God's presence endures and continues to enliven and sustain the community of faith. This assurance, this confidence, is embodied in the portrait of the eschaton. The hope that this revelation offers the community is tied to the transformation of human being and of the world,[66] a transformation portrayed in the images of peace, confidence, serenity, and

---

65. Collins, "Apocalyptic Eschatology," 27; see also Rev. 21–22; 4 Ezra 7:89–101; 10:25–28; 2 Bar. 49–52; 72–74.
66. Collins, "Apocalyptic Eschatology," 37.

restoration. This is the world of the end time.[67] This revelation extends the assurance that God is present in the world, that those who suffer do not suffer alone or without purpose. Apocalyptic revelation, therefore, is more concerned with opening the dilemma of the present situation to theological reflection, to a revelation that extends "from above," as it were,[68] in order to enlighten the world and human existence. This revelation is made within the rich and complex tapestry of the faith of Israel. The theodicy question serves as a focal point for that reflection.[69]

Furthermore, if apocalypticism is an essential part of the theological reflection of Judaism, then the attempt to place its origin at a specific point in history or within a specific historical epoch or context cannot but fail.[70] Apocalypticism is not a movement that took root in Judaism and that over time became more and more self-sustaining. It is one of the many threads of Israel's ongoing theological reflection. If Rowland is correct, one must not speak about an apocalyptic movement that arose at a particular point in history and that has a clearly definable history. One must speak instead of a number of apocalyptic movements that arose at various points in the history of Judaism.[71]

As we have seen, Hanson, Plöger, and others have offered a picture of apocalyptic that is couched in a particular understanding of the history of Judaism.[72] That is, apocalyptic is construed as a type of eschatology—as apocalyptic eschatology. Apocalyptic represents the final stage of prophecy (whether its flowering or its decline), a phenomenon that reaches back to the roots of faith. Yet if Rowland and

67. To this description we might add: trust, confidence, and reassurance. See, for example, the "woes" to the sinners in Sib. Or. 3:295-345; 1 Enoch 94:6—100:13; see also 1 Enoch 90:6-42; 95:3; 96:1; 97:1; 104:2; 2 Enoch 1-8; 4 Ezra 13:46-47; Sib. Or. 3:285 ("There is a certain royal tribe whose race will never stumble. This too, as time pursues its cyclic course, will reign and will begin to raise up a new temple to God"), 700-30, 767-95; 5:139-49; 14:351-60; 1 Enoch 10:18-19; 2 Bar. 29:5-8; 84:1-11. Also see David Aune's analysis of what he terms "Oracles of Assurance" in 1 Sam. 1:17; Isa. 41:8-16; 43:1-7; 44:1-5; Jer. 1:17-19; 15:19-21; 30:10-11; 42:9-12 (*Prophecy in Early Christianity* [Grand Rapids: Eerdmans, 1983], 94).

68. Collins, "Apocalyptic Eschatology," 37. Collins describes the worldview of apocalyptic reflection in terms of a two-story universe: a world above and a world below. See also 1 Enoch 72-82.

69. See, for example, 4 Ezra 4:22ff.; 7:61-62; 8:5-6; 43:113-14: 2 Bar. 14:1ff.; 1 Enoch 69:11-12.

70. Rowland, *Open Heaven,* 193.

71. Ibid., 193-97.

72. See, for example, Robert P. Carroll, *When Prophecy Failed* (New York: Seabury, 1979), 204ff.; M. E. Stone, "Apocalypses and Prophecy" and "Apocalypse and the Fulfillment of Prophecy," both in *Jewish Writings,* 384ff.

Collins are correct in their analyses, such an approach finally obscures our understanding of both apocalyptic and eschatology. According to Rowland:

> There can be no disputing the fact that the prophetic oracles concerning the future had a central role to play in the formation of various Jewish eschatologies which existed during the period of the Second Temple. The contribution of prophecy to the idea of apocalyptic, therefore, was very extensive and cannot be denied. . . . Of all the common elements in prophecy and apocalyptic . . . the shared conviction that knowledge of God comes through inspiration . . . is the most important contribution of the former to the latter. Confirmation of the contribution of prophecy to the ideas of apocalyptic is not an indication that apocalyptic is the child of prophecy.[73]

An appropriate metaphor of the relationship between apocalyptic and eschatology is the Cartesian coordinate system in geometry. On the one hand, there is the x axis, the horizontal dimension of eschatological hope. This dimension is oriented toward the future and sees the future as the resolution of the present experience of oppression and exile. Eschatological reflection looks forward in faith. On the other hand, the y axis, or the vertical dimension, represents apocalyptic reflection. Apocalyptic offers insight in seeking to open the present to the possibility of divine revelation in an effort to resolve the immediacy of suffering and death in the absence or hiddenness of God. Both dimensions are to be found in Judaism. These dimensions come together at the point where the relation between the human and the divine is weakest—in the presence of death.

Apocalyptic, then, is not a type of eschatology. They are two distinct but not unrelated phenomena that "come together precisely because the task of understanding God's will was particularly difficult as far as eschatology was concerned. Consequently it comes as no surprise that a dominant feature of the mysteries revealed to the apocalypticists is the secret of the future."[74]

From Collins's perspective, with which I am inclined to agree, it is not the secrets of the future but the depth of insight into the existence of human beings in history that is the subject and thrust of that revelation. This seems to be the thrust of the various accounts of the seer's

---

73. Rowland, *Open Heaven*, 245–46.
74. Ibid., 48.

journey through the heavens.[75] These journeys seem to offer a portrait of the power, presence, and purpose that underlie the universe and human existence, a portrait that is usually inaccessible to those who remain bound to the earth.[76]

If reflection upon the secrets of the universe is at all accessible within an eschatological perspective, the scope of that reflection would appear to be limited to a view of the restoration that lies beyond the present oppression of the community, whether that restoration is in this world or another, in transformation or in re-creation. The assurance that restoration is to be and remains a real possibility offers the community sustenance. How that restoration will occur, why it is delayed, and where God is are all issues that call for a revelation of purpose that can come only from God. This revelation lies beyond the portrait of the eschaton. Access to that purpose is given to the community via the reflection and revelation of the seer. Thus, while we find eschatological themes and concerns in apocalyptic texts, these themes and concerns do not in themselves define apocalyptic reflection.

In this sense, attempts to define apocalyptic as a type of eschatology seem doubly weak. First, this approach assumes that the definition of apocalyptic is contingent upon reaching an adequate understanding of eschatology. Second, this approach assumes that a consistent definition of eschatology can be formulated. Consistency of definition depends, to a great extent, upon the presence of historical information that can serve as the basis for conclusions drawn from such an analysis.

Given the vast and varied corpus with which we are dealing and given the actual lack of historical information needed to support a comprehensive and detailed analysis of the kind necessary to sustain

75. Not all apocalyptic texts contain journeys through the heavens. Those which do include the Apocalypse of Abraham, 1 Enoch 1–36, 37–71 (Similitudes of Enoch), 72–82 (Book of the Heavenly Luminaries), 2 Enoch, 3 Baruch, Test. Levi 2–5, the Testament of Abraham, and the Apocalypse of Zephaniah. Martha Himmelfarb has argued that journeys into the underworld are also not uncommon (*Tours of Hell* [Philadelphia: Fortress, 1985]). See, for example, the Apocalypse of Peter, the Apocalypse of Zephaniah, the Apocalypse of Paul, the Apocalypse of Ezra, Vision of Ezra, and 2 Baruch.

76. See 1 Enoch 17–36; Asc. Isa. 6–11 (though a later work); Dan. 7–12; Test. Abr. 10:1–15:15; Apoc. Abr. 15:1–29:21 (see esp. 23:3: "What you cannot understand, I will make known to you . . . and I will tell you what I have kept in my heart" [Rubinkiewicz trans.]; "If you can not understand it, I will explain it to you . . . and I will tell you the things laid up in my heart" [Pennington trans.]); Test. Levi 2–5; 3 Bar. 2–16 (esp. 1:8: "Come and I shall disclose to you the mysteries of God."). From a somewhat different perspective, see 4 Ezra 5:37: "I will explain the travail that you cannot understand." See also Ezra's driving questions in 4:22-25.

Hanson's position, at best we can offer only broad and fairly general definitions of eschatology and apocalypticism that are minimal in their claims.[77] Apocalypticism is concerned with the apprehension of divine will, insofar as the revelation of that will provides a context or purpose within which the life of the community, and its faith in God, is maintained and sustained. While the question of the justice of God's actions may never have arisen in prophetic texts, this question is implicit in apocalyptic reflection. That is to say, the need for divine revelation rests upon the experience of abandonment and estrangement from God. This experience is most acute at the point where human existence is pressed against its limits. That experience is embodied preeminently in the death question, which in turn cannot be raised without raising the issue of the justice of God's actions.

Eschatology, in contrast, is concerned with restoration, with transformation of the present crisis in or through the intervention of God. It is the sustained hope in future deliverance and restoration of the community of faith by God. That deliverance is to emerge through divine judgment at the end of time, it emerges beyond history, beyond human existence. Eschatological reflection holds open the possibility that conflicts that have no resolution in history ultimately find that resolution outside history. In this way, eschatology is the transformation of the immediacy of the prophetic promise of deliverance into a future possibility. Eschatology affirms and sustains the hope that the deliverance that is yet to be will be.

Eschatology promises redress for those who receive no redress in this world. Eschatology promises and affirms that God's presence endures even amid suffering and death. Furthermore, eschatology is an assertion made in faith about the ultimate righteousness and justice of God in the presence of historical events that seem to call that righteousness and justice into question. With the extension of faith in the triumph of God and deliverance of the faithful, eschatological reflection attempts to mitigate the issue of the suffering of the innocent, to provide a context within which the force of the theodicy question is softened, if not silenced, and within which faith in God is sustained.

Restoration of the community has two dimensions: On the one hand, there is the concern for the restoration of the power that was

---

77. The use of the word "apocalypticism" here is deliberate. It is not used to indicate the presence of an apocalyptic movement, as Hanson, for example, defines the term in his *IDBS* article. Rather, "apocalypticism" is used here instead of the phrase "apocalyptic reflection," as a mark of the integrity and unity this matrix of concepts and reflections has on its own, apart from the eschatological reflection of prophecy.

Israel's under David. On the other hand, the experience of oppression and exile is an experience of alienation and estrangement from God. This experience of estrangement, in a very real sense, is an experience of death, or at least is an experience of drawing near the edge of existence. Restoration is therefore a restoration of life, to the individual and to the people. As we noted earlier, the presence of God sustained life. The absence of God removed it. Part of the force of eschatological reflection, then, is the promise it extends for the return of the presence of God and thus for renewed life.[78]

Yet the promise of deliverance—the assertion that restoration will be—is not in itself enough to sustain faith or to resolve the death question. It cannot in itself resolve the issue of God's involvement in human suffering and death or quiet the possibility that there is no God there, that God's silence in the presence of our suffering and death speaks of our abandonment by God. Promise of deliverance is not enough. The promise of restoration and even the promise of resurrection are not enough. At some point only the emergence of God from the darkness, only a revelation of the purpose behind God's absence can overshadow the force of the death and suffering of the innocent. But as that suffering endures, the presence of death becomes more oppressive.

The more hidden the presence of God, the further into the distance that promised deliverance becomes and the less tenable and enduring seems the promise that eschatological hope extends to the community. Eschatological reflection, which itself provides suffering, oppression, and death with a perspective, is thus marked by an incompleteness that in turn calls faith, promise, and hope into question. Insofar as deliverance remains a distant promise and not an event in human history, eschatological reflection does not resolve the death question. Eschatological reflection intensifies it.

APOCALYPTICISM AND DEATH

The long tradition that stretches from Lücke to Hanson brings to these texts a passion for order, a singular commitment to a linear understanding of the historical development of Judaism, and a biblical hermeneutic that assumes that simpler ideas give rise to more complex

---

78. In this way, the case could be made that belief in resurrection, present in the intertestamental period, reflects more than simply Hellenistic influences. Such belief may well have its roots in eschatological reflection, which may in turn be drawn from the faith of Israel.

ones, that apocalyptic reflection owes as much to the demise of prophecy as it does to the circumstances in which the postexilic community found itself. In the previous section, I argued, first, that the relationship between text and event, which is a crucial part of the foundation of the tradition's understanding of the origin and development of apocalypticism, was not tenable; second, that the history of Judaism is not a linear process that began with the patriarchs, reached a climax with the prophets, and, with the dawn of apocalyptic, flowered and matured. To these a third point can be added: To speak of the flowering of apocalyptic as the final stage in the development of Judaism, to speak of a relationship between text and history in which each is constitutive of the other, is to introduce a structure and a systematic unity to these texts that, in the last analysis, is foreign to the texts themselves. Furthermore, these assertions finally obscure the rich and complex tapestry into which these texts have been woven. Such a tapestry takes shape not around a specific historical development or one or more concepts that are systematically explicated or even the demise of classical prophecy, but around a deep and lasting theological concern: Why in the presence of God is there death? This is the question that frames apocalyptic reflection. As we see in the Apocalypse of Abraham, in 4 Ezra, and in 2 Baruch, it is a question that speaks in many voices and textures, with a depth and a richness that is drawn from the heart of the faith of Israel.[79]

The Apocalypse of Abraham

As the apocalypse opens, Abraham is engaged in making idols. Each of the seven idols he makes suffers the same fate—they are broken (1:1—2:9). Abraham is troubled that Marumath, the god in whose image the statues were made, can neither stand up on its own nor recover from having fallen (3:1-8). How then, Abraham wonders, can a god whose head is made from one stone and its body made from another "be able to save a human, or hear a prayer, or reward humans?" (3:8). Upon his return to his father's house, Abraham confronts Terah. If the gods cannot help themselves, how can they help humans? (4:1-4). Terah is angered by his son's disrespect.

Terah orders Abraham to collect the shavings from statues of other gods that he was making so that Abraham might prepare dinner. In

---

79. In the interest of brevity, we examine here only the Apocalypse of Abraham, 4 Ezra, and 2 Baruch. Parenthetical references in the text are respectively to these books.

the shavings, Abraham discovers a statue of another god, Barisat (5:1-6). Abraham sets Barisat by the fire so that this god might use its power to sustain the fire. Instead, upon his return, Abraham finds that Barisat's feet have fallen into the fire. Eventually, Barisat is consumed in the fire (5:8-11). After Terah consumes the food that Abraham has just prepared, Terah praises Marumath. Abraham tells Terah that he should praise Barisat who was consumed in the fire, and not Marumath. Terah in turn praises Barisat and tells Abraham that he will make another statue the following day (5:12-17).

Angered and amused by his father's proclamation, Abraham challenges the idea that a god can be embodied in an image. Better fire than an image, and better water than fire, since fire is quenched by water (6:1—7:8). Determined to find the God, Abraham entreats his father to join him (7:9-12). Terah, his home, and all his possessions perish in a fire, apparently of divine judgment, (8:4-6).

Abraham is called by the God for whom no image can be made. Abraham offers sacrifice to God that hidden secrets might be revealed to him (9:5-9). With Iaoel as his guide, Abraham ascends into the heavens. Through seven visions the secrets of the heavens are revealed to him.[80] As part of that revelation, the events of human history that are yet to come appear before Abraham. The review of history concludes with the destruction of the Temple and the dawn of the eschaton. The history of the world is divided into twelve hours (29:2ff.). Each of those hours (or ages) of the world from the fall of Adam to the eschaton has anticipated the last hour, which is now at hand. In the last hour the righteous who have suffered unjustly at the hands of the wicked will be vindicated in their return from exile (see chap. 31). The wicked in turn will be punished or destroyed.[81]

There are several important issues here. Perhaps the two most important revolve around the conversion of Abraham from idolatry to "true faith" and around the problem of the suffering of the innocent and righteous (esp. chaps. 23–24). The issue of the nature of the proper expression of faith at least implicitly raises the question of how faith

---

80. Abraham has visions of fiery angels (15:5-7), fire (17:1-4), the throne (18:1-4), the heavens (19:4-9), the world (21:1-7), the seven sins of the world (24:3—25:2), and the destruction of the Temple (27:1-3).

81. Pronouncement of judgment is found in the plagues that are to be sent upon the Gentiles (29:1ff.). As Nickelsburg notes, a dualism between the saved and the damned is built into the cosmology of this text (*Jewish Literature between the Bible and the Mishnah* [Philadelphia: Fortress, 1981], 296).

is to be expressed. Clearly, proper faith is faith in the one God. That one God, of course, is the God of Israel.[82] This God is the author of creation (22:3), the source of all intentionality that underlies the created universe. Because of Abraham's faith, the whole course of human history is revealed to him. That revelation is startling because of its brutality.[83] This brutality is at the root of the second issue that troubles Abraham: If God is the source of all that is, the author of creation, the one whose intentions frame the universe, then insofar as there is both good and evil in the world, is not God lord over both?

> "Eternal Mighty One, why have you granted anyone like [Azazel][84] the power to destroy in this way the race of humans through what they do on earth?" And [God] said to me, "Listen, Abraham, I hate those who desire evil, because of what they do; and I have granted him authority to rule and be loved by them." And I answered, ". . . why have you willed that humans should desire evil in their hearts? For you are angry with what you have willed yourself when a person goes after things which have no place in your world." And [God] said to me, "It has been arranged like this as a wound to the nations for your race." (23:12—24:2)

Why has God allowed evil to be present in the world? In order to engender Israel's position among the nations. In point of fact, however, the presence of evil does not. Evil plagues Israel just as it does the nations. Nor, for that matter, does God distinguish between those who commit evil acts and are part of Israel and those who are not. All who are wicked suffer one fate. For Abraham, the logic of God's response is not apparent. Why would God use evil to accomplish good? In order to bring suffering into the world? In order to punish humans? If it is by the hand of God that evil enters the world, then is not God responsible for evil? If God is responsible for evil, then is not the suffering that is the consequence of evil also God's responsibility? If God is responsible for human suffering, why do the innocent suffer? Why in the presence of God is there death? In the Book of Job,

---

82. Nickelsburg suggests that in some way this is a comment on cultic practices (*Jewish Literature*, 298–99). If the author or authors are offering a critique of the cult or cultic practices, the point of that critique is lost to us.

83. For example, Cain's murder of Abel (24:5-9), the slaughter of many (26:6—27:12), and plagues (30:1-8).

84. Azazel is the name given to the embodiment of evil. It corresponds in form and function to the role assigned to Belial or Satan.

as we shall see, and in 4 Ezra 3:13-14 and 2 Baruch 4:5,[85] if there is an answer to the theodicy question, it remains inaccessible.

The revelation that is offered clearly attempts to remove the stain of guilt from God, to pronounce God not guilty, by establishing a reason or a purpose for God's actions, perhaps even by providing a context within which they are justified. In the last analysis, however, this revelation is made over against the question of God's responsibility. The revelation does not silence the theodicy question; it simply overwhelms us.

Fourth Ezra

As the text begins, a troubled and even angry God confronts Ezra. God is troubled by a people who has forgotten all that God has done on behalf of Israel (1:4-11).[86] Because Israel has forgotten what God has done on its behalf, the relationship between God and Israel has been broken. Exile and estrangement are the marks of the end of that relationship. Where there is exile and estrangement, death is close at hand. "Because you have forsaken me, I will forsake you. . . . You should be my people and I should be your God.[87] . . . But now what shall I do to you? I will cast you out from my presence. When you offer oblations to me, I will turn my face from you" (1:24-32).[88]

Human guilt, quite simply, implies divine innocence. But for Ezra, the relationship between human guilt and human suffering is neither simple nor to the point. Ezra is troubled by the desolation of Jerusalem and the wealth of the nations that oppress Israel (3:1-3).[89] Moved by what has befallen him, Ezra recounts the events from creation to the time of the patriarchs (3:4-19). On the one hand, by calling these events to mind, Ezra emphasizes both God's love for human beings and God's power over all creation. On the other hand, these events

85. John J. Collins argues for the distinctiveness of this text in relation to 4 Ezra and 2 Baruch (*The Apocalyptic Imagination* [New York: Crossroad, 1984], 186).

86. Much of the discussion of 4 Ezra that follows was presented to the Pseudepigrapha Section of the Society of Biblical Literature at its national convention in Anaheim in 1989. Pseudepigraphic translations here closely follow J. H. Charlesworth, ed., *OT Pseudepigrapha*, 2 vols. (Garden City, N.Y.: Doubleday, 1983–85).

87. See Jer. 7:23; 24:7; 32:38-39; 2 Sam. 7:24; Deut. 26:17-18; 29:13; Exod. 6:6; Ezek. 11:20; 14:11; 36:28; 37:26-28.

88. Also see Deut. 31:17-18; 32:20; Isa. 54:7-8; 57:17; 59:2; Mic. 3:4; Exod. 33:18-23; Ps. 69:17-18 (16-17); Ezek. 39:24-29; 1 Enoch 84:6.

89. In this case he is troubled by Babylon's wealth, as are also Job and Enoch. See 2 Enoch 1:3-4.

raise for Ezra a deep and troubling question: Despite all that God has done, God did not remove the shadow of evil from the human heart (3:20). Consequently, evil has overshadowed the promise of the law (3:20-27), and death has overshadowed life. To what end? (3:28-36). For what purpose?

For Ezra's questions, there is no answer. Instead the angel Uriel responds with more than a measure of contempt. "Your understanding has utterly failed regarding this world . . . do you think you can comprehend the way of the Most High?" (4:1ff.). But Ezra is not to be silenced. "It would be better," he says, "for us not to be here than to come here and live in ungodliness, and to suffer and not understand why" (4:12). Once again, Ezra's protest appears to fall upon deaf ears. This time Uriel offers a parable (4:13-21). Its point is that humans should not aspire to know what lies in the heavens. Such things can be known only by God. The assurance that the knowledge to which he aspires is God's alone does not move Ezra to silence. Instead he voices his protest again. "Why have I been endowed with the power of understanding? For I did not wish to inquire about the ways above, but about those things that we experience daily: why Israel has been given over to the Gentiles as a reproach; why the people you have loved have been given over to the godless tribes, and the law of our fathers has been made of no effect and the written covenants no longer exist; and why we pass from the world like locusts, and our life is like a mist, and we are not worthy of mercy" (4:22-25). Uriel does not seem to understand that Ezra does not aspire to know the secrets of the heavens. Ezra's question implies that until the question of the suffering of the innocent is answered, knowledge of the secrets of the heavens is inconsequential. Thus, despite Uriel's assurance that the end time is near (4:26-32), Ezra is not satisfied. Again Ezra's question finds no answer (4:33). In turn, Uriel tells him that his concerns are misplaced. For all things there is a time. Yet by humans that time is neither known nor hastened. What God does, God does in its own way and in its own time. This no human can change or comprehend (4:34-43).

As the next vision begins, Ezra is no less troubled than he was at the start of the first vision. Ezra prays to God, but that prayer quickly becomes a single question: Why? (5:21-30). Once again, Ezra's protest occasions another visit from Uriel. In the ensuing dialogue (5:31-55), Ezra again presses for an answer to his questions. Uriel's response is the same: The ways of God cannot be known (5:35-40). What God does, God does in its own time (5:41-55). Furthermore, as creation came from God, so will the end of all things (5:56—6:6). Everything that has happened, including exile and restoration, has been planned by God.

On the eighth day (6:35-37), Ezra is again troubled.[90] To the God that created all of creation (6:38-54) and that chose Israel as its firstborn and only begotten (6:58), Ezra again asks "Why? How long?" (6:59). Uriel's response is both complex and disquieting. Uriel tells Ezra that suffering is unavoidable, if not necessary (7:1-25). "Unless the living pass through the difficult and vain experiences," Ezra is told, "they can never receive those things that have been reserved for them. But now why are you disturbed, seeing that you are to perish? And why are you moved, seeing that you are mortal? And why have you not considered in your mind what is to come rather than what is now present?" (7:14-16). But this assertion, as disquieting as it appears, is at least counterbalanced by Uriel's contention that suffering is not in and of itself vain. For the righteous who suffer now, there is the fullness of the deliverance that is to come. For those who are not righteous, there will be only the emptiness of punishment (7:25).

When the signs Uriel has disclosed to him come to pass, Ezra is told, the hidden land will be disclosed. In those days the Messiah will be revealed (7:28). After four hundred years the Messiah and every human being shall die. For seven days the earth will lie in the silence of the primeval age undisturbed, and then the dead shall rise (7:30-32; see also Isa. 26:19). The last judgment will follow. To those who are righteous, paradise will be rewarded. To those who have sinned, hell will be disclosed as their inheritance (7:33-42).

Ezra is moved by this disclosure. But Ezra is also troubled by the promise of certain judgment. "But what of those for whom I have prayed? For who among the living is there that has not sinned, or who among men that has not transgressed your covenant? And now I see that the world to come will bring delight to few, but torments to many. For an evil heart has grown up in us that has alienated us from God,[91] and has brought us into corruption and the ways of death" (7:45-48). Ezra's companion attempts to console Ezra with a simple message: Two worlds have been created, one for the righteous and the other for the damned. To the world of the righteous few have

90. The third vision begins here (6:35—9:25).
91. The text here appears to read "from these" in the Latin, Syriac, and Ethiopic.

been called. To the world of damnation many will go. Over the fate of the wicked, Ezra's companion will not shed a tear (7:49-61). This pronouncement does not satisfy Ezra. "Let the four-footed beasts and the flocks rejoice, [for] it is much better for them than for us; for they do not look for a judgment, nor do they know of any torment or salvation promised to them after death. For what does it profit us that we shall be preserved alive but cruelly tormented? For all who have been born are involved in iniquities, and are full of sins and burdened with transgressions" (7:62-69; see also 7:46).

Uriel's response is to the point: Those who dwell upon the earth are tormented because though they have been endowed with understanding, they nonetheless violate the law (7:70-74).[92] Perhaps because Uriel's words offer no comfort, or perhaps because the finality of judgment appears overwhelming, Ezra again laments the fate of all that is human. "For what good is it to all," Ezra asks, "that they live in sorrow now and expect punishment after death? . . . What good is it to us, that an eternal age has been promised to us, but that we have done deeds that bring death? . . . For while we lived and committed iniquity, we did not consider what we should suffer after death" (7:117, 119, 126).[93] Uriel's response is that as long as one lives, one's

---

92. This statement appears to stand in the face of Uriel's assertion that human reason is inherently limited. How can human reason comprehend and live by the law if the law cannot be understood? No answer is offered. Uriel's response appears to satisfy Ezra, for his next question is about the fate of those who die before the day of judgment. Uriel outlines two separate paths, each with seven stages or ways. Notice that the corresponding stages are generally parallel.

The Way of Damnation	The Way of Deliverance
They have scorned the law.	They will see the glory of God that awaits them.
They cannot repent.	They will see that punishment awaits those who sin.
They will see the reward destined for those who obeyed the law.	They will see the witness concerning their righteousness.
They will see the torment that lies before them.	They understand the rest and glory that await them.
They will see the "habitations" of those who have been saved.	They will receive and enjoy their immortality.
They will witness the torment of the damned.	They will see how their faces will shine like the sun.
They will waste away in confusion and in shame.	They will rejoice because they will see the face of the one they served in life.

93. That Ezra, chosen for this revelation because of his righteousness, would here

fate is not written in stone. Every human is born with the freedom
to choose between damnation and deliverance (7:127-31). Upon hearing this, Ezra praises God (7:132-40). Uriel, however, does not sustain
Ezra's proclamation. Uriel instead sustains his earlier words—many
are created, but few are saved (8:1-3).

In words reminiscent of Job, Ezra responds to Uriel's pronouncement.

> For not of your own will did you come into the world, and against it
> you will depart, for you have been given only a short time to live. . . .
> You [God] have brought him up in your righteousness, and instructed
> him in your law, and reproved him in your wisdom. You will take away
> his life, for he is your creation; and you will make him live, for he is
> your work. If then you suddenly and quickly destroy him who with
> so great labor was fashioned by your command, to what purpose was
> he made? . . . What is man that you are angry with him; or what is a
> mortal race that you are so bitter against it? . . . Your goodness and
> righteousness will be declared when you are merciful upon those who
> have no store of good works. (8:4-36)[94]

Uriel's response is not comforting. Uriel does not care about those
who have sinned; only the righteous matter (8:37-41). Again Ezra asks
God for mercy (8:42-45). The response: Humans were not created to
suffer. Through the exercise of human freedom, however, many have
abandoned righteousness. The abandonment of righteousness leads to
suffering. The righteous do not suffer. From the righteous, death is
hidden and illness is banished. Furthermore, it is not for the righteous
to be concerned with the fate of those who have sinned (8:46-62).

The problem of suffering is addressed again in the appendix (15:1—
16:78),[95] which begins with the words: "The Lord says, 'Behold, speak

---

identify himself with those who have sinned seems strange. One would expect that
because Ezra is righteous, he would be able to detach himself from the fate that awaits
those who have sinned. Such seems not to be the case.

94. Note what appears to be a redaction seam in 8:19b: "The beginning of the work
of Ezra's prayer, before he was taken up. He said. . . ."

95. In form and content, the material in this section more closely parallels prophetic
texts than it does apocalyptic. Note, for example, the use of phrases such as "The Lord
says, 'Behold' . . .," or " 'Behold,' says the Lord . . . ," which resemble the prophetic
use of the phrase "Thus says the Lord. . . ." Furthermore, the tone of the material
contained in the appendix is harsh. The ironic tone that characterized many of Uriel's
comments to Ezra is absent here. Note also that nowhere in this section is Ezra mentioned. Cf. the use of the prophetic woe in the pronouncements that follow: 4 Ezra
15:24, 47; 16:1, 63, 77. For a detailed discussion of the use of the word "woe" in
prophetic texts, see Richard J. Clifford, "The Use of Hôy in the Prophets," CBQ 28

in the ears of my people the words of the prophecy which I will put
in your mouth . . . every unbeliever shall die in his unbelief' " (15:1-
4). Though all manner of evil and destruction are to be visited upon
the righteous, they will not be abandoned by God. Indeed, the innocent
and the righteous will be avenged (15:5-11).[96] At that time, there will
be no peace, pity, or prosperity. The crops will wither, violence will
be rampant, and there will be great tribulation throughout the world
(15:12-19). The presence of such misery and suffering may point to
the desertion of the righteous by God, but such is not the case. The
sinners will be punished (15:20-27). But, like gold that has been tested
by fire, the righteous shall survive punishment and exile (16:68-73).

The Ezrianic Turn

Ezra's encounter with human suffering is not without its consequences.
Out of the experience of suffering, Ezra is moved to press for an
answer that might resolve the problem of human suffering. Yet what
is revealed to Ezra appears to shed little light on the reasons for human
suffering. At no point—despite his pleas—is Ezra told why humans
suffer and die. This dilemma leaves us with three questions: First,
what is the relationship between this revelation and the problem of
human suffering? Second, how and to what extent does this revelation
provide a context for understanding human suffering? Third, how
might the presence—or absence—of a relationship between experience
and revelation provide insight into the origin of apocalyptic literature?
     This crisis of faith, which appears bound to the tension between
the promises of faith and the experience of suffering, demands a response from God.[97] The revelation of the secrets of the heavens made

(1966): 458–64; Erhard Gerstenberger, "The Woe-Oracles of the Prophets," *JBL* 81
(1962): 249–62. Also see Isa. 24:16; 28:1; 29:1, 15; 30:1; 31:1; 33:1; Amos 6:1; Mic. 2:1;
Nah. 3:1.
     96. See especially Isa. 53:7 and also Ps. 44:22.
     97. One scholar has concluded: "When God's care for his people falls short of
expectations, a crisis of confidence ensues, and all the more so when this shortfall is
compounded into outright disaster. The author of *IV Ezra* confronted just such a disaster
and his agony erupted into the searching dialogue that still stands as a significant attempt
to bridge the evident gulf between God's promises and the actual facts of Jewish history. . . . There is an undercurrent of discontent about the appropriateness or availability
of God's blessings, but his appreciation of them is restricted because of God's unwill-
ingness to control evil" (A. L. Thompson, *Responsibility for Evil in the Theodicy of IV
Ezra*, SBLDS 29 [Missoula, Mont.: Scholars Press, 1977], 1, 288).

to Ezra is intended to be that response. Note, however, that Uriel reminds Ezra that no human can comprehend the secrets of the heavens. In practical terms, then, of what use is this revelation? Little or none. What the human mind cannot comprehend, it cannot find comfort in. Despite the revelation, the innocent still suffer and die. Exile and estrangement still eclipse faith in God.

Thus, though perhaps intended to offer a context within which faith is not called into question by the experience of suffering and death, Uriel's revelation, as the revelation made to Job, overwhelms but does not silence Ezra's protest. Uriel's revelation is intended to offer the assurance that human suffering is neither wanton nor arbitrary. Within the context of the hidden mystery of the whole, known only by God and shown to Ezra, all things have a reason, a purpose. But for Ezra, neither the context nor the assurance appears to be enough to resolve or to still the theodicy question. Ezra thus turns the question of human suffering and death back upon God. This Ezrianic turn is born in the knowledge that the revelation made in the name of God does not soften or mitigate the experience of exile and estrangement. The facticity of human suffering remains unchanged. The possibility remains that the God of love and the God of death are one and the same.

Insofar as Uriel's revelation is made in response to human suffering and exile, there is de facto a relationship between that experience and the revelation. Furthermore, insofar as apocalyptic reflection is an apocalypse (i.e., a kind of revelation), what is revealed and what elicits that revelation are inexorably bound together. In this way, the experience of suffering and death and of estrangement and exile provides both the occasion and the basis for apocalyptic reflection. Apocalyptic reflection, therefore, attempts to pronounce a verdict of not guilty over God, despite all the evidence to the contrary. But human suffering remains, despite that revelation. The cries of the dying are not stilled. Thus does human suffering turn the death question back upon God. The Ezrianic turn has at its heart the realization that as long as the silence of God enshrouds human existence, human suffering implies divine guilt. And as long as humans suffer and die, as long as in the course of events God appears detached from the course of human existence, the shadow of divine guilt continues to threaten to eclipse faith.

Second Baruch

We first meet Baruch on the eve of the destruction of Jerusalem.[98] Baruch is told by God that the remaining two tribes are to suffer exile because they have sinned. Indeed, their suffering is to be greater than those ten tribes because these people have forced their kings to sin (1:4). Baruch is overcome with sorrow and asks God to take his life, for he can bear neither the sins of Jerusalem nor the thought that he might witness the city's destruction (3:1). While Baruch appears to grant that God's anger against Jerusalem is just, he fears that God's anger will destroy the city forever (3:5ff.). "How long," he asks, "will this exile endure? Will Jerusalem vanish forever?"

God's response to Baruch is interesting. On the one hand, God offers Baruch comfort and reassurance: The exile will last "for a time" (4:1). On the other hand, Baruch is rebuked by God for even thinking that God could—or would—forever desert Jerusalem (4:2-7). Here, however, God does not speak of this Jerusalem, but of the vision of the city of paradise, promised first to Adam and later revealed to Abraham and Moses.[99] Though God then commands Baruch to go to the city and do as God has commanded, Baruch protests again. This time Baruch argues that Jerusalem be spared because, without Jerusalem, YHWH's name would be forgotten. Again this protest falls upon deaf ears. God assures Baruch that the name of God will last forever (5:1-4).

In the valley of Kidron, Baruch announces the judgment that has been revealed to him, to Jeremiah, and to the leaders of the people. Then, that evening, after he has withdrawn from the city, he witnesses in a vision the interment of the sacred vessels from the Holy of Holies in the earth (6:7ff.). After these vessels are buried, the destruction begins.[100] Once the angels have broken the walls of the city, Jerusalem is plundered by the Chaldeans, Zedekiah is sent to Babylon, and the people are carried off into captivity (8:5). Overcome with sorrow, Baruch and Jeremiah fast for seven days (9:1-2).

After seven days, the "word of God" comes to Baruch, and he is instructed to tell Jeremiah to follow the captives to Babylon. Baruch

---

98. Nickelsburg observes that in this text Baruch is portrayed as a prophet who is superior in stature to Jeremiah (*Jewish Literature,* 281); see also 2 Bar. 2:1.

99. The author implies that the Jerusalem that is to emerge from the exile, with the second temple restored, is this paradise.

100. Note that according to 2 Bar. 7:1, the city is destroyed not by the Chaldeans or any human enemy but by four angels carrying torches. This destruction or punishment by God then enables the Chaldeans to enter the city. See 2 Bar. 3–4.

is to remain behind so that God might reveal to him "what will happen at the end of days" (10:3). Following Jeremiah's departure, Baruch sits by the door of the temple and weeps. That lamentation raises the theodicy question (10:6—12:5). "Blessed is the one who is not born, or the one who was born and died. . . . And those who have no children will be glad, and those who have children will be sad. For why do they bear in pains only to bury in grief? . . . Would that you had ears, O Earth, and would that you had a heart, O Dust, so that you might go and announce in the realm of death and say to the dead, 'You are more happy than we who live' " (10:6—11:7). Baruch's lament is moving—and bitter—for it speaks of the inevitability of suffering (12:4) and of the certainty of incurring the wrath of God. Having offered his lament, Baruch fasts for seven days.

Later, while standing on Mount Zion, a voice "from the high heavens" speaks to Baruch. The voice addresses Baruch because he has been surprised by the destruction of Jerusalem. Baruch is told that because he has been surprised he will "be preserved until the end of times to be for a testimony" to the nations (13:2-3). The testimony that Baruch is to offer is about the force and power of divine retribution (13:6). Once the issue of the inevitability of retribution has been raised, Baruch asks: "What have they profited who have knowledge before you? . . . O Lord, my Lord, who can understand your judgment? Or who can explore the depth of your way? . . . For we all have been like breath. For as breath ascends without human control and vanishes, so it is with the nature of men, who do not go away according to their own will, and who do not know what will happen to them in the end" (14:5-12).

God's reply does little to comfort Baruch. Instead, Baruch is told that if the law had not been given, human beings would have been unable to understand the reasons for judgment. But, having been given the law and understanding, human beings are held accountable by God for the consequences of their actions (15:1-7). The consequence of human failure is human suffering. The glory and the destiny of the righteous lie in their suffering (15:8); the end of the world is coming on their account. Baruch is also told that a long life does not profit a human (17:1-4). Even if everyone were happy, despite the brevity of human life, all would be in vain because "the day death was decreed against those who trespassed," all humans die (19:8). The conclusion: The flow of time will hasten, the years will pass more quickly as the end of time approaches. Baruch is to remember what has been revealed

and prepare for what is to come (20:1ff.). Appropriately, Baruch retires
to a cave in Kidron and fasts for seven days (21:1-2).

At sunset, perhaps on that seventh day, Baruch again speaks to God.
Baruch's words are moving, and his concern is simple: How long?
How long will the corruption remain? How long will it be until mortals
can be happy? How long until death is forever sealed? (21:19-26).
Again God's response seems to offer little comfort: To all that has been
and will be there is an appointed time. "For when Adam sinned and
death was decreed against those who were to be born, the multitude
of those who were born was numbered. And for that number a place
was prepared where the living ones might live and where the dead
might be preserved. No creature will live again unless the number
that has been appointed is completed. For my spirit creates the living,
and the realm of the dead receives the dead" (23:4-6). Baruch is to
take heart because the day of judgment is almost at hand. At that time,
the suffering of God will be revealed (24:2). Baruch is to be preserved
until that time. These are the signs of the end time: chaos, loss of
hope, horror, and great torment (25:3-4).[101] After the torment, the
earth will again be fruitful (29:1ff.), and the Anointed One will come.
At that time, "those who sleep in hope of him will rise," and the
wicked "will the more waste away" (30:1-5).

Having received this revelation, Baruch again returns to address
the elders and leaders in the Kidron Valley. Baruch's message is simple:
The end is near. Prepare. Do not fear (32:1ff.). Upon concluding this
revelation, Baruch again returns to the ruins of the Holy of Holies
and weeps. Among the ruins, Baruch falls asleep. While asleep, Baruch
receives another vision. He sees a plain covered with trees and surrounded by mountains. In the midst of that forest there is a vine, and
under the vine a fountain. Waves from the fountain destroy all but
one cedar (36:6). Eventually even that cedar is overcome. The vine
condemns the cedar for its role in having fostered evil. As the cedar
burns, the vine grows (37:1). The following chapters contain a lengthy
explanation of this vision. In short, Baruch is told that the Anointed
One is the vine and the fountain. The last remaining cedar is the last
of many evil rulers. The evil ruler is to be brought to Zion and killed
by the Anointed One. This will mark the beginning of the rule of the
Messiah, and it will last until all corruption is brought to an end (40:3).

---

101. See the so-called apocalypse of the twelve calamities (2 Bar. 27:1-15). Cf. A.
J. F. Klijn, "2 Baruch," in *OT Pseudepigrapha*, 1:615–52.

As the interpretation of the vision comes to an end, Baruch is instructed to communicate what he has learned to the people. In response to this command, again Baruch gathers the elders of the people together and addresses them (44:1—46:7). Once again, Baruch's message is simple: "Prepare your heart so that you obey the law and be subject to those who are wise and understanding with fear. And prepare yourself that you shall not depart from them" (46:5-6). Once again Baruch withdraws from the people and fasts for seven days.

After his fast, Baruch again prays. Many of the themes that dominate Baruch's earlier prayers are present here: the brevity of human existence, the power of the divine, and the transience of existence. Unique to this prayer, however, is the force of Baruch's statement of faith (48:22-24). God's response is to the point: Only the wicked will be destroyed (48:29). Following this assurance, Baruch is again offered a picture of the events that will mark the days before the Anointed One is to come (48:32-41). Those who have forgotten the "law of the Mighty One" will be condemned by the Judge (48:39).[102] Having been assured that the righteous will not be destroyed, Baruch then asks God to describe the shape of human existence after the final judgment. Baruch is told that the dead will rise from the earth (50:2), after which both the righteous and the wicked will be transformed. The appearance of the wicked will be deformed, but the appearance of the righteous will be glorified. The mysteries of those things now hidden will then be revealed (51:9).

Again Baruch receives a vision while he sleeps. Klijn aptly names this the apocalypse of the clouds. For in his dream Baruch sees a cloud coming across the sea (53:1ff.). During the ensuing storm there is devastation and destruction. Accompanied by lightning, twelve rivers emerge from the sea. Again Baruch asks God to explain the meaning of the vision to him. Toward the end of his prayer, a new dimension is added to the discussion. Where in earlier dialogue Adam bears full responsibility for the condition of the world, Baruch here argues that "each of us has become our own Adam" (54:19). Unlike Baruch's other visions, the apocalypse of the clouds is interpreted not by God but by Ramael, the angel of true visions (55:3). Baruch is told that the black waters that fell represent those transgressions that brought evil into

102. The identity of this Judge is not known. The Judge and the Anointed One may be one and the same, but without more certain textual evidence, no conclusion can be reached regarding the relationship between them.

the world (56:4–17).[103] The bright waters represent those moments when human beings draw nearer to God (57:1ff.).[104] Again Baruch is told of the devastation that will accompany the final days (70:2–10). Baruch is then told of the dawn of the rule of the Anointed One (70:7—74:4). With the dawn of his rule, the whole of creation is to be transformed. As the revelation draws to a close, Baruch proclaims the glory of god. Ramael offers Baruch a final revelation: that of Baruch's own fate. Baruch is told that he will be removed from the world in forty days. He will not die but will be kept by God until the world ends (76:2–5).

So Baruch returns to his people and instructs them in all that he has learned (77:2ff.). The people respond by asking Baruch to write a letter so that his instructions might not be forgotten. This Baruch does. The text says that Baruch wrote two letters—one to the nine and one-half tribes lost in exile, and another to those in exile in Babylon (77:19–20). Of these letters, only the letter to the nine and one-half tribes survives in the text (78:2—86:1). This is a moving letter, one that recalls earlier times before the tribes were divided by enduring exile. The letter is also a call to obedience despite the exile (84:7–11). The apocalypse ends with the conclusion of the letter.

Throughout the text, Baruch looks to God for comfort and compassion. At each critical point, however, God's reply does little to comfort Baruch. Instead, Baruch is offered a revelation that is intended to replace his concerns with a sense of the greater purpose of God's actions and to put an end to the question of the suffering of the innocent within the context of that purpose. But in the last analysis, God's revelation does not answer or directly address the death question. Instead, the burden of guilt is passed from the divine to the human: Baruch is told that, in the last analysis, human suffering is not God's responsibility. It is ours. Having been given the law and understanding, human beings are held accountable by God for the consequences of their actions (15:1–7). The consequence of human failure is human suffering.

Yet, as Baruch sees, both the just and the unjust suffer the same fate—with or without the law, with or without God's revelation, with or without insight into God's hidden purpose. That the just and the unjust suffer the same fate serves to disarm the force of the revelation

<hr/>

103. See also 58:1-2; 60:1-2; 62:1-8; 64:1—65:2; 67:1-9; 69:1-5.
104. See also 59:1-12; 61:1-8; 63:1-11; 64:1-10; 68:1-8.

and diminishes the possibility that suffering is a consequence of human actions. As long as the just and the unjust suffer the same fate, the possibility remains that it is by the hand of God that we suffer and die. As long as the innocent and the guilty suffer the same fate, the death question stands open.

Revelation and Discontent

In the shadow of death (here understood in a broadly inclusive sense), faith cannot stand. The experience of death seems to have included exile, oppression, and separation from God, whether corporate or individual. Death is the experience of radical separation of the divine from the human. Apocalyptic reflection, with its concern for the revelation of divine purpose and presence, seeks to overcome the incompleteness of eschatological hope and to press back the shadow of death. Apocalyptic reflection thus seeks to provide the context within which the distance between promise and fulfillment, between eschatological hope and historical reality, is eclipsed. Apocalyptic reflection offers a context within which eschatological expectation is supported and sustained. Apocalypticism is that revelation that seeks to bring the infinitely distant promise intimately near. Apocalyptic reflection seeks access to the presence of God through the disclosure or revelation of the divine purpose. Apocalypticism "is concerned with knowledge of God and the secrets of the world above, revealed in a direct way by dreams, visions, and angelic pronouncements. . . . Many would have echoed the cry of the unknown prophet who, in Isaiah 64:1, pleads with God to rend the heavens to solve the many riddles of human existence which present themselves. The answer to this desperate plea is found in apocalyptic."[105]

In the words of 4 Ezra, "I do not wish to inquire about the ways above, but about those things that we daily experience: why Israel has been given over to the Gentiles as a reproach; why the people whom you loved has been given over to godless tribes, and the law of our fathers has been made of no effect and the written covenants no longer exist; and why we pass from the world like locusts, and our life is like a mist, and we are not worthy to obtain mercy" (4:23). And, "because of my grief I have spoken; for every hour I suffer agonies of the heart, while I strive to understand the way of the Most High

---

105. Rowland, *Open Heaven,* 9–11.

and to search out part of his judgment" (5:34).[106] Where eschatological reflection extended the hope or promise of deliverance, apocalypticism offers the hope for transcendence of death in the disclosure of the mysteries that shroud the world and human existence. That disclosure carries with it the promise that God will emerge from the darkness in which it has hidden itself.

Apocalypticism seeks to overcome, then, the overwhelming sense of the mystery of the universe. Since it is from the hand of God that the universe comes, apocalypticism seeks to lay bare to the faithful the deeper truth of divine purpose. Apocalypticism seems to begin with the conviction that what is wrought by the hand of God is wrought with a purpose. Apocalypticism also begins with the realization that that purpose, however incomprehensible, is not totally inaccessible. The mystery of the divine purpose can be revealed to the faithful. Apocalypticism is that revelation.[107] However, apocalypticism is concerned with more than the revealing of the secrets of the universe and rendering the order of the heavens intelligible. It is essentially concerned with revealing to human beings what it means for a human being to exist within the world and before God. Thus, apocalypticism is a human revelation. That is, it is a revelation to human beings about human being.[108]

Because theological reflection takes as its starting point the intimacy between the human and the divine, suffering and death, the hope for redress and restoration in the presence of exile and oppression, become a problem. The reflection that marks apocalyptic revelation takes as its starting point the dilemma raised by the discontinuity between faith and history, between the promise of life in the presence of YHWH and the shattering reality of suffering and death. At issue, then, in the theological reflection offered by apocalypticism is a resolution of the theodicy question, not in the hope for resolution and redress in the future but in an immediate revelation of divine purpose and truth that hopes to secure, at the same time, the presence of God. In the revelation made in apocalypticism, the hidden ways of God are brought out of the darkness and made accessible to the faithful.

---

106. Also note the importance of the revelation of secrets in 1 Enoch (see 40:3; 41:1, 3; 49:4; 52:1, 3; 60:10-11; 65:11).

107. 1 Enoch 71:3-17; Apoc. Abr. 14:1-14.

108. Here we might add that for the faith of Israel, being human was inseparable from being before God. See von Rad, *Old Testament Theology,* 1:355ff. (1:352ff.); Eichrodt, *Theology of the Old Testament,* 2, pt. 3, pp. 231ff. (3:20:1ff.)

Eschatological proclamation holds open the possibility that redress will come, the faithful will not be abandoned. But eschatological reflection does not answer the deeper question: Why? Why in the presence of God is there suffering, death, and tragedy? The death question is not answered by the expectation of future deliverance, for the future cannot resolve the intensity of suffering here and now. Moreover, the faith that deliverance will certainly come in the future holds open the possibility that the suffering that is now endured, the death that is now close at hand, and the separation from the presence of God that marks exile and failed restoration are marked and caused by the willful absence of God. The faithful who suffer and endure oppression now, who stand in the presence of death now, do so by the will of God. In the presence of death, the faithful stand abandoned by God. Why in the presence of God is there death? "While the problem of theodicy achieves focus in death . . . the issue is much broader than that. Indeed, every phenomenon that brings into question an assumption of harmony undergirding human existence presents additional evidence . . . against God. We may thus define theodicy loosely as the attempt to pronounce a verdict of 'Not Guilty' over God."[109]

But for those of us who live in a world where all things die, God's silence speaks of God's complicity in our death. Complicity implies guilt. Death points to the absence of God, to the radical and total separation of the faithful from the presence of God forever. The enduring presence of death raises the possibility that those who suffer do so by the will of God. It is the issue of God's involvement in and responsibility for human suffering and death that apocalypticism attempts to resolve by pointing to deeper revelations about the hidden purposes of God, about the mysteries of the universe, that can provide human suffering, oppression, and finally even death itself with a perspective.[110] At least in theory, the problem is resolved by pointing to deeper truths that reveal the reasons behind God's actions. This revelation in turn absolves God of involvement or complicity in our death. Apocalypticism attempts to establish God's innocence.

Ideas such as life after death and the resurrection of the righteous offer tenable explanations, or perhaps graspable hopes, which ease but do not resolve the problem of death. For the mystery is not resolved.

109. J. L. Crenshaw, ed., *Theodicy in the Old Testament* (Philadelphia: Fortress, 1983), 1.

110. Ibid.

It is simply given a context. This context in turn supports the eschatological promise of restoration. Apocalyptic reflection provides the theological context within which belief in final restoration is sustained and made tenable. By pointing to the transcendence of death, apocalyptic reflection seeks to ease the crisis that faith experiences in the presence of death.

As von Rad has noted, the experience of death was, in the context of the faith of Israel, inseparable from the experience of God. The experience of what death means was "not a matter of mere neutral empirical fact: It was not established once and for all on the basis of a definition common to all humanity. Rather, it was YHWH who apportioned death for all humans, and what death was and was not Israel came ever again to learn anew from YHWH. . . . Death begins to become a reality at the point where YHWH forsakes a person, where [YHWH] is silent."[111]

Death is not to be transcended—not by divine revelation or by the promise of eschatological restoration—until the death question is answered or resolved. And for the faith of Israel, death was not known or understood "as in any way an independent mythical force—the power of death was fundamentally YHWH's own power. Death was no last enemy, but a way in which YHWH acts toward human beings.[112] This is the line taken by the most decisive of Israel's statements about death. . . . YHWH sentences a person to death."[113] Apocalypticism cannot overcome this death sentence. It can, however, provide

111. Von Rad, *Old Testament Theology,* 1:388 (1:386–87). See also Eichrodt, *Theology of the Old Testament,* 1:258–69 (*Theologie des Alten Testaments,* 1:168–76; cf. 2:491–92, 3:146): "the mystery of the problem of suffering can only be overcome on the basis of the category of revelation, that which is sheer miracle and of which the origin can never be traced, not on the basis of the ordinary, or on the basis of rational human thought. From this it follows that any theodicy whatever has become intrinsically impossible. . . . For the sake of this God the world with all its mysteries, even suffering, can be affirmed; for by speaking [God] emerges from [its] hiddenness" (2:491–92). Though there is much to say in favor of Eichrodt's analysis, I would argue that the experience of suffering and death finally precludes affirmation of God.

112. The German here reads: "sondern ein Handeln Jahwes am Menschen," which could be translated literally as "but a way/power of YHWH toward humans." The connotation, however, strongly suggests a disposition or attitude and an exercise of power that YHWH adopts toward humans. According to Lou Silberman, "Whatever ideas about and attitudes toward death the Israelites held . . . stood in some crucial relationship to what they believed about life; and that in turn was related to other spheres of interest until . . . these were ultimately connected to a way of understanding God" ("Death in the Hebrew Bible and Apocalyptic Literature," in *Perspectives on Death,* ed. Liston O. Mills [Nashville: Abingdon, 1969], 14).

113. Von Rad, *Old Testament Theology,* 1:390 (1:388). Christoph Barth has com-

death with a context and a perspective that extend a kind of assurance
and expectation that it is not by God's hand that we die. But apocalypticism cannot silence the presence of death. Apocalyptic reflection
cannot answer the death question; apocalyptic can only offer a context
within which the question takes shape so that the possibility that God
is responsible for our death can be silenced. Only God can answer the
question of its involvement and complicity in our death. Only God
can establish its innocence and guilt. And God has chosen to remain
silent. As long as God remains silent, the death question remains
unanswered and unanswerable. As long as the death question remains
open and unanswered, the reality of God remains problematic. Here
again, the words of Ezra seem particularly important: "You cannot
understand the things with which you have grown up; how then can
your mind comprehend the way of the Most High?"[114]

Part of the human tragedy is that we cannot comprehend the ways
of God. Even when revealed by the seer, pondered by the sage, and
proclaimed by the prophet, the reason (which the faithful pray underlies divine action) remains more than we can comprehend. As long
as God's purpose remains incomprehensible, the possibility stands open
that there is no purpose there, that the world and the God that created
it are marked by a kind of purposelessness and meaninglessness that
render our suffering and death all the more unbearable. And beyond
the incomprehensibility of the "way of the Most High" veiled in the
darkness, the face of God remains hidden. The confidence and prayer
of the seer is that the promise of his revelation will be fulfilled and
God will emerge from the darkness. Faith will transcend death.

---

mented, "Starting from the axiom of the almighty God, to which there is no equal,
[one is constantly forced] to comprehend the power of death as God's own responsibility. . . . Good and evil, life and death, heaven and hell, are both aspects of the
Godhead" (Die Errettung vom Tode in den individuellen Klage- und Dankliedern des Alten
Testaments [Basel: Evangelischer Verlag, 1947], 69). The phrase "God's own responsibility" in German reads "Gottes eigene Macht." Macht, from machen, means "force,"
"power," "responsibility," "strength," etc. Macht appears earlier in this quote with
reference to the power of death as well. Here, however, the point is not so much that
death is a power of God or a power that emanates from God as it is that death, having
come from the hand of the almighty God, is God's responsibility. As such, the almighty
God is the God of life and death. See also Th. C. Vriezen, An Outline of Old Testament
Theology (Oxford: Basil Blackwell, 1958), 162–68; also Deut. 11:26–32; 30:15–20.

114. 4 Ezra 4:10; also see 5:34–35: "Because of my grief I have spoken, for every
hour I suffer the agonies of the heart, while I strive to understand the way of the Most
High and to search out part of his judgment. He said to me, 'You cannot.' And I said,
'Why not, my lord? Why then was I born? Or why did not my mother's womb become
my grave, that I might not see the travail of Jacob and the exhaustion of the people of
Israel?' "

In this way, the words of the seer extend a twofold invitation. On the one hand, the revelation of the seer calls the community of faith into the darkness that shrouds the presence of God. On the other hand, the words of the seer call to God to come out of the darkness in which God has hidden itself. Yet while the community can enter into the darkness, the darkness remains darkened, defying comprehension. The darkness denies enlightenment. And the God that is there in the darkness remains darkened. In the darkness, the question of the reality of God stretches across our existence. Where apocalypticism promises presence, there remains absence. Where apocalypticism promises light, there is darkness. Where apocalypticism promises intimacy and life in the presence of God, there is only distance. Indeed, so distant is the presence of God, that those who follow the seer into the darkness cannot be sure that there is anyone or anything there. Again, while the revelation of the seer is intended to defuse the question of the reality of God, that revelation instead intensifies that question. Where the seer expects intimacy, there is distance. Where the seer expects presence, there is absence. Where the seer expects vision, there is blindness. Where the seer expects resolution, there is uncertainty. Where the seer expects an end to the death question, there the question stands.

four | DIVINE SILENCE AND HUMAN FAITH

Job, Qoheleth, and the Darkness of God

*For certainly we will die, like water poured out upon the
ground which cannot be gathered up.*

2 Samuel 14:14

*Jewish wisdom (like Egyptian) was directly concerned with
affirming a meaningful order in reality. Wisdom itself was the
principle of order by which the earth was founded and the
heavens established (Prov. 3:19). Humans were wise by
participation in the same wisdom which gave order to the
universe. . . . The ordered reality of the wisdom tradition . . .
could be called into question by the inescapable phenomenon of
death.*

John J. Collins,
"The Root of Immortality:
Death in the Context of
Jewish Wisdom"

In the previous chapter we examined apocalyptic literature within the context of the long and complex
scholarly tradition that has surrounded its study. No
such tradition seems to have taken shape around wisdom literature. As one might expect, there have been
rather sharp differences of opinion regarding the origins of wisdom literature and its place and function
in Hebrew Scripture. But those differences always
seem to occur within a nexus of assumptions that
appear to leave little room for variance.

Many scholars, for example, share the opinion that
wisdom could have arisen only during the monarchy,
when Israel was exposed to strong foreign cultural
influences. Hengel, as a case in point, argues that the

origin of Qoheleth is to be placed in the rise of a "scribal school" during the monarchy.[1] Though each might find grounds for disagreement with the others, von Rad, McKane, Eichrodt, Crenshaw, Pedersen, R. B. Y. Scott, and Gordis, among others, would all support this analysis.[2] Because its origin is placed in the period of the monarchy, wisdom literature is regarded as a late development. Once it is seen as a late development, wisdom is bracketed from what is usually termed normative or orthodox Judaism.[3] That is to say, wisdom literature becomes a late development that owes more to cultural and religious influences outside Judaism than to Judaism itself.[4]

A further issue emerges. In a scholarly tradition that defines orthodoxy in terms of the prophetic tradition, the questions that wisdom literature raises are seen as a challenge to orthodoxy. These questions, it is argued, mirror a deep internal crisis in Judaism. Often this crisis is described in terms of a growing sense of personal identity and mortality that eventually replaced the older prophetic sense of corporate personality. This rise of an individual sense of identity is usually attributed to the growing influence of Hellenism. With the rise of Hellenism and its strong sense of personal identity came an equally strong sense of skepticism and cynicism about older, more orthodox expressions of faith.

This analysis is brought to bear on the texts themselves. Qoheleth, for example, is described by Gordis as a gentle cynic largely because his reflection seems to question many aspects of the understanding of God normally associated with orthodox Judaism.[5] Hengel speaks of

1. See Martin Hengel, *Judaism and Hellenism* (Philadelphia: Fortress, 1981), 1:78–79.
2. Gerhard von Rad, *Wisdom in Israel* (Nashville: Abingdon, 1971), 206–39, and *Old Testament Theology,* 2 vols. (New York: Harper and Row, 1962–65), 1:418–59 (1:439–57); William McKane, *Prophets and Wise Men* (London: SCM, 1965), 13–62, esp. 48ff.; James L. Crenshaw, *Old Testament Wisdom: An Introduction* (Atlanta: John Knox, 1981), 11–29, esp. 28–29; R. B. Y. Scott, "The Study of Wisdom Literature," *Int* 24 (1970): 20–45, and *The Way of Wisdom in the Old Testament* (New York: Macmillan, 1971), 12–18, 23–47. Hengel provides an adequate review of most prominent positions. See his "Koheleth and the Beginning of the Crisis in Jewish Religion," in *Judaism,* 1:115ff; also W. Zimmerli, *Old Testament Theology in Outline* (Atlanta: John Knox, 1978), 156–57.
3. Perhaps the proper term here is "Yahwism," insofar as "Judaism" is usually used with reference to postexilic times. Though "Yahwism" and "postexilic Judaism" are not one and the same, these terms are used more or less interchangeably here.
4. J. L. Crenshaw, "Method in Determining Wisdom Influence upon 'Historical' Literature," *JBL* 88 (1969): 129ff.; Roland E. Murphy, "Assumptions and Problems in Old Testament Wisdom Research," *CBQ* 29 (1967): 104; von Rad, *Old Testament Theology,* 1:429ff. (1:451–57).
5. See R. Gordis, *Koheleth: The Man and His World* (New York: Bloch Publishing, 1955).

Qoheleth's "cool, assertive skepticism."[6] This cynicism is seen as a rejection of faith, or at least as a questioning that makes faith untenable. Crenshaw offers an analysis similar to that of Gordis in that he stresses the pessimism, if not cynicism, associated with wisdom literature.[7] Similarly, the structure, redaction, and formation of Ecclesiastes have all been subject to much debate. Some, like Addison Wright, find a very rigid and strict structure in the text.[8] Others, like Roland Murphy, R. K. Johnson, or even Zimmerli, have offered analyses that have varied in scope and degree of order.[9] But in the last analysis, Qoheleth has been assigned relatively little importance in biblical theology.[10]

Job has suffered a similar assessment.[11] For example, the present text of Job seems to be a composite formed by the inclusion of a poetic text within a narrative framework.[12] Many scholars seem to think that the poetic material, now located in the block of material that forms 3:1—42:6 in the present text, was an addition to the older narrative text, which may have been of Babylonian origin.[13] It is usually argued

6. Hengel, *Judaism,* 1:109.

7. James L. Crenshaw, "The Shadow of Death in Qoheleth," in *Israelite Wisdom: Theological and Literary Essays in Honor of Samuel Terrien,* ed. John G. Gammie et al. (Missoula, Mont.: Scholars Press, 1978), 205–16.

8. See A. Wright, "The Riddle of the Sphinx: The Structure of the Book of Qoheleth," *CBQ* 30 (1968): 313ff., and "The Riddle of the Sphinx Revisited: Numerical Patterns in the Book of Qoheleth," *CBQ* 42 (1980): 38ff.

9. R. Murphy, "Form Criticism and Wisdom Literature," *CBQ* 31 (1969): 475–83, and "A Form Critical Consideration of Ecclesiastes VII," in *SBL Seminar Papers, 1974,* ed. G. W. MacRae (Cambridge: SBL, 1974), 1:77–85; R. K. Johnson, " 'Confessions of a Workaholic': A Reappraisal of Qoheleth," *CBQ* 38 (1976): 14–28; W. Zimmerli, "Das Buch Kohelet: Traktat oder Sentenzsammlung?" *VT* 24 (1974): 221–30. Also see Timothy Polk, "Wisdom of Irony," *StudBT* 6 (1976): 5–6; and G. T. Sheppard, "The Epilogue to Qoheleth as Theological Commentary," in *Wisdom as a Hermeneutical Construct* (New York: de Gruyter, 1980), 182ff.; H. L. Ginsberg, "The Structure and Contents of the Book of Koheleth," in *VTSup* 3 (1955): 138–49; Santigo Breton, "Qoheleth Studies," *BTB* 3 no. 1 (1973): 22–50.

10. J. L. McKenzie, "Reflections on Wisdom," *JBL* 86 (1967): 1–9; Walther Zimmerli, "The Place and Limit of the Wisdom in the Framework of the Old Testament Theology," in *Studies in Ancient Israelite Wisdom,* ed. J. L. Crenshaw (New York: KTAV, 1976), 314ff. According to Zimmerli, "Wisdom has no relation to the history between God and Israel. . . . Wisdom has to do with man" (p. 315).

11. R. Polzin, "The Framework of the Book of Job," *Int* 31 (1974): 182–200.

12. Norman C. Habel, "Naked I Came . . . : Humanness in the Book of Job," in *Die Botschaft und die Boten: Festschrift für Hans Walter Wolff* (Neukirchen-Vluyn: Neukirchener Verlag, 1981), 372–92; J. W. Whedbee, "The Comedy of Job," *Semeia,* no. 7 (1970): 1–39; Morris Jastrow, *The Book of Job* (Philadelphia: Lippincott, 1920), 13–14, 39–40, 64–86; David Robertson, "The Book of Job: A Literary Study," *Soundings* 56 (1973): 446–69; Edwin M. Good, "Job and the Literary Task," *Soundings* 56 (1973): 470–84; Scott, "Study," 147–52; Crenshaw, *Old Testament Wisdom,* 100–116.

13. Scott, "Study," 143; Crenshaw, *Old Testament Wisdom,* 38; James B. Pritchard,

that the original text has been given a new context by the poetic material, which now forms the heart of the text. That reformation of the text, it is argued, calls into question the retribution doctrine and thus challenges orthodox Judaism.[14]

For example, von Rad has argued that the poetic material raises a serious hermeneutical problem: How did the poet intend this material to be heard?[15] To what extent does the later poetic material modify or alter the theological concerns of the original text? The second question cannot be answered, since neither the original text nor its definitive theological perspective can be recovered. Given the present shape of the text, the poetic material is the focus of reflection, not the older narrative material. The narrative material has been appropriated by the Joban poet in order to lay the foundation for his own theological reflection. To reverse the current relationship between the poetic and narrative material is to obscure the issues raised by the current shape of the text, in which only literary style seems to distinguish the poetic material from the older narrative text. Rather than see the appropriation of the narrative material as discontinuous with the poetic material, the theological reflection of the poetic material should be seen as appropriating that earlier reflection. This is the approach taken here. The following discussion, then, is forced to take shape less around a scholarly tradition and more around the texts themselves. In response to the established understanding of wisdom literature, it will be argued that the wisdom tradition's concern for the suffering and death of the innocent is part of a long-standing concern for a resolution of the death question—a concern that finds expression throughout Scripture.

THE DEATH QUESTION AND
THE SHAPE OF SCRIPTURE

To raise the death question is to raise for reflection the depth of the experience of abandonment by God. The experience of abandonment

---

ed., *The Ancient Near East*, 2 vols. (Princeton: Princeton University Press, 1975), 2:148–67.

14. See Jastrow's analysis, for example, in *Job*, 11–12. See also 88–91, 109–47; and Scott, "Study," 152–64.

15. Von Rad, *Wisdom in Israel*, 217, 225–26, and *Old Testament Theology*, 1:408–18 (1:405–55); see also Nahum N. Glatzer, *The Dimensions of Job* (New York: Schocken Books, 1969), 1–48. Glatzer provides a good history of the interpretation of Job.

lies at the heart of the experience of God's concealment or hiddenness.[16] If our being in the presence of God defines our humanity, the feeling that God has abandoned us speaks of its end. For when God abandons the faithful, death is not far away. The experience of abandonment, therefore, is like being given over to death by God's withdrawal of itself. It is like a child's experience of abandonment by its parent, or like the experience of loss of breath. For while the presence of God is the breath of life, abandonment by God steals that breath away.[17]

Throughout Scripture, the threat of abandonment is juxtaposed against the promise of life that the presence of God offers. This contrast is summarized, as it were, by the "law of the heart." "But the word is very near you; it is in your mouth and in your heart, so that you can do it. See, I have set before you this day life and good, death and evil. If you obey the commandments of the Lord your God which I command you this day, by loving the Lord your God, . . . then you shall live and multiply, and the Lord your God will bless you in the land. . . . But if your heart turns away, and you will not hear. . . . I declare to you this day that you shall perish."[18] In the presence of death, there is no innocence. Death implies guilt. The innocent do not die. That absence of innocence, that shadow of guilt, raises a further question. Do we die because we are guilty? Is our death indicative of our inability to love God, and of our failure to remain faithful to God?[19] Or do we die despite our innocence? Are we put to

16. On abandonment, see Samuel Balentine, *The Hidden God* (Oxford: Oxford University Press, 1982), 9, 171–73; also Deut. 31:17-18; 32:20; Ps. 10:11; 13:2(1); 22:25(24); 27:9; 30:8(7); 44:25(24); 51:11(9); 69:18(17); 88:15(14); 102:3(2); 104:29; 143:7; Isa. 8:17; 54:8; 59:2; Hos. 5:15; 6:4-6; Ezek. 39:23-29; Mic. 3:4; Jer. 33:5; Job 13:24; 34:29; cf. the refrain in Ps. 80: "Let your face smile on us, and we will be safe." See also BDB, 736d–737d; Marcus Jastrow, *A Dictionary of the Targumim, the Talmud Babli and Yerushalmi, and the Midrashic Literature* (New York: Traditional Press, 1975–76), 1516d–1517a; Isa. 54:8.

17. See Gen. 2:7; 2 Sam 24. In Lamentations, abandonment by God is synonymous with the experience of desolation.

18. Deut. 10:12-13; 6:4ff.; 30:8ff.; see esp. 30:14-15.

19. See Walther Eichrodt, *Theology of the Old Testament*, 2 vols. (Philadelphia: Westminster, 1961), 1:258–69, "The Wrath of God." It should be noted that Eichrodt wishes to restrict Israel's experience of the wrath of God in judgment to what he terms the "*sphere of retributive justice*, which metes out reward and punishment." He also argues that YHWH's anger was never despotic or capricious. See his "Faith in Providence and Theodicy in the Old Testament," in *Theodicy in the Old Testament*, ed. J. L. Crenshaw (Philadelphia: Fortress, 1983), 31–32, for a similar analysis. Note his insistence that wisdom is marked by an attempt to confront a "rational" understanding of retribution (pp. 33–34). Also see von Rad, *Old Testament Theology*, 1:384ff. In contrast to Eichrodt, von Rad argued that retribution "is not a new action which comes upon the person

death by the hand of God? Do we die because the law of God is
oppressive and more than any human can fulfill? Do we die because
YHWH is a jealous, lustful God, a God for whom no love is enough?
If we die in innocence, is God not guilty of our death? If God is guilty
of our death, if we cannot proclaim God's innocence, then what are
we to make of God's guilt? Can we believe in a God who takes our
life?

The claim that YHWH is just, or that every human act has consequences for which we bear full responsibility, breaks down at the
point where the innocent suffer and at the point where we are forced
to conclude that no human is righteous before the law. It makes no
sense to speak either of a just God or of human culpability in the
presence of a cruel God. As long as the innocent suffer in innocence,
the issue of human innocence and guilt is inseparable from the issue
of God's innocence and guilt. Either God is innocent and we are guilty,
or God is guilty and we are innocent. Either we can love God with
all our heart and with all our lives, or we cannot—either because our
humanity is our occasion to sin, or because God wants more than the
human heart can give. Either God's love brings life, or God's lust
consumes us in death. The issue of the reality of God is inseparable
from the issue of the reality of death.[20]

In either case, faith in God may well be untenable. If we argue that
we are indebted to God because the human is "ontologically deformed," then it seems to make no sense to speak of loving God with
all our heart. Human love is imperfect, deformed, perhaps even motivated by fear of punishment, by an attempt to placate God for our
own selfish reasons. Humans are unable to love God, except insofar
as love of God is made possible for human beings by God. Thus,
human beings are in debt to God because of this guilt, because the
human desire and ability to love and serve God has been deformed as
a consequence of the sin of Adam. But indebtedness precludes love.
In our indebtedness human beings can fear God, but humans cannot

---

concerned from somewhere else; it is rather a last ripple of the act itself which attaches
to its agent" (1:385). This approach seems to be shared by K. Koch (see his "Is There
a Doctrine of Retribution in the Old Testament?" in *Theodicy in the Old Testament,* ed.
Crenshaw, 57–87). He argues that Hosea is "compelled . . . by the view that actions
have built-in consequences and it is in this vein that he proclaims the onset of disasters"
(66).

20. On the encounter between wisdom and death see Zimmerli, "The Place and
Limit of Wisdom in the Framework of Old Testament Theology," in *Studies in Ancient
Israelite Wisdom,* ed. Crenshaw, 324.

love God. Insofar as fear precludes love of God, fear only nurtures a
sense of guilt and indebtedness. The more pressing our sense of guilt,
the more difficult fulfillment of the law becomes.

Yet even in this analysis, the question of who this God is cannot
be silenced. For if, on the one hand, the law is given in order to
transform the human so that it might love the divine, the giving of
the law increases the human debt to God.[21] Insofar as the law stands
against human nature, the human propensity to fail to love God is
engendered by the law.[22] We cannot be what we are not. If, on the
other hand, God must redeem us from our humanity by dying on the
cross, our debt to God would seem insurmountable. In effect, since
God does for humans what no human can do for itself, in ransoming
humans from their sins, human beings owe God more than just their
lives—humans owe God their heart.[23] We are in debt to the one who
has bought our freedom. In either case, failure and guilt, anger and
punishment, are inevitable. Love cannot be bought or secured by
indebtedness. God's pursuit of our heart, then, leads not to life, which
is its promise, but to death. The God whose love is meant to sustain
life engenders our suffering. In either case, the question of God's
complicity in our death is not diminished.[24] The face of God remains
darkened by our death. The presence of God remains oppressive.[25]
Because the presence of God remains oppressive and dark, the death
question endures.

The force of this dichotomy of life and death, freedom and indebtedness, seems to mark the whole of the relationship between Israel
and YHWH.[26] In the presence of the tension between freedom and
indebtedness, life and death, love and lust, the relationship between
the human and the divine remains unstable and fragile. God's love

---

21. In light of Ezek. 20:25 it could be argued that the law was often the occasion
of its own violation: YHWH could use the law to punish Israel, and it also became an
end in itself, thus further driving Israel away from YHWH's presence.

22. Prov. 10:22, 27; 12:28; 13:13; 14:27; 19:16, 23; 22:4; 28:5-9; Sir. 2:1ff.; 24:23, 32-
33; 32:15, 24; Deut. 6:10-13; 8:1-6; 11:13-17; 30:6-10, 15-20; Jer. 29:11-12. See also von
Rad, *Old Testament Theology*, 1:370–83; Eichrodt, *Theology of the Old Testament*, 1:240–
47; Walther Zimmerli, *Old Testament Theology in Outline* (Atlanta: John Knox, 1978),
141–45.

23. Here "heart" is to be understood in the sense of the Hebrew *nephesh*.

24. R. J. Williams, "Theodicy in the Ancient Near East," *CJT* 2 (1956): 14–26.

25. See James L. Crenshaw, *A Whirlpool of Torment: Israelite Traditions of God as an
Oppressive Presence* (Philadelphia: Fortress, 1984).

26. Once again note the way in which this either-or forms the heart of the argument
in Deuteronomy.

seems indistinguishable from God's lust, human infidelity inseparable from human finitude,[27] human love from human fear, and God's presence in life from God's absence in death. As long as this transience and instability remain lodged within the tension between the either and the or, the relationship between the human and the divine remains fragile. A relationship that remains fragile is destined to be broken.

While that relationship was broken often by Israel, that relationship could just as easily be broken by God.[28] On the one hand, Israel often withdrew from its relationship to God.[29] There were times when Israel turned its back on what YHWH wanted and whored after other gods. The judgment that ensued was often swift and without mercy.[30] Indeed, judgment is expected insofar as YHWH is a righteous God.[31] Those who die go to their death because they have rejected YHWH.[32] On the other hand, in raging anger, in a kind of bitter fury, YHWH could judge Israel or withdraw into the darkness. Once YHWH was hidden in the darkness, Israel was given over to death. In the absence of the presence of God, human existence could not be sustained. Yet despite the abandonment of that relationship by the human or the divine,

27. An important point needs to be made here. Human finitude and human guilt are not the same phenomenon. See Paul Ricoeur's analysis of the difference between fallibility and guilt in *Symbolism of Evil* (Boston: Beacon Press, 1969), 100–150, "Guilt," esp. p. 45: "The fear of not loving enough is the purest and worst of fears . . . only perfect love casts out fear." As one might expect, such a perfect love for Ricoeur and for the Christian tradition as a whole is God's love for us. Human love is always fearful and thus finally flawed and guilt ridden. Also see Ricoeur, *Fallible Man* (Chicago: H. Regnery, 1967), 201–21, where innocence is defined as fallibility without fault; guilt is a consequence of human fallibility. Human fallibility is taken by Ricoeur to be the consequence of an ontological deformity. See his essay "The Image of God and the Epic of Man," in *History and Truth* (Evanston, Ill.: Northwestern University Press, 1965), 110–28. The link to the idea of original sin is clear. Ricoeur's insistence on a propensity toward guilt undermines the power of his concept of fallibility.

28. As far as the prophetic texts are concerned, human actions were far more likely to cause a breach in the relationship between the human and the divine than were God's actions. This point was discussed in greater detail in chapter 3.

29. Ezek. 20:1-44; Deut. 7:6-7; Exod. 3:8-9; Hos. 4:12-13; 9:15-16; 12:12, 15(11, 14); Mic. 13:1-2; Jer. 7:21-22, 31-32; 11:15-16; contrast with Jer. 7:21; 22:3-4; Mic. 6:8; Hos. 6:6; Zech. 7:9-10.

30. See Jer 4:4: "Circumcise yourselves . . . lest my wrath should leap out like a fire and burn with no one to quench it, in return for the wickedness of your deeds." See also 6:11-15; Ezek. 20:33-44; 21:1-12; Hos. 6:4-6; Isa. 42:18-19; 2 Sam. 24:10-11.

31. See Peter R. Ackroyd, *Exile and Restoration* (Philadelphia: Westminster, 1968), 43–49, "The Recognition of Divine Judgement"; Hans Walter Wolff, *Joel and Amos* (Philadelphia: Fortress, 1977), 100–6; Walther Zimmerli, *Ezekiel*, 2 vols. (Philadelphia: Fortress, 1979–83), 1:315–16, 379ff.; Ezek. 14:13-20; 18:5-32.

32. Deut. 30:14-20; see also Lev. 11:44-45; 19:2; 20:26; Deut. 11:26; 26:19; 28:9; 29:6-13.

despite the fragility and instability of the relationship, the possibility that that relationship could be reestablished, that the wayward heart or the distant God might return, provided a sense of continuity in the presence of brokenness and discontinuity.

At one point, however, this sense of radical continuity is overshadowed by an equally powerful sense of discontinuity. In the presence of death, the promise of restoration is itself broken. For in death there is only separation, brokenness, and discontinuity. In death, the human can no longer be in relationship to God.[33] Insofar as it is this being before God, this being in relationship to God, that defines what it means to be human, death is more than the end of our relationship to God. Death is the end of our humanity. Because it is the point at which our humanity is at its end, death precludes continuity. Moreover, at the end of our humanity, the dichotomy between love and death, presence and hiddenness, freedom and indebtedness, is suspended forever without answer. As long as the end of our humanity is death, radical discontinuity threatens to overshadow and eclipse the radical continuity that the relationship, sustained by God's love, promises.[34] God's withdrawal into the darkness, God's hiding its face, broke the relationship that sustained life and kept death at a distance.

The problem is that the promise of the relationship between YHWH and Israel is a life filled with love for God. The promise of the covenant, of this relationship, is that Israel will return YHWH's love, and in returning that love, Israel will draw close to God. Israel will see God's face.[35] Having looked upon the face of YHWH, Israel would live in God's love forever. Israel would know the wisdom of God's ways. Knowledge and wisdom, love, life, and prosperity (see Prov. 22:3-4) are the promises of the relationship between Israel and YHWH and of the covenant in which that relationship was embodied. But the suffering of the innocent and the death of the righteous are not. The end of our humanity and the discontinuity of death are not. That both the wise and the foolish both suffer the same fate, that no one is

33. Acording to N. N. Glatzer, "Death not only terminates life; it penetrates life; it destroys life in the very process of living" (*The Dimensions of Job,* 9).

34. Hence the importance of the biblical image of the face of God. Hebrew uses the preposition *lip na,* literally "to the face of" or "in the face of." To be before God was to be face-to-face with God.

35. See Exod. 33:18; Ps. 4:6-7(5-6); 13:2(1); 27:8-9; 28:8; 30:8(7); 31:17(16); 34:4, 25(3, 24); 51:11(9) 67:2(1); 69:17-18(16-17); 78:34; 80:4-8, 20(3-7, 19); 88:15(14); 98:9; 102:3, 29(2, 28); 104:29; 105:4; 107:6; 116:9; 143:7; Hos. 5:15; Isa. 8:17 ("I will wait for the Lord who has hidden [its] face from the house of Jacob"); Lam. 5:20.

blameless before God and before the law, and that death remains our
fate likewise are alien to the promise of the relationship between Israel
and YHWH.[36]

Here we come to the heart of the problem. Only when God emerges
from the darkness can the death question be answered. In death we
are forever barred from the presence of God and from certain knowledge of good and evil. As long as we die, we cannot know the ways
of God or love God with a love that knows no fear. For in the presence
of death and in the absence of God, there is only fear—fear of God
and of death; fear that our ignorance, assured by our death, will
consume us in violation of the law; fear that our inevitable disobedience
will win for us certain judgment. The presence of death is the long
and brutal shadow that falls between the human and the divine. Though
we seek presence, we find only absence. Where we seek intimacy,
there is only estrangement and loneliness. "Whatever God plans God
carries out. No doubt then that God will carry out my sentence, like
so many other decrees that God has made; that is why I am full of
fear before God, and the more I think, the greater grows my fear of
God. God has made my heart sink; Shaddai has filled me with fear.
For darkness hides me from God, and the gloom veils God's presence
from me" (Job 23:13-17).

JOB

Perhaps of all those who suffer in innocence, none is better known to
us than Job. Job is a man of integrity and righteousness, a man who
fears God and avoids evil (1:1).[37] He has taken great pains to fulfill

---

36. Job 4:6-7, 17; Prov. 11:4, 19; Eccles. 8:12-15; 9:3; also see Ezek. 20:25: "I even
gave them laws that were not good and observances by which they could never live."
According to von Rad, "The saving event whereby Israel became YHWH's is indis-
solubly bound up with the obligation to obey certain norms which clearly mark out
the chosen people's sphere, particularly at its circumference" (Old Testament Theology,
2:391–92; see Deut. 10:12-22; Exod. 20:1-21). Note that in Deut. 11:13-15, loving
YHWH and obeying the commandments are seen as distinct. Note also that in the
Shechemite Decalogue (von Rad's name for Deut. 27:9ff.) obedience to the law rests
upon Israel's having been chosen by YHWH. The law was to be the visible sign of
Israel's love of God and a mark of the special relationship between YHWH and Israel.
Yet the law could just as easily become the vehicle of judgment—either because ob-
servance of the law surpassed love of God or because the law was used by God to
punish Israel. See Isa. 10:2; 29:13-14; 43:22-28; Mic. 6:6-8; Hos. 6:6; 8:11-12; Amos
5:25; Jer. 7:5, 21-28; Zech. 7:9.
37. Text references in this section are to the Book of Job.

both the spirit and the letter of the law. In his desire to remain righteous before God, he has atoned for his transgressions and for those of others as well (1:3-5). Despite the weight of his tragedy, Job's faith in YHWH and his confidence in his own innocence remain untouched.[38] "Naked I came from my mother's womb, naked I shall return. YHWH gave. YHWH has taken back. Blessed be the name of YHWH. . . . If we take happiness from God's hand, must we not take sorrow too?" (2:10).

Yet despite—or perhaps even because of—his righteousness and his integrity, Job suffers. The Joban poet presses the issue of the suffering of the innocent to its limit by juxtaposing Job's innocence against the claim that guilt is an inseparable part of our humanity. Job pleads his case before those for whom human innocence is not a possibility. Job is assured by his interlocutors that the righteous do not suffer. Those who suffer cannot claim innocence. Job's interlocuters offer no middle ground;[39] those who break the law of God are punished by God in accordance with the severity of their offense. The innocent do not suffer.[40] Only the guilty do. If Job suffers, then he too must be guilty. This becomes Job's dilemma: Job is innocent. Job is righteous. Job fears God. Yet he suffers. Either Job suffers in his innocence, or he suffers because of his guilt. If Job is innocent and still suffers, then the theodicy question is turned back upon God. That is to say, if the innocent and the righteous do indeed suffer, then the righteousness and justice of God are called into question. Either God is righteous and just, or God is not. If the righteousness and justice of God are called into question, so too is faith in God. Again there seems to be no middle ground. For we cannot believe in or love a God that seeks to take our lives. We cannot believe in a God that is capricious and whose capriciousness is the source of our torment. The Joban poet seeks to dismiss the idea that those who suffer, suffer because they are

38. Actually, as Job's suffering endures, his patience with his interlocutors—and with God—diminishes.

39. For many scholars, Job's argument is seen as an attack on the relationship between suffering and guilt. The systematic formulation of this relationship is referred to as the retribution doctrine. It is argued (for example, by Zimmerli, von Rad, and Eichrodt) that the Book of Job represents an attempt to question, rebuke, or challenge that doctrine. Clearly, there is a relationship between guilt and punishment in Hebrew Scripture, but whether that relationship was simply understood or was formulated in terms of an actual doctrine is another matter. Indeed, the assumption that such a doctrinal formulation ever existed in Hebrew Scripture or in Judaism is quite questionable.

40. Sir. 2:10-12, 20; Prov. 14:27; 16:6, 20; 22:3; 28:5; Ps. 1:1-4; contrast with Eccles. 7:19-20.

guilty by virtue of their humanity, or guilty of some offense or violation of the law.

Job's suffering is made all the more incredible and the capriciousness of God is made all the more alarming by the description of the circumstances within which Job's suffering arises (1:6-12; 2:1-7). YHWH, the God of Israel, the God of gods, the Lord of lords, appears to succumb to the temptation of the Accuser.[41] The Accuser appears to convince God that Job's righteousness is a result of the good favor YHWH has shown him. If Job is tested and suffers the loss of all he holds dear, he too will curse God and die. In cursing God, Job will come to deny the very God by whose favor he has previously prospered. The Accuser claims that no human can remain righteous in the presence of adversity. There is a kind of twisted logic here: Righteous Job is not guilty and enjoys God's favor. The Accuser's wager is that Job is righteous only because God has kept him in its favor. The Accuser implies that Job's innocence is not so much a matter of his own choice as it is a consequence of God's favor. So long as he remains in God's favor, Job will remain righteous. Thus, should he be denied divine favor and forced to endure suffering, Job will curse God. Once Job curses God, Job will have sinned. At that point, Job will no longer be innocent, and all his suffering will be just. Job, then, is to suffer in innocence.

This is not what we expect. Either one is innocent, or one is guilty. Either one prospers in righteousness, or one languishes in guilt. Yet Job the innocent suffers the fate of the wicked, and he suffers that fate without just cause. He suffers that fate because of a cruel and arbitrary wager. Paradoxically, righteousness does not guarantee that one will be free from suffering. Righteousness does not guarantee freedom from death. It would seem that righteousness only guarantees immense suffering. After all, Job's only "sin" is his faith in God. It is not Job who has deserted God; it is God who has deserted Job.

Job's proclamation of his innocence, however, is overshadowed by his concern for his death. Job does not simply search for vindication

---

41. The Hebrew uses the phrase *ha satan*, which is usually translated "Satan." The Hebrew term seems to refer to one who is like a prosecutor in a court of law. Note that the Hebrew uses the definite article *ha* before the noun *satan*. Also note that the Accuser is described as one of the *bene ʾelohim*, that is, as one of the sons of God. Job's righteousness is tested by the Accuser, not by Satan, where Satan is understood to be the embodiment of the power or presence of evil. BDB offers "adversary" as a likely translation (966b–c).

or forgiveness. Job's search is the search for the meaning of life, for the reason why humans suffer and die. His quest is the quest for an answer to the paradox of our existence. Job's longing is a longing for an end to the discrepancy between the promise of faith and the experience of abandonment, between life and death, between God's presence and God's absence. Job's search remains unfulfilled, for he never discovers the reason why humans suffer and die. Throughout the whole of the text, no reason is given.[42] YHWH addresses Job twice. Each time God stresses its power over creation and over human being. God never answers Job's lament. Nor does God address the issue of the suffering of the innocent. YHWH's display of power and might forces Job to repent despite his innocence (42:5-6). Job repents not because he is guilty or because he deserved punishment but because he is overwhelmed by the power of God.

Furthermore, although Job is restored in the end, that restoration does not mitigate the arbitrary and apparently purposeless suffering that he endured. In the end, despite his restoration, Job still dies. His restoration, his faith in God, his willingness to accept guilt even though he was in fact innocent, are not enough to deliver him from death. While Job's refusal to admit guilt in the face of inhuman suffering provides him (and in effect all human beings) with a kind of dignity, the portrait of God offered by the Joban poet is far less flattering. Job's God is a God without love. Job's God is arbitrary and fickle in its dealing with human beings. Job's God is a God without compassion—Job's restoration is a mark or demonstration of God's power, not an expression of God's compassion or mercy. Yet what Job sought was not God's power and glory but God's love and compassion.

This concern is not shared by Job's interlocutors. In fact, it seems as though Job and his interlocutors are engaged in dialogue on two different levels. For Job, the issue of innocence and guilt is inseparable from the death question. The death question, in turn, raises the issue of what kind of a God it is that we believe in. For Job's interlocutors, the issue is simply innocence and guilt, defined in terms of obedience to the law. For these people, innocence is a relative term. "Can you recall a guiltless person that died, or have you ever seen good people brought to nothing? Was ever there a person who was blameless in

---

42. Examine what is often termed the epilogue of the Book of Job (42:7-17), as well as the section that contains the speeches of YHWH to Job (38:1—42:6).

the presence of the creator?"[43] Their logic is clear—since death is a punishment that befalls the wicked, and since no one is blameless before the law, then death is the inevitable end that must of necessity come to all humans.[44] Note, first, that Job's interlocutors portray a God that is angry, vindictive, and vengeful. Second, God's vindictiveness is rooted not in the divine but in the human, insofar as that vindictiveness is a response to human actions. Death is our responsibility, not God's. God's anger and vindictiveness are just. It is because we sin that we die. Once again, God's justice overshadows—or even precludes—compassion. Third, while we are responsible for our death, we are denied innocence. Guilt, like death, is our fate. We are caught in a paradox from which we cannot emerge. On the one hand, the law cannot be fulfilled. Since we cannot fulfill the law, our lives are taken. On the other hand, despite our confidence in our innocence, the possibility remains that we have broken the law. Again we encounter a paradox: Either the law cannot be fulfilled because of some tragic flaw or weakness in human being,[45] or God placed the burden of an unfulfillable law on us.[46] Either we fail because God wants us to, or we fail because we are human. In either case, guilt, suffering, and death are our fate, and a kind of tragic blindness that clouds our existence. Only God knows what lies in our hearts. God has the last word, we do not.[47] If we suffer, we can only assume that God has found us guilty. Our fate is just.[48] In the last analysis, however, no one is really innocent before God.

As far as Job is concerned, this position is unacceptable. For Job, the issue is not the relative degree of guilt all humans endure before the law and before God. Innocence is a real human possibility that stands in sharp contrast to the guilt and to the violation of the law

43. Job 4:6-7, 17; 8:1-22; 11:1-20; 15:1-35; 22:1-30; 25:1-6; cf. Prov. 17:15; 20:9; Eccles. 7:19-20. Note the role of human failings in the tragic end that comes to such figures as David, Saul, Solomon, Absalom, Abimelech, and Moses.

44. This conclusion is echoed in Prov. 11:4; 12:28; 19:16; 20:9.

45. This possibility is akin to the supposed ontological defect associated with "original sin."

46. Cf. Paul's attack on the law, which is finally not a reflection upon the law, as if the law is malevolent and God benevolent, but upon God itself. Cf. Rom. 3:28; 7:1-25; 10:4; 1 Cor. 9:3-14, 19-23; Gal. 2:15-21; 3:5, 10-29; 4:4-7; 5:1-6; 1 Tim. 1:8-11.

47. Prov. 15:3, 11; 16:1; Job 26:5; 28:24.

48. Job 42:16; Gen. 25:8; 35:29. Guilt seems relative—note the way in which length of life is associated with faithfulness and obedience to God. Insofar as all humans die, all are guilty; by implication, however, those who live longer are theoretically less guilty.

that Job's interlocutors find at the heart of human existence. For Job, the choice is clear: innocence or guilt. To choose innocence is to choose life. To choose guilt is to choose death. Job is haunted by the fact that both the innocent and the wicked suffer by the hand of God (9:22; see also Eccles. 9:2-3). Job is innocent and righteous. Yet neither innocence nor righteousness is enough to change his fate. In this sense, Job's critique of his interlocutors is also a critique of God, insofar as God finds all humans guilty through the imposition of a law that cannot be fulfilled. Job can no more accept a God that condemns all human beings to death with a kind of arbitrary imposition of guilt than he can relinquish his claim to innocence.[49] Although Job's interlocutors affirm YHWH's righteousness and justice, Job cannot. While Job's interlocutors place the burden of suffering and death upon human shoulders, Job cannot. For Job, the presence of suffering and death raises the possibility that God is not just. The God of Job's interlocutors is arbitrary, perhaps even cruel, almost certainly vengeful. But that God is not just. If God were just, innocence and guilt would be real human possibilities. If God were just, the innocent would not suffer and die.

Yet Job's call to God is not just a protest against God's apparent injustice but is a call born in innocence is a call to God to come out of the darkness so that the death question might be answered. Only God can absolve itself of guilt in our death. Only God can establish its innocence. We cannot. In this way, Job overturns the argument offered by his interlocutors. Where they argued that human innocence and guilt could be established only by God, Job argues that divine innocence and guilt can be established only by God. At issue in human suffering and death is not human innocence and guilt but God's innocence and guilt. In faith Job asks God to establish its innocence. In faith Job asks God to reveal the reason why the innocent suffer and die. What are God's reasons? Why in the presence of God is there death? (30:20-27). "I cry to you and you give me no answer; I stand before you, but you take no notice.[50] You have grown cruel in your dealings with me, your hand lies on me, heavy and hostile. . . . I

49. The experience of divine injustice is made far worse by Job's experience of the prosperity of the wicked: "Why do the wicked still live on, their power increasing with age? They see their posterity ensured and their offspring grow. The peace of their houses has nothing to fear; the rod that God wields is not for them. . . . They end their lives in happiness, and go down to Sheol" (Job 21:7-13).

50. The Hebrew seems to be corrupt here. The Jerusalem Bible follows the Septuagint. The RSV reads, "Thou dost not heed me."

know it is to death that you are taking me. . . . I hoped for happiness, but sorrow came, I looked for light, but there was darkness" (30:20-26). In the shadow of death God remains concealed (23:16-17). In the presence of death and amid the silence of God, YHWH appears to be cruel, brutal, arbitrary, and unjust (30:21). Though we may have eaten of the tree of knowledge of good and evil, the presence of death precludes understanding the ways of God.[51] In his protest Job calls into question the claim that for all things under the sun there is a purpose that comes from the hand of a God that shapes and guides the whole of creation and human existence. Job's faith leads him to protest against an arbitrary existence lived in light of an arbitrary God (see 42:1-6). In part, human existence and divine activity seem arbitrary because death bars human being from comprehending the ways of God. Because Job has faith he cannot accept the possibility that God's actions are arbitrary and without just cause. Job calls to God to emerge from the darkness and reveal its ways so that God's innocence might be proclaimed and God's purpose revealed.

Once again, the promise of the law and the possibility of faith seem mitigated by the presence of death. In the presence of death and in the presence of a law that cannot be fulfilled, the face of YHWH appears to be blackened, distorted, twisted by our suffering and death. How can a lustful God be a loving God? How can a holy God be a vengeful God? How can we draw near to the presence of God and see God's face if we cannot understand the ways of God? How can we embrace God if God remains hidden? How can we speak of innocence and guilt, of righteousness and wickedness, if all human beings suffer the same fate? How can the God who has given us life condemn us to death? What kind of a God speaks of love and offers death?[52] "Job's miserable condition soon extinguished the philosophical question, 'Why does God permit me to suffer?' and set afire the bold formulation, 'Why does God *make* me suffer these injustices?' The shift from suffering to God as the real problem reveals the depths of Job's agony. Torn by the discrepancy between past memory and present reality, Job strove mightily to reconcile the two faces of God."[53] For Job, then, the problem of death is the problem of God.[54]

---

51. Insofar as the dead no longer exist in the world, they are separated from the presence of God. Once separated from God's presence—however distant that presence might be—it is no longer possible to understand the ways of God.

52. Crenshaw, *Old Testament Wisdom*, 109–10.

53. Ibid., 119.

54. See John Briggs Curtis, "On Job's Witness in Heaven," *JBL* 102, no. 4 (1983):

The promise of wisdom, however, is that the ways of God will be opened, unveiled to human being, so that we might understand and grasp all that is hidden from us. Implicitly, the promise of wisdom is that in grasping the ways of God, in seeing the order that underlies human existence and the world, the presence of God will itself emerge from the darkness. Understanding is the prelude to knowledge, which is the threshold of revelation. Revelation opens the darkness that enshrouds God and obscures its face from human being. Where there was darkness and mystery, wisdom seeks to offer certainty and knowledge. Where there was hiddenness, wisdom seeks to offer presence. Where there was the possibility that we suffer and die by the hand of God, wisdom seeks to proclaim God's innocence. Yet, as Job discovers, the pursuit of righteousness and wisdom ends not in revelation but in darkness. "Job is left in darkness and the divine speeches do not touch the point. . . . The righteousness of God, as he in common with his friends had always understood it, cannot be detected in the world as God rules it. And he exhibits the terrible perplexity into which the discovery threw him. . . . To miss God's righteousness in the world is equivalent to missing God Himself."[55]

The lesson offered by Job goes even further: The attempt to find meaning in suffering is itself vain, for we suffer without reason. We go to our death for no purpose. Indeed, our death even calls into question our ability to love God.[56] Wherever human existence is drawn to its limit, the question of the reality of God and the issue of God's complicity in our death become most pressing. Furthermore, the experience of suffering and death calls into question not only the meaning of human existence and the reality of God but our ability to love God

---

552, 562. Curtis stresses Job's belief in a personal God as the solution to Job's anger. That is, Job's complaint is with the God of the universe or with the corporate deity that is too busy to be concerned with the death of one righteous person. Curtis follows the traditional approach to wisdom literature, which sees Job and Ecclesiastes as works that mark the movement from belief in a corporate deity to a more personal God. This transition is often linked to the growing influence of Hellenistic philosophy. While I would argue against the dichotomy Curtis and others see between Job's personal God and the impersonal corporate or cosmic deity, his argument in favor of interpreting Job's lament as a judgment against a murderous God is to the point. Also see his "On Job's Response to YHWH," *JBL* 98 (1979): 497–511.

55. A. B. Davidson, "The Book of Job," in *The Voice out of the Whirlwind,* ed. Ralph E. Hone (San Francisco: Chandler Publishing, 1960), 72. See also von Rad, *Wisdom in Israel,* 312.

56. See Job 7:6-21, esp. 21; 10:18-19; 14:5-17; Ps. 39:6-7(5-6); 104:29-30; Eccles. 1:3-11; 3:21-22.

as well. Faith cannot be sustained in the presence of death. A God that is feared can be obeyed—hence perhaps the frequent attempt to obey the law—but that God cannot be loved. The God of death can be feared, but it cannot be loved. Insofar as fear casts out love, God cannot be loved. In the absence of love, of a heart that is given completely and without question to God's love, God's call inevitably remains unrequited and unsatisfied. That unrequited love becomes the occasion for YHWH's bitter rage, vengeance, and fury.[57] Faith meets its death in the presence of a God that is always angry, bitter, cruel, and lustful.

Israel's experience of the boundless love of God is tied to its experience of its inability to satisfy that love. In many ways, YHWH's anger is an expression of its love for Israel, a love that, however powerful the human love for God may in turn be, finds no satisfaction. God's unrequited love becomes God's lust for human being, and that lust consumes us. Paradoxically, inasmuch as the history of the faith of Israel speaks of a God whose face is darkened by our suffering and death,[58] of a God whose lust consumes the object of its love, that history also speaks of a God whose love persists and endures with compassion, kindness, warmth, and even patience. This God suffers in its love for Israel. YHWH suffers rejection, indolence, and desertion by the one it loved. In this sense, YHWH's lust is rooted in a love that has no bounds. Yet this very boundlessness becomes the seed of YHWH's anger and vengeance. We are not divine. We are human. We can love only as humans love. Our tragedy—and God's—is that this relationship cuts both ways. The triumph of love is our tragedy, but the tragedy of love is not our triumph. It is our suffering.

The faith of Israel takes shape within the ongoing tension between love and death, obedience and fidelity, lust and compassion, permanence and transience, meaninglessness and totality. Within the world

57. See, for example, Isa. 29:1-4.
58. The use of the phrase "history of the faith of Israel" is certainly problematic. Since Wellhausen's *Prolegomena*, written more than a century ago, the use of this phrase has almost always called to mind attempts in the nineteenth and early twentieth centuries to apply modern historical-critical analysis to Hebrew Scripture so that the "historical events" behind the text might be uncovered. Such reconstructions, however, are hypothetical at best and probably bear little resemblance to the events they claim to uncover.

Here the phrase "history of the faith of Israel" refers to the theological reflection that occurred within Judaism. This reflection has a history insofar as successive generations appropriate it as their own. The tradition has a history insofar as it is the mark that identifies the community to which it belongs. The history of the faith of Israel in this sense is not a series of events but a pattern of reflection sustained over time.

in which human being discovers itself, the world that is bound by our birth and our death, love is often inseparable and indistinguishable from death, obedience from fidelity, lust from compassion—and the God of life from the God of death. The sage, like the seer, is moved, and even consumed, by the apparent contradiction between the promise of faith and the reality of death, by the force of the absence of God amid the suffering of the innocent, by the strength of the possibility that God's vengeance and lust are without reason. For the sage, death raises the possibility that there is no God there in the darkness, that all that is human passes into meaninglessness in the presence of death, that the God who has written its presence upon the human heart, who has filled the human heart with a desire for its presence, is the same God whose face can never be seen, whose heart can never be embraced, whose presence extends beyond the touch of a human hand.

ECCLESIASTES

Ambiguity. Futility. Meaninglessness. The endless search for the face of God. The passionate and persistent quest for comprehension of God's ways. The enduring search for the resolution of the death question. The complex matrix of reflection that surrounds these concerns forms the rich and perplexing tapestry we know as the Book of Ecclesiastes.[59] To read this book is to stand alongside the enigmatic Qoheleth, immersed in the mysteries that cloud and overshadow our existence. To read the Book of Ecclesiastes is to suffer the eclipse of human existence by the death question and to stand overshadowed by the search for meaning in the presence of futility. Most of all, to read the Book of Ecclesiastes is to search for the presence of God behind our suffering and death. For it is in the presence of God that the futility of our suffering and death, the vanity of our search for meaning and purpose, finds its reconciliation. Yet, to read the Book of Ecclesiastes and to take Qoheleth's words to heart is to understand

59. Gordis has expressed the sense of mystery that surrounds Qoheleth in this way: " 'Like a great and dark riddle is this little book to us, from its cry of victory over the nothingness of the world to the silent words of sadness at the end, at the sadness of man at his inevitable doom.' . . . Whoever has dreamt great dreams in his youth and seen the vision flee, or has loved and lost, or has beaten barehanded at the fortress of injustice and come back bleeding and broken, has passed Koheleth's door and tarried beneath the shadow of his roof" (*Koheleth,* 3).

just how far from the world of even the most pressing human concerns is the presence of that God.[60]

Qoheleth asks, Where is YHWH's judgment? Why do the righteous appear to suffer, while the wicked prosper? (3:16; 4:1-3; 5:7). Why do the wise and the foolish, the wicked and the just, all suffer the same fate? Does not faith promise that the righteous shall prosper and live, while the wicked suffer and die? These questions plague Qoheleth because as long as our existence is inseparable from our death, the ways of God cannot be discerned. So Qoheleth's questions cannot be answered. Knowledge of the world and of the ways of God eludes the grasp of even the sage (7:24-25).[61]

Though we have within our hearts the seed of eternity, which is the source of our desire for the presence of God and for discernment of its ways (3:11),[62] in our mortality we can have neither the presence nor the knowledge we seek (5:15).[63] Our quest for understanding and for the presence of God is in vain. They are ours to seek, but they are not ours to find.[64] We can no more understand the ways of God than

60. No less mysterious is Qoheleth himself. References in the text to Qoheleth are few. They occur within what is usually recognized as the body of the text (Eccles. 1:1-2, 12; 7:27) and in the epilogue (12:8). In the body of the text, Qoheleth occurs in a single form: *qohelet*. We cannot be sure if the word here is used as a proper name or as a title. K-B, 829a–d offers "speaker in assembly," even for 1:1. While it is usually translated in English as a proper name (as Qoheleth or Ecclesiastes), *qohelet* here may be a title, official designation, or office. BDB, 875b, for example, translates *qohelet* as "collector" (perhaps of sentences or proverbs), "convenor," "gatherer" (as perhaps one who would call an assembly together, either in the court or in the temple). Aside from the fact that this noun is rooted in the verb *qahal,* which means "gather, assemble," its meaning is unclear and unattested in the rest of Hebrew Scripture.

In 12:8, however, the Hebrew reads *ha qohelet.* Here a *vav* appears between the initial *qoph* and the letter *he.* The leading *he,* which functions like the definite article in English, would indicate that *qohelet* in this instance is being used to designate a person's function and not as a personal name. Clearly, *ha qohelet* is the collector, gatherer, or assembler—the one who calls others to assemble—but is not a specific personal name. It could also be argued that 12:8 is a play on the name Qoheleth and establishes a parallel between Qoheleth's search for wisdom and the tedious task of collecting proverbs and the writing of books, both of which are mentioned in the epilogue. Certainly this is possible, but not very likely. The ambiguity of the word *qohelet* adds to the enigmatic nature of the book.

61. See also Job 28:12-28; Sir. 1:6.

62. Isa. 55:6-9; Sir. 11:4; 18:5-6.

63. Job 1:21. A similar reflection can be found in an ancient Babylonian text (which some scholars feel may be the source of the text we know as Job): "The mind of the god, like the center of the heavens, is remote; knowledge of it is very difficult; people cannot know it" (Pritchard, *Ancient Near East,* 2:165).

64. We perhaps could argue that we can no more not seek the face of God and understanding of God's ways than we can stop being human. See Eccles. 7:15, 24-25; 8:17.

we can master the wind (8:8). If we cannot understand the ways of God, then it seems we can either have faith that what God does, God does consistently, or we can find the ways of God to be without reason or purpose. Qoheleth's search is the search for that hidden purpose. The promise of wisdom is its revelation.

For only an arbitrary God punishes the innocent and the guilty, rewards the just and the unjust, without apparent cause or reason. The sage seeks to dismiss the possibility that God acts arbitrarily by discovering meaning and purpose—by answering the death question. Either God's actions are righteous, or they are not. Either God acts arbitrarily, or God does not. If God's actions are not righteous, neither is God. If God acts arbitrarily, then God is arbitrary. What is arbitrary is without purpose or meaning. A universe subject to the whim of an arbitrary God is itself arbitrary and without purpose. An existence lived in an arbitrary world, subject to an arbitrary God, is futile and vain.

In the presence of the death question, neither God nor God's actions appear righteous or less than arbitrary, and human existence is stripped of meaning and purpose. A God by whose whim we suffer, a God that is not righteous, is a God that is responsible for our death. We cannot believe in a God that is responsible for our suffering and death. Questions raised by the sage about the righteousness and justice of God are raised in order to resolve the question of God's innocence and guilt in favor of God's innocence. In raising the death question, the sage desires to understand the ways of God and to discover a reason that establishes God's innocence, that stills the possibility that we suffer at the hand of an arbitrary God, and that silences the possibility of God's complicity in our death.[65] Thus, the sage's call to God to come out of the darkness is an invitation extended to God in faith to establish its innocence, to reveal its purpose.

Much is at stake here, including the possibility of faith itself. These questions plague Qoheleth not because he lacks faith but because he is a person of deep faith. He would not be troubled by God's absence if he did not expect God to be present; he would not be troubled by the possibility that God acts without reason or purpose if he did not expect God's presence to imply order and purpose. The suffering and

---

65. God's innocence implies human culpability. The traditional understanding of a human nature deformed by original sin, the stress placed upon salvation *sola gratia,* and the need for redemption from our sin by the suffering Messiah all represent attempts to establish God's innocence at our expense.

death of the righteous trouble him only because he expects the promise of enduring life in the presence of God to be a real human possibility. He would not be troubled by the hiddenness of God's ways, by the apparent incomprehensibility of divine purpose, if in faith he did not expect God to reveal itself to the righteous and the wise. Thus, Qoheleth's crisis is not a crisis of faith. It is a crisis of knowledge, of understanding born in the desire to comprehend a God whose purpose cannot be perceived and whose face cannot be seen. If there is a "dark side" to Qoheleth's reflection, it lies in the sharp contrast between the expectation offered in faith that questions addressed to God will not fall on deaf ears, and the experience of God's silence. The shadow of God's silence renders all that is human vain.

Against the vanity of human endeavors stands the poem of appointed times (3:1-8).[66] The pronouncement that there is an appointed time for all things rests upon the conviction that for everything there is a purpose, a time, which places that event within the context of the hidden mystery of the whole.[67] The tension between the assurance that for all things there is a purpose and the experience of futility is mirrored in the contrast between 'olam and hebel. As Williams has noted, 'olam has a broad semantic range.[68] Because of the richness of its semantic range, a wide variety of translations has been offered.[69] For example, 'olam has been translated as "enigma,"[70] "love of the world,"[71] "the hidden," or "the forgotten,"[72] and even as "the flow

66. Von Rad, Galling, and others have argued that this section represents a "doctrine of the right times." This doctrine stresses the appropriateness of human actions within the scope of divine purpose and the hidden mystery of the whole. See von Rad, *Wisdom in Israel*, 138; K. Galling, "Das Rätzel der Zeit im Urteil Kohelets," *ZTK* 58 (1961): 1ff. That such a doctrine was part of the sage's reflection seems questionable. Eccles. 3:1-8 could just as easily be the fruits of simple reflection.

67. S. G. Williams, "What Does It Profit a Man?: The Wisdom of Koheleth," in *Judaism* 20 (1971): 179–83. Eccles. 3:11 reads: "God has made everything beautiful in its own time; God has even put eternity in their heart so that humans cannot discover the things that God has done from the beginning [presumably creation] to the end [presumably to the end of time or up to the present moment]." On the difficulties in translating this verse, see BDB, 795d–796a. BDB postulates that *ha ma'aseh* may mean an act of judgment or deliverance. See Judg. 2:7-10; Josh. 24:31; Ps. 28:5; 33:4-22; 92:5(4); Isa. 5:12; Eccles. 7:13; 11:5. In such an understanding, our longing for eternity precludes comprehension of the hidden mystery of the whole. See K-B, 739d–741c.

68. Williams, "What Does It Profit a Man?" 182.

69. The richness is rooted in what appears to be the ambiguity of the word itself. No single English word captures the breadth and depth of its meaning.

70. R. B. Y. Scott, *Proverbs and Ecclesiastes*, Anchor Bible, vol. 18 (Garden City, N.Y.: Anchor Doubleday, 1965), 220–21.

71. Gordis, *Koheleth*, 56, 231ff.

72. See O. S. Rankin's article in the *Interpreter's Bible*, 5:46–49. Rankin stresses the

(or passing) of time."[73] Generally, these translations seem to fall into two more or less distinct ranges of meaning. The first range of meanings seems to highlight the more temporal aspects of ʿolam. Here the word connotes temporal existence or continuity. The second range of meanings seems primarily to connote hiddenness, absence, or distance.[74] ʿOlam is our longing for eternity, and yet, paradoxically, it is also the mark of our separation from the eternal. Williams offers this analysis: "However the word ʿolam may be translated, more important is it that it is whatever lies at the core of existence. . . . It appears to be that which moves man, that which makes him distinctive as a creature. It moves him toward God, yet he cannot fathom God's works."[75]

In part, God's person and purpose are enigmatic because human beings are not eternal. We do not exist ʿad ʿolam. Qoheleth is barred from understanding God's ways because he is barred from eternity. As is noted above many times in 4 Ezra, we cannot comprehend the ways of God precisely because our existence is limited by our death. The limit of our existence is the limit of our discernment. Furthermore, the desire to know God and to understand God's purpose is rooted in our longing for ʿolam, for eternity, a longing that is written upon our hearts by God. The things that are secret are hidden because we cannot be forever.[76] Eternity is as hidden from us as are the ways of God.

If Williams is correct and ʿolam is best described as that which lies at the heart of our existence, as that which most characterizes us as human, Qoheleth's paradox seems clear: Our being takes shape not around presence but around absence, not around what is revealed but around what is hidden. What is hidden? The presence, purpose, and face of God.[77] Without access to ʿolam, human existence becomes vain,

---

importance of the use of the definite article in Eccles. 3:11 (the Hebrew reads ha ʿolam, not simply ʿolam). Hence, Rankin's translation is supported by the fact that ʿolam may also mean "conceal, forget, hide," or "obscure."

73. As Williams notes, Galling uses the German Zeitablauf, which is itself difficult to translate. The verb ablaufen means "pass, ebb, flow," or "move."

74. BDB (761–63a) associates each range of meaning with a different root—although each is spelled the same way and presumably was pronounced alike. K-B (709a–b) does not share this analysis.

75. Williams, "What Does It Profit a Man?" 182.

76. Thus Rankin's translation is not without merit.

77. Crenshaw argues that Qoheleth is convinced that God is unknowable. In place of the presence of God, Qoheleth offers a theology of mystery (Old Testament Wisdom, 137–39).

futile, fleeting. In the presence of death we cannot understand the rhythm of the appointed times. We can only be subject to them. All human concerns, actions, attempts to discern the appointed time, and attempts to understand why the innocent and the wicked seem to suffer the same fate—all must end in failure. This searching and this striving, in Qoheleth's own words, are vanity and a chase after the wind.

In contrast, because ʿolam has been written upon our hearts we cannot rest until we see the face of God. We can affirm that what God does, God does in its own way and in its own time. We can affirm the judgment of all by God, that for all things under heaven there is a time and a purpose. Yet we cannot see YHWH's judgment, touch God's face, discern YHWH's ways, or overcome our death. While ʿolam is the word for the presence of God upon our heart, it is also the word for the mystery and the darkness that shroud the face of God. ʿOlam expresses both the awareness that for all things there is an appointed time as well as the inaccessibility of God's ways. Thus, ʿolam connotes both awareness and mystery, the call to search and that which obscures the search, the presence and the absence, that which reveals and that which conceals. Thus, Williams,[78] Galling, and others, who see Qoheleth's fear of God as motivated by a kind of prudent skepticism that thinly veils his iconoclastic attack on Judaism, are wrong. Qoheleth is not hedging his bets. He is not a nihilist. Rather, he is concerned with finding or establishing the limits within which faith is possible and within which existence endures and has meaning.

The presence of ʿolam upon our hearts carries with it not only an awareness of the presence of God and a sense of the rhythm of God's ways but also an acute and pressing sense of the breath that is human existence. The search for ʿolam is made vain and futile by the presence of death. For Qoheleth, the transience of human existence makes the search for the face of God all the more pressing. That sense of transience is bound by the shadow of death, a shadow that draws ever closer. The further away the sustaining presence of God seems, the stronger grows our awareness of the certainty of our death and our distance from God. Conversely, the closer the shadow of death, the more pressing the search for God. Yet, the more we press for the presence of God, the further away God seems, and the more vain our quest.

If we could but look upon the face of God, our longing would be satisfied. As long as our death separates us from God, that longing

---

78. Williams, "What Does It Profit a Man?" 184.

cannot be satisfied. And that longing for ʿolam haunts us as long as we live. ʿOlam is not only the awareness of the presence of God but is also the awareness of the inevitability of death and the hiddenness of God. Insofar as ʿolam is the source of our longing for God, of our desire to know and understand, it is our greatest joy. Insofar as it is the source of our awareness of death, ʿolam is the source of our greatest sorrow. In the end, Qoheleth's search for the presence of God has brought him no nearer the presence of God or an understanding of the ways of God. Instead, his search has only brought him nearer his death. Thus, our longing for life is inseparable from the certainty of our death.

That longing for life juxtaposed against the certainty of our death renders all that is human futile and vain. This juxtaposition is captured or embodied in the word *hebel,* which expresses the vanity or purposelessness of human existence and the futility of human actions.[79] It characterizes both the search for the hidden mystery of the whole and the nature of human existence. Human existence is futile, or vain, because like a mist, it passes quickly from the earth. Human existence is also futile because humans are destined to chase after the wind— we will forever pursue the presence of God and the hidden mystery of the whole. Like the wind through our hands, both the presence and the mystery will elude us forever. We search for what cannot be found. We reach out for what cannot be touched. In a world where all things die, human beings long to live. Confronted with the limitations imposed upon human existence by death, all that we hope, desire, and dream passes away before our eyes like dew on the grass at dawn. All our desires pass with us, and the world, untouched by our passage, remains as it was before us.[80] Human actions and the totality of human expectations and aspirations—human being itself— are vain.

79. BDB (210d–211a) offers "breath" or "vapor" as the translation for *hebel*. K-B (223c–d) translates it as "dust, vanity, wind, breath." As with ʿolam, the semantic range of *hebel* is broad; it evokes images of wind, mist, smoke, breath, and even emptiness. Thus, *hebel* means more than what is usually associated with the words "futility" or "vanity." It more conveys the sense of transience, passing time, mortality, and diminishing existence that marks human existence. Part of the richness of this word is mirrored in Qoheleth's usage. Almost without exception, every occurrence in the text stresses one or another aspect of *hebel*'s complex of meaning. Even the phrase for which Qoheleth is best known—"Vanity of vanities"—occurs in slightly different contexts throughout the book. Thus, it is not possible to offer one and only one translation for *hebel,* as Williams, Ginsberg, Scott, and others do.

80. This observation finds elegant and powerful expression in Eccles. 1:3–11. Note the power assigned the presence of death in the final poem (11:1—12:8).

Transience, impotence, and distance all mark the futility of human existence. *Hebel* is all these things. It is the acute sense of the passage of time, the pressing awareness of the fate that must befall us all. *Hebel* is the realization that our grasp of our existence is tenuous at best. It is the experience of estrangement and alienation from the world and from God. Yet *hebel* is also the passionate longing, the determined quest, for the presence and face of God. It is the passionate search for eternity in a world where all things pass too quickly away. *Hebel,* then, is that which marks us as most human, and yet that which marks the end of our humanity. It is the paradox of being that shapes our existence and secures our death.

Insofar as human being is defined by its relationship to the divine, the impermanence and transience that mark human being call into question not only the being that is human. It also calls into question every aspect of the relationship between the human and the divine as well. If *hebel* characterizes the shape of human existence, it also characterizes the relationship between the human and the divine. While Qoheleth is certainly troubled by the transience of human existence, it is the futility of the pursuit of the presence of God that seems to plague him the most. The search for *ʿolam* presupposes that there is something there to be found. Yet the search for the hidden mystery of the whole, the search for the presence of God, finds that apart from the darkness, there is nothing there. Here between the expectation and the reality, between everything and nothing, *hebel* is born.

To be human is to be before God, to have one's face turned toward God. Human being is defined by its radical openness to God. A kind of nakedness characterizes our openness to God. Apart from the presence of God, our being ceases to be human. Yet, to be human is to be apart from God, to experience and to live in the distance between the human and the divine. For there to be a relationship, the human and the divine must stand face-to-face, so to speak. But the presence of God is more than conspicuous in its absence. Where the human is naked before God, the face of God remains elusive, and God's presence always mediated. YHWH is never present to. YHWH is always present through[81]—through its word (see Jer. 1:4; Ezek. 1:3); through Torah,

---

81. The descriptions of YHWH's appearances in Hebrew Scripture are of interest here. Moses, for example, encounters the burning bush. Ezekiel encounters what appears to be the chariot of God. Elijah is confronted by the thin voice of silence. In part the human pursuit of the face of God is mirrored in Exod. 33:12-23. While Moses sees the "hind parts" of God, he is barred from looking upon God's face. Also see Exod. 20:19. Ironically, we long for the face of God, but if we look upon that face, we are condemned to death.

the prophets, its glory (Ezek. 1:28); and even through our death. However mediated the presence of God might be, that presence calls for a response to the person of God. Trust, confidence, humility, faith, and even fear are responses to that presence (Eccles. 5:6b; 10:16-19). For Qoheleth, fear is the proper stance one must take in relationship to God, even in the presence of corruption and wickedness.[82] Where Deuteronomy proclaims, "You shall love the Lord your God," wisdom declares, "Those who fear the Lord keep their hearts prepared and humble themselves in God's presence."[83] Fear of God is a kind of radical humility, a kind of anxious anticipation, perhaps of God's wrath, of judgment. It is an abiding sense of the uncertainty about the ramifications of one's actions. Fear in this sense characterizes the way in which a human being stands in the presence of God. Here there is a further problem: Insofar as we are human, we cannot love what we cannot know. We can, and frequently do, fear what is unknown to us. We can be overwhelmed by the darkness and mystery that shroud the presence of God. Thus we can fear God, but an unknown, faceless God, we cannot love.[84]

In the absence of the possibility of loving God, fear of God is more than prudent. It is the only mark of dedication we can offer. That fear of God is most often expressed, even in Ecclesiastes, in terms of obedience to Torah. The promise of wisdom, born in fear of God,[85] is this: Those who stand in proper relationship to God will see God's face;[86] Torah will be understood; the mysteries of the universe, of God's ways, will be revealed; the rhythm of the appointed times will become clear; the sage will transcend the limits of human reason and come to understand what is now hidden in darkness; love of God, which had been cast out by fear, by the limitations that bind our existence, will in turn cast out fear. But this promise is to remain

---

82. Yet, fear of the Lord is not enough to overcome or even to diminish wickedness and injustice. They endure despite the righteousness of the sage.

83. Sir. 2:17; cf.1:14-20; 19:20; 24:23-28/32; Prov. 1:7; 22:3.

84. Note that Qoheleth does not speak of love of God, a topic avoided generally in wisdom literature.

85. Detailed discussions of fear of God can be found in Eichrodt, *Theology of the Old Testament*, 2:268–76; von Rad, *Old Testament Theology*, 1:433–44; and Roland E. Murphy, "Qoheleth's Quarrel with the Fathers," in *From Faith to Faith: Essays in honor of Donald G. Miller*, ed. Dikran Y. Hadidian (Pittsburgh: Pickwick Press, 1979), 240–42.

86. Again see Exod. 20:19; 33:12-17.

unfulfilled.[87] For the sage is human, and his humanity precludes comprehension of all that is not human. What is not in the world exceeds
our grasp. The sage's search must fail.[88] The wisdom that should have
brought joy, instead has brought sorrow.[89] The promise of wisdom
remains nothing more.[90] Insofar as that promise remains unattainable,
wisdom serves not to comfort but further to burden the human search
for ʿolam. Thus wisdom heightens the sage's sense of the futility of
human existence. It fails to lessen it. This search Qoheleth labels the
vanity of vanities (1:13-15).[91] According to Murphy, the "advantage
of wisdom over folly is cancelled . . . by the reality of death (2:15-
17). . . . Just as Job complains about God's failure to honor human
integrity, Qoheleth complains that human wisdom is not achieving
the goals she should."[92] Murphy's insight is to the point and well taken.
However, the problem lies not in human wisdom but in the inaccessibility of God. The ʿolam that the sage seeks is inseparable from the
person and presence of God. As long as God remains hidden and
concealed, the human mind cannot grasp ʿolam. Again, the God who
has written its presence upon our hearts has withdrawn that presence
from our grasp.

Still the specter of death remains. In the presence of death the
advantage of the righteous and the wise over the foolish and the wicked
is diminished if not eclipsed (2:15-17). In death, even the distinction
between what is human and what is not is lost (3:18-21). If God is
responsible for all things under the sun, is not God also responsible
for suffering and death?[93] For the ambiguity that shrouds our existence
in darkness and the futility and transience of our lives? How could the
God that is the author of our existence and that has written its presence

87. Those who tend to see Qoheleth as a rebel or as an iconoclast argue that Qoheleth
may well have intended to demonstrate that God's purpose for the world transcends
human reason. See, for example, Eichrodt, *Theology of the Old Testament*, 1:263.

88. Eccles. 3:11-21; 7:24; 8:16-17.

89. Eccles. 1:18; Prov. 14:10; Wis. 8:16.

90. See Eccles. 4:13-16; 9:13-16.

91. This passage may provide a key to understanding the importance of Torah for
Qoheleth. In the absence of the presence of God, and given wisdom's inability to unveil
the presence of God, Torah seems to become all the more binding. Torah seems to
offer insight into the how human existence is to be lived in the absence of God (von
Rad, *Wisdom in Israel*, 228–29). Von Rad wrote: "Behind the problem of the future,
there lies for Koheleth the still more difficult question of death which casts its shadow
over every meaningful interpretation of life. Whenever Koheleth speaks of fate (*miqreh*),
death is always invisioned at the same time" (p. 228).

92. Murphy, "Qoheleth's Quarrel," 237.

93. Von Rad, *Wisdom in Israel*, 305.

upon our hearts condemn us to death? Qoheleth does not offer an answer. If there is a reason, it is not ours to know.

Much of the text of Ecclesiastes concerns itself with the incongruities of human existence. Qoheleth does not amend these incongruities or soften their presence. He is not able to answer the death question or to make our suffering and death more reasonable. No matter how desperately we seek the face of God or try to understand its ways, both the face of God and the mystery of its ways remain hidden. Only our death seems assured and certain. Indeed, the presence of death haunts our life. From the moment of birth the mourners are already in the street. In the presence of this death, all things are vain. All things pass like a mist.[94] Our advantage? "The living know that they will die.[95] Those who have died know nothing. For them there is no more reward. Their memories are forgotten. Their loves, their hates, their desires, these have all perished. There is no share for them in what is done under the sun" (9:5-6).

Despite his faith in YHWH, or perhaps because of it, Qoheleth is not able to overcome the incongruities that plague human existence. Those incongruities, Qoheleth argued, as Crenshaw noted,[96] rest in the hand of a God that actively and intentionally concealed knowledge of its ways from human beings. But to stand before God in faith and in love is to open oneself in toto to God. To stand before is to stand open. Openness to implies not only that one has opened oneself but also that one is open to the other. Openness calls for a response to oneself. Clearly, the God to whom we have opened ourselves, the God that demands that we open ourselves to it, has chosen to stand back. The promise of faith is eternity, but the reality of God's concealment, distance, and silence is death. Between the promise and the silence lies the incongruous. These incongruities will not be silenced and are not mediated or softened. Their persistence is chilling. In the presence of these incongruities, Qoheleth finds himself caught in a web of paradox that pursues and plagues him. The longer he lives,

94. Qoheleth comments, not without bitterness, that it is better to be a live dog than a dead lion (9:5). Life, even in the presence of death, is preferable to death.

95. The Hebrew here is difficult to translate: literally, "the ones who live [are] the ones who know that they will die." Both participles are usually translated as nouns in English. In Hebrew it seems that an equation is being drawn between the ones who live and the ones who know. That is, the living, in contrast to the dead, are the ones who know at least that they will die.

96. See Crenshaw's "The Eternal Gospel (Eccl. 3:11)," in *Essays in Old Testament Ethics*, ed. Crenshaw and John T. Willis (New York: KTAV, 1974), 23–55.

the more deeply entwined he becomes in its web. Qoheleth remains
caught between his faith in God and the lingering presence of death,
between the transience of our existence and the desire for permanence,
for eternity.

Qoheleth's quest is not just a search for justice and restitution for
those who suffer unjustly. Qoheleth's search is the search for the end
of the paradox of human existence. He seeks to satisfy the longing
for eternity that has been wrought upon our hearts. While this longing
turns our hearts toward God, it also reminds us of our mortality. It
speaks to us of the passing of time. As beings in time, we share the
fate that is the destiny of all that live upon the earth. This is more
than unjust. It is more than ironic. It is empty. It is bitter. It is cruel.
Yet it is our fate. It is our paradox. Out of the bitterness of this paradox
we cry out to God for compassion, mercy, and deliverance. But God
remains silent. And the silence of God overpowers us.

In the silence of God we are left to live our lives, to eat, drink, and
find whatever measure of happiness we can embrace. For these too
come from the hand of God.[97] This is not a call to hedonism.[98] Rather,
it is an acknowledgment of the limitations of our existence. We are
to live, as brief as that life might be, and we are to take what is given
us[99] from the hand of God, until the silver cord is snapped (12:6). In
the presence of a fate we can neither alter nor change, this is all that
we can do. Indeed, this need not be the mark of a deep-seated pessimism. This confidence is not simply a mark of our blind acceptance
of our death. For Qoheleth, quite the opposite is true. It is an act of
faith and trust in God. Despite the absence of any clear purpose or
reason, despite the absence of the face of God, Qoheleth stands fast
in faith. And faith in YHWH promises transcendence of death. For

97. Eccles. 2:24-25; 3:12-13, 22; 5:17; 8:15; 9:7-8; Sir. 14:14.
98. Hengel, *Judaism*, 1:122-27; Hengel offers a detailed analysis of the impact of
Hellenistic thought on Qoheleth—including the influence of an Epicurean carpe diem
approach to life in the presence of death. This approach obscures Qoheleth's argument.
While I do not deny that Qoheleth might have been influenced by Greek philosophy,
I do question the analysis of any text in terms of a culture or philosophy that is foreign
to it. While Qoheleth might have been influenced by Hellenistic thought, he remains
a Jew. Any impact of Hellenistic philosophy on his thought would be reflected within
the context of his culture and faith, not in estrangement or opposition to it. A similar
path is taken by Crenshaw, who argues that the experience of the futility of human
existence and the pursuit of pleasure go hand in hand (*Old Testament Wisdom*, 141–42).
99. Eccles. 9:9-10. The Hebrew word here is *heleq*, which means "portion, share,
tract, territory." It is what is inherited, that which is given us to live out—in short, our
"lot in life."

Qoheleth, all things—love and death, wickedness and righteousness, wisdom and folly, remembrance and forgottenness[100]—come from the hand of God; and what God does, God does consistently. What God does, God does with a purpose. "To this nothing can be added. From this nothing can be taken away" (3:14).

Even this confession of faith does not ease our pain or resolve the paradox of our existence. It does not make death any easier to bear. Rather, it makes our tragedy and our trauma, suffering, and death all the more difficult to accept. It makes the paradox of our existence all the more consuming and the presence of the shadow of death all the more unnerving. While faith promises that death will be overcome, death remains. Death persists. In the presence of death, the silence of God is impossible to carry in our hearts. "YHWH my God," wrote the psalmist, "I call out for help all day, I cry out to you all night. May my prayer reach you, hear my cries for help, for my soul is troubled, my life is on the edge of Sheol. . . . Alone, down among the dead, with the slaughtered in their graves, among the ones you have forgotten, those deprived of the protection of your hand . . . I am here, calling for your help, praying to you every morning. Why do you reject me? Why do you hide your face from me? . . . Slowly dying since my youth, I have endured your terrors; now I am exhausted. . . . Now darkness is my companion" (Ps. 88).

These words speak of an unending anguish and sorrow. These words come from the depth of a heart committed in faith to a God that has withdrawn into the darkness, and they capture the heart of the shadow of the person we know as Qoheleth. The psalmist, the sage, and the seer all speak the name of God even unto death. But where is the God to whom they called? Where is God while the innocent and the righteous die? Why has God chosen silence and absence? In the presence of God's silence and hiddenness, the paradox of our existence endures. As long as that paradox endures, the God of love seems inseparable from the God of death. Indeed, as long as that paradox endures, the shadow of death threatens to call into question all that is human. Once our humanity is called into question, so too is faith in God. Yet despite our death, despite the vanity of our existence, despite even the triumph of death, our faith stands.

But without the face of God, we cannot defuse the paradox of love and death or free ourselves from the possibility that it is by the hand

---

100. See Ps. 31:13(12): "I have passed out of mind like one who is dead."

of God that we die. Furthermore, without the face of God even our faith becomes vain and our wisdom folly. In the presence of the paradox of love and death, of eternity and mortality, the sage stands open in the silence waiting for God to speak, waiting for love to overcome death, for eternity to eclipse mortality, for the reality of God to over-shadow the reality of death. The sage waits unto death, and still God does not speak. The sage waits until the last breath passes from his lips, and the passing of that breath carries a final prayer to the unknown God that stands silently in the darkness. In death, the breath of life passes from our lips forever, and with the passing of the breath of life, the vanity, the futility, the breath that is our existence also passes away. In death the sage offers the unknown God his innocence, faithfulness, love, and even humanity. Then, consumed by death, his dreams, loves, expectations, and faith are all cast upon the wind, scattered like dust upon the water. And yet, despite the stillness and futility, despite death, though the almond tree blossoms while the pitcher lies shattered by the spring, even while the dust of our lives consumes our days, it is the face of YHWH that is our breath.

five | THE PROTEST AND THE SILENCE

Once again,
Lest I withdraw more distant and turn my eyes
onward,
In loneliness I turn my hands upward,
To you to whom I retreat,
To whom I have solemnly consecrated altars in the deepest,
most intimate embrace
For your voice has always called to me in turn.
Thereupon does the deeply written phrase glow:
"To the Unknown God."
It is I though I am still left in the
outrage of the herd.
It is I—and I feel the traps which pull me down struggling,
and I wish to flee.
Yet I compel myself to a delicate situation—
I desire to know you,
you who are unknown,
you who put your hands deep into my soul,
you who wander through my life like a storm,
you who are incomprehensible,
you who are kin to me.
I desire to know you,
as you know yourself.

Friedrich Nietzsche,
"To the Unknown God"

Confronted with death, the human from the very depths of its
soul cries out for justice. Historical Christianity has only
replied to this protest against evil by the annunciation of the
kingdom and then of eternal life which demands faith. But
suffering exhausts hope and faith and then is left alone and
unexplained. The toiling masses worn out with suffering and
death, are masses without God . . . the only original rule for
life today: to learn to live and to die, and in order to be a
human being, to refuse to be a God.

Albert Camus,
The Rebel

DEATH AND HEBREW SCRIPTURE

It is a fact of our existence: To be human is to die. In death we realize
the telos, or completion, of our humanity. Death both defines our
humanity and proves to be its end, for when we die, we cease to be
human. Yet death is not a distant figure we encounter at the edge of
our world. Death is not an end that suddenly and unpredictably comes
upon us. Death lingers before us. As long as we are human, we exist
in and beneath the shadow of death. The moment of death always
stands before us (Eccles. 12:1-8). That moment shapes our existence
and colors our world. From the moment of birth, we are already old
enough to die.[1] Death is always a possibility that draws ever nearer
with age, illness, or abandonment by God. As long as we are human,
we are given over to death (Ps. 88:16-19 [15-18]). Once given over
to death, we are separated from the world, from God, and even from
ourselves. To this fate the seer, the sage, or the prophet never could
take exception.

In death the *nephesh,* the life force,[2] becomes separated from the
body. This union of dust and breath, of *nephesh* and flesh, that forms
the living being is broken in death. Once broken, that union is dissolved
forever. With the dissolution of that union, the human becomes separated or alienated from its very being. In death, the body returns to
the dust from which it was formed.[3] The *nephesh* in turn is scattered
into a kind of eternal dispersion, an enduring dissolution. *Nephesh* is
like air enclosed in a bottle. While the bottle remains sealed, the air
remains within. When the bottle is opened or broken, the air within
escapes. Once removed from the bottle that gave its presence shape
or form, the air scatters. The longer it remains unbound, the more it
drifts and dissipates.

The tragedy of death is not that life ends but that while death is
the end of life, it is not the end of existence.[4] Despite the return of

---

1. Job 7:1-21; Ps. 39:6-7 (5-6); Eccles. 2:22; 4 Ezra 4:22-25; 7:61.
2. *Nephesh* is the breath of life YHWH is said to have breathed into the dust of the
earth in order to create living beings. The idea that there is a soul that makes our body
"human" and qualitatively different from an animal or plant is absent here. That the
nephesh separates from the body does not imply a dualism of mind or soul and body.
As Lou Silberman notes, dualism of soul and body is foreign to Hebrew Scripture
("Death in the Hebrew Bible and Apocalyptic Literature," in *Perspectives on Death,* ed.
Liston O. Mills [Nashville: Abingdon, 1969], 16). The *nephesh* is not a soul. Humans
do not possess a soul. A human does "not have a *nephesh,* he is a *nephesh,* an animated
being, a total person" (p. 17).
3. Silberman, "Death," 20, 25-26.
4. Clearly, the use of "existence" here is problematic. Within the context of exis-

the body to the dust of the earth, the *nephesh* endures. "Death is the spilling out of life. The dead are the echo of life; they are not part of creation, but its shadow."[5] Here Qoheleth's metaphorical play on the word *hebel* is to the point. *Hebel*, as we noted, means "breath" as well as "vanity" or "futility." Life is futile and vain because life is like a breath, like the wind. That is, life is fleeting, and like all that passes quickly, the breath that is our life scatters and disperses without apparent end—further and further into nothingness. The breath of life, like water spilled on the ground (2 Sam. 14:14), like leaves scattered by the wind, like the mist that rises with the dawn (4 Ezra 4:22-25; 7:61), drifts and disperses for eternity.

Yet despite that dissolution, the *nephesh* endures and is sustained. Thus, the dead continue to be—they are not "dead." Yet neither are they alive. The dead are empty shells that exist in nothingness, in isolation from the world of the living and in separation from all that is human. They have not passed into nothingness. Like dark shadows that linger at the edge of the horizon of our world, their presence endures, even though their humanity does not. The dead are shadows of what is human, but they themselves are no longer human.[6] This eternal dispersion, this endless loss of identity and humanity, this perpetual separation from the presence of God marks the tragedy of death in Hebrew Scripture. The tragedy that befalls those who die is existence in forgottenness, darkness, sheol, condemned to remember and to long for what can no longer be theirs. The lament of the psalmist, the sober questions of Qoheleth, the probing anguish of 4 Ezra, and the sorrow of Job are borne upon the hearts of those who fear, not a death that is the end of existence, but a death that is not.

Deprived of their humanity, the dead can no longer be in relationship to God. The dead exist forever in a kind of exile from God. "The dead have no experience either of God or of anything else. They are shadows gone from the scene where God and man are related in event."[7] Denied the presence of God, the dead are left alone, abandoned and deserted, in an existence that knows only absence and emptiness.

---

tentialism and certain forms of phenomenology, existence is a technical term that refers to a life authentically lived within the world. Existence here does not mean authentic being unto death. Rather, it means something more like being after death, or enduring presence after death, or even a kind of continued being without continued life.

5. Ibid., 25.

6. Ibid., 21-25.

7. Ibid., 25; H. Wheeler Robinson, "Hebrew Psychology," in *The People and the Book,* ed. Arthur S. Peake (London: Oxford University Press, 1925), 378-79.

For the living, however, continued existence offers the possibility that the presence of God can emerge from the darkness and fill human being. To be, to live—even in the presence of an elusive, hidden God—is to exist in relationship to God. To exist before and in relation to God is *not* to exist under the watchful eye of one who is off in the distance, much like a parent watches a child as the child plays. To exist before God is to exist face-to-face with God. To exist in the fullness of one's being is to exist with, by, and in, the presence of a God that has stepped out of the darkness and revealed itself. Fullness of life implies God's disclosure of itself. As the dead endure God's absence eternally, the living are sustained by the promise that God's face will not be hidden forever.[8] For those who live, the promise and expectation that the face of God will emerge from the darkness and sustain life forever arises within the context of life as it is lived in a world bound both by total absence and by total presence.[9]

FULLNESS AND EMPTINESS

We can speak, therefore, of a kind of spectrum of existence. This spectrum stretches from the shadowy existence of the dead to existence in its fullness. In this sense, life is dynamic—the movement between the full presence of life and its complete absence in death is continuous. To be human is to be in between eternal life and absolute death, to move incessantly from one edge of the horizon of our existence to the other, and to struggle to attain life in the presence of death. This dynamic movement between the extremes of total presence and total absence actually continues "past" or "through" death. However, death marks a point of no return. The dead cannot cross back into the world of the living. Those who have died cannot press their existence toward God. Alone, abandoned, the dead endure eternal exile. To that exile there is no end. In exile the dead exist forever. The psalmist writes: "YHWH, come back, rescue me, if you love me; save me, for in death there is no remembrance of you. Who can sing your praises in Sheol?" (Ps. 6:5-6 [4-5]).[10]

8. Silberman, "Death," 25.
9. Again, this hope or expectation can be most vividly seen in the great either-or of Deuteronomy: be faithful and live, or be rebellious and die (30:15-28).
10. Also see Ps. 30:8-10 (7-9); "You hid your face and I was terrified. . . . What do you gain by my blood if I go down to the pit [i.e., to Sheol]? Can the dust praise you or proclaim your faithfulness?"

In this sense, without a concept of death as end, there can be no concept of life after death. Death is another type or form of existence, one marked by total alienation and separation from all that is human and from God. For those who exist in Sheol there is no hope other than restoration and deliverance. The dead call to God to raise them out of the darkness, to deliver them from nothingness, to restore them to the world of the living, and to renew their presence in the world by raising their bodies out of the dust from which they came and to which they have returned. This restoration implies a resurrection of the body. In resurrection the *nephesh* would return to the world of the living and to the presence of God. Resurrection is return from eternal exile.[11]

However much the hope for restoration from death is embraced and proclaimed by the seer and awaited and sought by the sage, the facticity of human suffering and death remains. The hiddenness of God continues. Like the God whose presence the sage and the seer seek, restoration and deliverance remain distant, beyond the reach of our hands. In the distance between the presence of that hope and the absence of its fulfillment, the dead remain dead. In this sense, the faith of the sage is not sustaining enough. The lament of the psalmist is not powerful enough. The revelation of the seer has not strength enough. At that point where existence and faith are discontinuous, where the death question emerges between the human and the divine, the presence of death and the absence of restoration again raise the issue of God's complicity in our death.

Perhaps nowhere is the discontinuity between faith and death more pronounced than at the point where humans appear to suffer and die in innocence. At the point where the discontinuity between faith and death is most pronounced, God seems unmoved by, if not indifferent to, the human cry for deliverance. We do not know whether God is indifferent to our cry for deliverance, or if God's anger precludes compassion for our suffering. Whether we have been abandoned by a distant God that has given us over to death, or left to die by an impotent God, we do not know. In any case, the force and the power of that discontinuity is not lost in Hebrew Scripture. On the one hand, the portrait of Jerusalem offered in Lamentations certainly leaves little doubt about the magnitude of the destructive power and force of God's

---

11. No idea of the existence of a "soul" outside of or apart from this world is implied or understood here.

anger.[12] "Look, YHWH, and consider: whom have you treated like this? Why, women have eaten their little ones, the children they have nursed in their arms! Why, the priest and the prophet have been slaughtered in the sanctuary of the Lord! Children and old men are lying on the ground in the streets; my virgins and my young men have fallen by the sword; you have killed on the day of the wrath of YHWH, you have slaughtered without pity" (Lam. 2:20-22).[13]

On the other hand, the kind of malevolent abandonment Job experiences offers an equally powerful expression of human abandonment by God. In Job's case human suffering and death are without cause and without justification. Job simply suffers in his humanity. Yet however violent the suffering that God unleashed against Israel, pronouncement of judgment was almost always accompanied by the promise of restoration.[14] However long Job endured a most senseless suffering, Job was restored. Likewise, exile was always coupled with the promise of restoration.[15] With restoration of the nation and of life, there is restoration of humanity. With restoration of our humanity, there is restoration of faith. That restoration is always framed in terms of a return to life in this world. But those who suffer and die remain dead. For them restoration and deliverance are impossible.

At those moments where human beings were pressed to the limits of their existence, the relationship between YHWH and Israel was also pressed hard.[16] Insofar as the relationship between YHWH and Israel constitutes the life and faith of Israel, that relationship was the focus of an ongoing exegesis: Who is this God? Where is this God? Why have we been chosen? Furthermore, the promise of having been chosen, the promise of God's love for Israel and of Israel's love for God, is life,[17] eternity, and prosperity. Yet, the force of the promise, the strength of the love, and the power of the relationship are all eclipsed

12. As we noted earlier, the force of the prophetic texts lies in part in their powerful and disarming pronouncements of judgment. See, for example, Isa. 5:25; 34:1ff.; 42:24ff.; 44:24ff.; Mic. 6:9-14; Amos 5:1-6; 8:9—9:4; Hos. 5:8—6:1; 6:4—10:15.

13. This translation is adapted from the Jerusalem Bible; see also Hos. 9:15ff.

14. The promise of restoration is absent in some of the judgment oracles in Isaiah. See, for example, Isa. 29.

15. See chapter 3.

16. See the preceding chapters on wisdom and apocalyptic.

17. As we noted earlier, the promise of life advanced in Deuteronomy is formulated in terms of a kind of either-or: either love God and live, or turn away and die (see Deut. 11:26-32; 13:2ff.; 28:8-14; 29:8-28; 30:1-10, 15-20). In either case, the choice offered to Israel emerges within this world and not another. No concept of life after death is offered or implied.

and called into question by the shadow of death. If God is there, if God has given us its love, if God has opened itself to us, why in the presence of God is there death? To this question the sage could find no answer, the seer could find no revelation, the psalmist could find no prayer. With this question upon his lips, Jesus died.

DEATH AND THE IDENTITY OF GOD

That God would have offered to Israel life and prosperity in exchange for our hearts and would have held before us the promise of life in a world where all things die says as much about God as it does Israel.[18] The choice between life and death is no choice at all.[19] We would gladly give our hearts to God in order to ransom our lives from death, were our hearts ours to give. That God would use the power of death as a means of securing our love and of winning our hearts raises anew the question of what kind of a God this is. What kind of God threatens us with death in order to secure our love or offers us a choice between love and death? Certainly not a loving God. Not a benevolent or merciful God. The face of the jealous and lustful God of death is very dark. Thus, the cross as often traditionally construed is not the sign of God's love. It is the sign of God's anger and lust, just as much as it is the sign of our humanity. The power of the cross lies in the fact that it is at once the sign of our humanity and the sign of the lust of God. In this way, the death of Jesus says as much about the lust and jealousy of God as it does about the finality of human existence.

In this sense, the whole of the relationship between Israel and YHWH, between the human and the divine, can be understood in terms of a love affair gone sour: God wanted our love, but our love was not love enough. We could love God unto death, but that love was not sustaining enough. Because our love was not love enough, God's love became a consuming, jealous, and even lustful fire that burned our humanity on the altar of our existence. The threat of death, the experience of exile, and the abuse suffered at the hands of a jealous

18. The promise of life is extended to all who have given their hearts to God, a promise that figures prominently throughout Hebrew Scripture (Deut. 4:29; 6:4; 10:12; 11:13; 30:6; Mic. 6:8; Amos 5:4-6; Hos. 6:6; Ps. 15:1; 51:8 [6]; Jer. 7:21-23).
19. As we saw in chapter 4, part of Job's dilemma is that he is caught, as it were, between God and death, neither of which he can change or overcome.

God can lead us to fear God. But a God that is feared cannot be loved.[20] The more unable we are to love God, the more we try to placate it, whether through offerings and sacrifices or through the assertion of our sinfulness and unworthiness to be loved and to love. Thus, we say no human is righteous before the law; that one never really loves God with one's whole heart, soul, and mind; that without the grace of God, we are condemned to our sinfulness. In the presence of our suffering and death, we proclaim our guilt that God's innocence might be maintained. In turn, this attempt to placate God does not satisfy God's lust for our hearts. Instead, it intensifies God's lust and anger, until the objects of God's love become the objects of God's anger and revenge.[21]

THE CROSS AND DEATH

Thus, the death question comes to stand near the heart of the faith of Israel, and insofar as we take as our sign the cross of Jesus, that question is written upon our hearts as well. For in death upon the cross, faith in Jesus of Nazareth is broken with his body, broken by the silence of God, broken under the weight of the cross.[22] Beneath the shadow

20. According to Aldous Huxley, "Love casts out fear; but conversely fear casts out love. And not only love. Fear casts out goodness, casts out all thought of beauty and truth . . . in the end fear casts out even a man's humanity" (*The Ape and the Essence* [New York: Bantam, 1971], 38). Huxley's point—indeed, the whole point of this book— is that fear of God overshadows and precludes love of God. That fear renders human being impotent, and leads to what we call "evil" (pp. 92–95). Furthermore, this impotence possesses us, and once so possessed, we can no longer be possessed by God. "From the second century onward, no Orthodox Christian believed that a man could be possessed by God" (p. 95).

21. This fate is often manifest in prophetic oracles of judgment. See Isa. 1:10-16; 24:1-18; 29:1-6; 4 Ezra 1:26-27; 2:1-14; Jer. 4:5-31; 5:15-17; 6:1-8, 16-19; 9:9-11; Ezek. 7:15-27; 21:1-37; 24:1-14; 36:29-36; Hos. 5:1-7; 6:3—10:15; Amos 1:3—2:16; 3:1-8; 6:8-14; Mic. 6:1; Zeph. 1:14-18; 1 Enoch 60:6-7; 89:51-67; 100:1-13; Jub. 5:8-11; 23:22-32; 36:10-20; Pss. Sol. 15:3-13; Hist. Rech. 8:1-6; Lives Proph. 10:10-11; Sib. Or. 1:389-400.

22. "We should, therefore, not speak about Jesus' non-Messianic history before his death, but rather of a movement of broken Messianic hopes, and of one who was hoped to be the Messiah, but who not only at the moment of failure, but in his entire message and ministry, disappointed the hopes which were placed in him" (Günther Bornkamm, *Jesus of Nazareth* [New York: Harper and Row, 1975], 172; see 169–71, 179ff.); "Confronted with the historical rejection of Jesus' message and eventually with his person, the first Christians were moved by the renewal of their own lives after the death of their master and recalling the fellowship they had enjoyed with him to confess this Jesus as crucified and risen lord in whom they had experience of definitive and final salvation" (Edward Schillebeeckx, *Jesus* [New York: Seabury, 1979], 545).

of the cross, the sign of his desolation and abandonment and of our humanity, Christian theology begins.[23] It begins at the point where human being is pressed against its limits, where the presence and person of God seem most distant, alien, and hidden.[24] The sign of that theology is the sign of the cross. Inasmuch as it is the sign of our humanity, the cross embodies the agony of our existence and the certainty of our death. The cross embodies the death question. The cross is the point at which the death of one human being becomes the sign of all that is human. In the shadow of the cross, his death and ours are raised as an issue before and to a God whose silence, distance, and hiddenness can no longer be borne upon the heart in silence. The cross is the moment when all that is human cries out to God, enraged by God's distance, angered by God's silence, even embittered by God's absence.[25] Thus, death not only calls our being into question, it calls into question the being and reality of God as well. Once the issue of the reality of God is bound to the question of what it means to be human, the possibility and tenability of faith in turn are bound to the death question. The death question stands because God's silence endures.[26] The God that was silent then is silent still. As long as the death question stands, we do not know what to make of God's silence. Does that silence mean that we suffer and die by the hand of God? Or does that silence mean that we suffer and die because God is powerless in the presence of death?[27] Does God's silence mean that there is no God

---

23. Jürgen Moltmann, *The Trinity and the Kingdom*, (San Francisco: Harper & Row, 1981), 39–40, 52. In Moltmann's *Crucified God* (New York: Harper and Row, 1973), he concludes the chapter "The Historical Trial of Jesus" by saying, "Thus in the end the basic problem and the starting point of christology is the scandal and the folly of the cross. In this sense M. Kähler is right: without the cross there is no christology, and there is no christology which does not have to demonstrate its legitimation in the cross" (p. 125). See also Nils A. Dahl, *The Crucified Messiah and Other Essays* (Minneapolis: Augsburg 1974), 13, 34, 72.

24. "The death of Jesus on the cross is the center of all Christian theology" (Moltmann, *Crucified God*, 204).

25. Moltmann, *Crucified God*, 119, 124. The cross, then, is more than the sign of the end of our humanity. It threatens also to be the sign of the end of our faith.

26. While Christian Scripture attempts to offer a sense of the mediated presence of God insofar as God "speaks" through the community of faith, Hebrew Scripture looks to the emergence of the unmediated presence of God from its darkness. Faith invites presence—not stillness and distance, nor mediated presence. Against the backdrop of Hebrew Scripture, the tragedy of the death of Jesus is framed by the distance between the desire for intimacy and presence and the reality of our distance and estrangement from God.

27. Ludwig Feuerbach, *The Essence of Christianity* (New York: Harper and Row, 1957), 207.

there in the darkness? Despite the power of our desire to believe, God's silence remains.

SILENCE

What are we to make of God's silence? If God is there, why is God silent? In the presence of God's silence, three possibilities are open to us. Perhaps God is silent because God is not there. Perhaps God is silent because it is by God's hand that we suffer and die. Or perhaps God is silent because God cannot change our fate. On the one hand, we cannot believe in a God that is not there. If God is not there in the darkness, there is nothing in which to have faith. On the other hand, we cannot believe in a God that is responsible for our death; such a God is to be denied. Yet neither can we believe in a God that promises life in return for our love if that God cannot change our fate. In the end, whichever way we turn, the enduring presence of death presses the affirmation of faith to its limit. Since there is no faith where there is no humanity, in death there can be no faith. Until God emerges from the darkness and answers the death question, God's silence remains. The agnostic passes over the silence of God in silence. That is, the agnostic finds the silence of God inconclusive and insurmountable because there seems to be no way for the human to penetrate the darkness in order to disclose either the presence or absence of God. Until the presence or absence of God can be disclosed, the agnostic finds the evidence in favor of both God's presence and absence inconclusive. Faith is possible only insofar as God actually exists and that existence is both tenable and accessible. Until God speaks, and in speaking offers some proof of its existence to us, the agnostic remains unable or unwilling to move toward a resolution of the problem of God. For the agnostic, the death question overshadows and precludes the possibility that faith in God might be affirmed or denied.

ORTHODOXY

Orthodox Christianity has sought to explicate and mitigate the silence of God, first, by binding the death of Jesus to the resurrection of the Christ, and second, by placing the responsibility for the death of Jesus the Christ not upon God's hands but upon our own. In effect, orthodox Christianity has answered the death question for God: We die because we sin. The facticity of death remains because the facticity of our sinfulness endures. This is not to say that the death and resurrection of the Christ have left human being unaffected. Even though death remains, its character has been changed by the force of the event of the death and resurrection of the Christ.

The death of the Christ, the Son of God, in obedience for our sake, has altered forever the human experience of death. We die, but death is no longer the end of our being. We die in order to enter into a new life with God—a life that forever stands free from death. "God gives life," wrote Barth, "only through death. . . . Consequently in Jesus . . . atonement occurs only through the faithfulness of God. By his death he declares the impossible possibility of our redemption."[28] Death is a metamorphosis—the means by which we come into the presence of God. The Deuteronomistic promise of life in this world won by openly and freely giving one's heart to God becomes transformed. That hope is now expressed in terms of the resurrection of the dead at some future moment. That promise is expressed in terms of the immortality of the soul, of the righteousness and graciousness of God, which suffered our humanity even unto death that we might be saved. "If the curse of death that separates man from God is abolished in the death of God, natural death remains. . . . In the cross of his Son, God took upon himself not only death, so that man might be able to die comforted with the certainty that even death could not separate him from God, but still more, in order to make the crucified Christ the ground of his new creation."[29]

This move toward a concept or doctrine of "new creation" seems to have replaced the sense of eschatological urgency that so fills the work of Paul and subsequent generations. This sense of renewal points to a more distant eschaton than the first Christians might have been inclined to accept. The concept of new creation sees the death and resurrection of Jesus as the point at which God begins a second creation, one that will replace the world deformed by the sin of Adam. Moltmann writes: "Ultimately we hear in [the] voices of Christian theology that proclaim Jesus Christ and faith as the end of history . . . the universal saying that for Israelite and Christian faith, history is experienced as the horizon of hope for the fulfillment of God's promise."[30]

28. Karl Barth, *Epistle to the Romans* (London: Oxford University Press, 1963), 105.
29. Moltmann, *Crucified God*, 217. See also Karl Rahner, *Foundations of Christian Faith*, (New York: Seabury, 1978), 400–4; Barth, *Romans*, 30, 105. Tillich's discussion of the humanity of the Christ as the advent of new being and new creation is relevant (*Systematic Theology*, 3 vols. [Chicago: Univ. of Chicago Press, 1966], 2:79–95).
30. J. Moltmann, "Das Ende der Geschichte," in *Perspektiven der Theologie* (Munich: Kaiser Verlag, 1968), 234, 241. Much of Moltmann's work embodies this sense of a more distant eschaton that will be the climax of the re-creation of the world.

This new creation begins with the death and resurrection of the Christ. For Jesus as the Christ, true God and true human, cognizant of both his divinity and humanity, went to his death for our sake. This death for our sake once again opens the world to God's presence, grace, and love. The innocent, sacrificial lamb offered himself to God in our stead that the sins of the world might be forgiven. In that death for our sake, that death wrought by our hands, by our sins, God humiliates itself that we might share its love for us.[31] The question of divine innocence and guilt is resolved by placing responsibility for sin and death upon our shoulders.[32] God's innocence implies and calls for human guilt.[33] God died on the cross for us. We put God there. We drove the nails into its flesh. We pierced its side with the lance of our humanity. And God, out of the depth of its love for us, nonetheless transformed that suffering and death into the vehicle of our salvation. Huxley wrote, not uncritically, "Either man, in his theology, prefers to see a God of absolute good perpetually in conflict with a Devil or supernatural being of evil nature; or else . . . he ascribes to God wisdom and kindness infinitely transcending our own, so that evil of all sorts, including pain and misfortune, but especially moral evil . . . is to God's absolute knowledge a necessity for our spiritual development, to his transcendent wisdom an obligatory move in the working out of the cosmic plan."[34]

Thus if God suffers with and for us, the death question ought not to arise. Moltmann, for example, begins his analysis of the problem of theodicy by raising the question of God's involvement in human existence. Either God is apathetic, or God is pathetic—in the sense that God has pathos for human beings. If God is apathetic, distant, uncaring, and hidden, then the question of theodicy is very real. Indeed, at the point where the experience of suffering is separated from God, the existence of God and the tenability of faith are called into

31. Karl Barth, *Church Dogmatics,* IV.1 (Edinburgh: T. and T. Clark, 1980), 79.

32. Ibid., 82, 93–95, 202–3.

33. Julian Huxley, *Religion without Revelation* (New York: Mentor/New American Library, 1957), 182–212.

34. Ibid., 109. According to Aldous Huxley, "The problem was very troublesome indeed. God as a sense of warmth about the heart, God as exultation, God as tears in the eyes, God as a rush of power or thought—that was all right. But God as truth, God as $2 + 2 = 4$—that wasn't so clearly all right" (*Antic Hay* [New York: Bantam, 1962], 1). Nietzsche asserted, "Christianity presupposes that human being does not know, is incapable of knowing what is good for it and what is evil—God alone knows" ("Twilight of the Idols," sec. 5, *Sämtliche Werke* [Berlin/New York: De Gruyter, 1980], 6:113–14).

question.[35] This separation leads to the eclipse of faith, and to what Moltmann terms protest atheism.[36]

Conversely, the theodicy question is answered, in a sense before it can be asked, if God is intimately present in and to the world, if God makes our suffering its own.[37] Moltmann offers this analysis: "A man who experiences helplessness, a man who suffers because he loves, a man who can die, is . . . richer than an omnipotent God who cannot suffer, cannot love, and cannot die."[38] Thus, Moltmann argues, in its love for us, God has entered into our history, into our world, into our death, and therefore into our being, via the life, death, and resurrection of the Christ.[39] The God that loves us passionately, passionately suffers its love for us. God's suffering with us precludes the possibility that it is by the hand of God that we suffer. It also excludes the possibility that we suffer at the hands of an impotent God.[40] By excluding the possibility that God is impotent, Moltmann attempts to free God from complicity in human suffering and death.[41]

The death and resurrection of the Christ, then, definitively answer the death question. Death remains in the presence of God because sin remains, because death, no longer the sign of the end of our humanity, now marks the transition, the metamorphosis, from being "here" in the absence of God before death,[42] to being "there" in the presence of God after death. The God of love replaces the God of lust. The God of mercy and compassion replaces the God of anger and vengeance. The gracious God overcomes the bitter God. Divine guilt is replaced by divine innocence, human freedom by human indebtedness, and human love by divine grace. The God that has everything to do with the way in which we live has everything to do with the way in which we die. In effect, the death of God for our sake is meant to carry with it the assurance that God is neither impotent nor responsible. Insofar

35. Moltmann, *Trinity*, 48–52.
36. Moltmann, *Crucified God*, 223–24.
37. Moltmann, *Trinity*, 25–32.
38. Moltmann, *Crucified God*, 223. Also see "Gott und Auferstehung," sec. 4, "Wer ist Gott?" in *Perspektiven und Theologie*, 55–56.
39. Moltmann, *Trinity*, 40–41.
40. Moltmann, *Crucified God*, 216–17.
41. Moltmann, *Trinity*, 22–25.
42. Thus, while God remains in the distance, God remains indirectly present. In the "in-between time," the time after the ascension of the Christ into heaven and before the end of the world, orthodox Christianity would argue that God's presence is mediated by the third "person" of the Trinity and by the existence of the church as the body of Christ.

as God endures death for our sake, it would appear that God has done all that it can do to alter the finality of our death.

But the facticity of our death remains unaltered. Our death is no less final, troubling, terrible, or unacceptable.[43] And we might add, our refusal to accept our death has given us the crucified God, whose death for us nevertheless leaves the facticity of our death unchanged. If God can do nothing to alter the facticity of our death even by suffering death itself, then God would appear to be unable, if not unwilling, to overcome our death. In that case then again God is impotent, and God's impotence remains bound to our death. An impotent God can be pitied or can be the object of our anger or bitterness—but not of our love. If we cannot love God, faith would appear to be without purpose.

If, however, God is unwilling to change the facticity of our death, then God's culpability seems certain. A God that is able to overcome the facticity of our death but chooses not to is guilty of our death— as guilty as if it were by the hand of God that we died. Again, a God that is guilty of our death is a God in whom it does not make sense to have faith. We can fear such a God. We can even hate or resent such a God. But we can neither trust nor love such a God. All that we can do is to seek to free ourselves from the hand of death and from the God that is unmoved by our cries for deliverance.

ATHEISM

This critique of orthodoxy becomes the basis for another response to the silence of God: atheism. Here God's silence implies God's absence. Feuerbach argued, for example, that God never was. God is an illusion. It makes no sense to speak of faith in a God that does not exist. Christian faith is marked by a deep-seated contradiction: "God" is simply the name we give our alter ego.[44] In the absence of God, we have made

43. According to Arthur Koestler, "The refusal to accept death either as a natural or as a final phenomenon [has] populated the world with witches, ghosts, ancestral spirits, gods, demi-gods, angels and devils. . . . In all mythologies [the dawn of civilization] is steeped in fear, anxiety and guilt, dramatized by the fall of angels, the fall of man, by floods and catastrophes but also in comforting promises of eternal survival; until even that consolation was poisoned with the fear of everlasting tortures" (*The Ghost in the Machine* [New York: Macmillan, 1968], 311).

44. Feuerbach, *Essence of Christianity*, 195.

a God in our own image and likeness.[45] "Religion is the relation of man to his own nature . . . knowledge of God [is] nothing else than knowledge of man!"[46] Here Feuerbach's argument can be taken a step further: Confronted with the death question, we have chosen to resolve the issue of God's presence and absence, innocence and guilt, by creating an image of God that embodies all that is noble, all that we respect and desire—and all that we are not. Whether God is an illusion we have conjured because the force of our impending death is too much or because we cannot accept the loneliness of our existence, in the final analysis, the vanity of faith stands. The power of the death question lies in the fact that it presses the question of the reality of God to its limit.

ANTITHEISM

Antitheism is perhaps best represented by the Death of God Movement.[47] The word "movement" is not normally used to describe those who advanced the death of God theology in the early 1960s. Much like the Biblical Theology Movement before it, the Death of God Movement was less a movement and more a loose collection of individuals of similar but distinct positions. Still, a kind of common consensus brought these theologians together. At the heart of this consensus was the belief that the God of Christendom had died. Generally, proponents of the movement traced their intellectual heritage through Bonhoeffer and Nietzsche. Theologians generally associated with the Death of God Movement include Vahanian, Altizer, Hamilton, van Buren, and Ogletree. The work of Gilkey and Cox brackets the beginning and end of the movement.[48] Like the Biblical Theology Movement, the Death of God Movement was short-lived. The passing

45. Feuerbach's critique can be applied to Moltmann insofar as Moltmann's emphasis on the need for God to be "pathetic" (in the sense of having pathos for human beings) is characteristic of attempts to overcome God's silence by ascribing human characteristics to God. See Moltmann, *Crucified God*, 210–60, and *Trinity*, 22–60.

46. Feuerbach, *Essence of Christianity*, 197, 207.

47. Moltmann refers to antitheism as protest atheism (*Crucified God*, 219–27). Also, Moltmann uses this term with reference to Nietzsche's critique of Christianity. Here the term "antitheism" is expanded in its application and thus represents a modification of Moltmann's analysis.

48. Gilkey was not actually a proponent of a death of God theology, although the movement would not have been possible without his critique of biblical theology. I have included Cox in this group because his work is clearly in debt to the movement and because his analysis presupposes the basic premises of the movement.

of the movement has not brought about the end of Christian theology. Instead, after the secularization of Christianity in the 1960s and early 1970s, there has been a resurgence of traditional orthodox theology coupled with the development of liberation theology.

Antitheism denies the necessary link between God, the world, and death that marks the orthodox response to the death question. Where orthodoxy had sustained the intimacy between the human and the divine in the suffering of the Christ, antitheism seeks to embody the distance between God and the world. For the antitheist, God has nothing to do with the way in which we live and die. "To say that God is dead or to assert an infinite qualitative difference between God and man means not only that no ladder leads from man to God; it also means that there is no identity of substance between man and God, and accordingly, that the problem of human existence is independent of the problem of God."[49] God has nothing to say about what it means to be human. If God exists, God exists in the distance, far beyond the horizon of our world. God is a being off in the distance whose presence we might some day encounter, a being that stands away, unmoved and unmovable. Indeed, it is the God that emerges within the world—the God of immanence—that is dead. Where orthodox Christianity had sought to assert the union between the human and the divine at the point where human being is brought up against its limits, the death of God theologians sought to hold the human and the divine apart. That distance between the human and the divine is intended to silence the possibility that God—either in absence or presence, in impotence or force of will—is responsible for our death. Thus, however the death of God is understood, whether that God died upon the cross or was simply an illusion formed to hold the universe in place, that death has left us alone. That aloneness is a fact of our existence—just as our death is. The task at hand, then, is to determine what humanity and Christianity without Christ and God might mean.[50]

---

49. Gabriel Vahanian, *The Death of God* (New York: George Braziller, 1967), 210.
50. The death of God theologians relied heavily upon existentialism. Chief among its "ancestors" were Nietzsche, Camus, Kierkegaard, and Heidegger—or so their analysis would have one believe. As we shall soon see, their claim upon these "existentialists" is unfounded.
    The work of Harvey Cox can be seen as an attempt to formulate a "Christian theology" after the death of God. See his *Seduction of the Spirit* (New York: Simon and Schuster, 1973), esp. 123–43, "Beyond Bonhoeffer." See also his *Secular City* (New York: Macmillan, 1966, 1967, 1978), esp. chap. 11, "To Speak of God in a Secular

Given the death of God, then, we must find our humanity for ourselves.[51] For Cox at least, finding our humanity means accepting the hiddenness of God, whether that hiddenness rests in God's absence or in God's death. "In Jesus of Nazareth," says Cox, "the religious quest is ended and man is freed to serve and love his neighbor."[52] "In Jesus God is teaching Man to get along without Him."[53] Through Jesus and his experience of the hiddenness of God, we become mature once we are freed from our dependence upon God. "In Jesus God does not stop being hidden; rather He meets man as the unavailable 'other.' He does not appear, but shows man that He acts, in his hiddenness in history."[54] The portrait of secular Christianity that Cox offers thus calls for a turning away from God toward our humanity. It is a call for responsibility and maturity, a call to fashion our own destiny by our own hands for ourselves. God has chosen to let us be until we can enter into an "I-Thou" relationship with it. The whole of biblical faith thus becomes a history of our maturing. Maturity means being responsible for oneself alone. Christian responsibility replaces Christian theology as that which is properly the most human of concerns. God is no longer the issue. It is human being. It is living faithfully despite and even because of the distance. This sense of the distance of God does not imply the end of faith. Indeed, faith in a hidden God liberates both the human and the divine to be as they must be and to do as they must do.

We should note that the gospel of liberation and social concern that was so much a part of the secularization of Christianity in the last two decades finds its root here. Cox's theology of hiddenness holds that in Jesus we are freed to be alone. If God is hidden and we cannot discern how—or if—God is acting in history, we must act for ourselves. As Cox notes, the Christian faith has three dimensions: social, political, and theological. Of these, only the theological traditionally has dominated. The recognition that what God does, God does in its own way

---

Fashion." This chapter begins with a quotation from Bonhoeffer: "We are proceeding toward a time of no religion at all. . . . How do we speak of God without religion? . . . How do we speak in a secular fashion of God?" (quoted from *Prisoner for God* [New York: Macmillan, 1959, 123). According to Cox: "The world has become man's task and man's responsibility" (*Secular City*, 1).

51. To find one's humanity for oneself is to define what it means to be human apart from being in the presence of God.

52. Cox, *Secular City*, 232.

53. Ibid., 226; see also J. Huxley, *Religion without Revelation*, 113.

54. Cox, *Secular City*, 226.

and in its own time is not a restriction upon our actions but a kind of call to arms on behalf of God for ourselves. In effect, God's distance from the world strengthens both the political and the social aspects of faith and frees us to assume responsibility for ourselves and for our world.

For Vahanian, as for Cox, we must fashion our humanity for ourselves. The death of God is liberating. Unlike Cox, Vahanian sees no room for the hiddenness of God. God—and faith—are both dead. The God that is dead is the God whose existence was tied to its immanence in this world. Vahanian, like Cox, holds open the possibility that God does exist, but that God and that existence are inaccessible and not hidden. Inaccessibility implies infinite distance, and infinite distance in turn implies, entails death. Both the freedom of God and the freedom of human being presuppose and necessitate the immense distance that separates the human and the divine. "What is taking place on the stage of Western culture is not 'a struggle against God for God,' to use Jaspers's phrase in describing the Book of Job. In order to struggle against God for God, man needs faith. Such a struggle ceases as soon as faith dies. This faith has died from its own application."[55]

The death of God and the death of faith are both rooted in Christianity itself. Vahanian and Ramsey speak of our culture as "post-Christian." That is to say, the history of Christianity as the history of a religion that stresses immanence has brought about the death of God.[56] With the death of God, Christianity has come to an end. As Ramsey puts it, God has become superfluous.[57] We are faced with a twofold challenge: First, we are freed to discover for ourselves what it means to be human; second, while the God of Christianity, the "biblical deity," to use Ramsey's words, remains dead, the presence of living beings presupposes or implies the presence of a transcendent God that has freely chosen to let us be. If that God stands apart from the world and remains distant from our existence, what purpose would faith in such a God serve? The answer is none. Yet still the need to acknowledge that distant presence remains.

As long as the existence of God is part of the fabric of the world in which we live, God's existence overshadows human being. If God

55. Vahanian, *Death of God,* 146.
56. Ibid., 137–62.
57. Paul Ramsey, "Preface," in ibid., xxi.

"is" in this world, there is a sense in which we cannot "be." Conversely, if we "are," God cannot "be." If God exists in this world, it would be necessary to kill God. This does not mean that ultimately there is no God. It means that if God is, God is beyond and outside of the horizon of this world. It is this world to which our attention is drawn. It is to our place in that world that our reflection is given. If human beings are to take this responsibility seriously, then we and not God must accept the consequences of our actions. Once we have accepted responsibility for the world and for our actions, faith becomes superfluous—as does God. As a result, "man has declared God not responsible and not relevant to human self-knowledge. The existence of God, no longer questioned, has become useless to man's predicament and its resolution."[58] Insofar as God and faith are dead, they have no place in the world of human affairs.[59] If we are alienated and suffer and die, it is not because we are alienated from God by sin or because it is the will of God. We suffer and die, we experience anxiety and estrangement from the world and from others, because we are human.[60] Essentially "the self is a dialectic element between life and death, between possibility and necessity, or between finitude and infinitude."[61] Because God is dead, we are responsible for the world and for ourselves. We are responsible for overcoming our anxiety, our estrangement.[62] We are responsible for uncovering the sense of immanence that binds us to the world.[63]

Yet, this new sense of responsibility, this new awareness of immanence, born in the death of God, does not free us from anxiety and

58. Ibid., *Death of God,* 147.

59. In Vahanian's analysis it is just as correct to argue the converse of this statement: namely, that since God and faith have no place in the world of human affairs, they are dead. Vahanian seems to use these arguments interchangeably.

60. Ibid., 146–48, 227. Thomas Altizer describes the experience of estrangement and exile as follows: "We can say God only by embodying exile in our voice, only by making openly manifest our exile from eternal silence and presence. . . . God is the name of the source or origin of our estrangement from the source of eternal presence" (*The Self-Embodiment of God* [New York: Harper and Row, 1977], 31). For Vahanian, the source of that presence or immanence is not God but the world itself. A similar position is taken by Sartre: "The passion of man is the reverse of that of the Christ, for man looses himself as man in order that God might be born" (*Being and Nothingness* [New York: Philosophical Library, 1956], 615).

61. Vahanian, *Death of God,* 212.

62. While the responsibility is ours, it is clear that the promise of overcoming that sense of estrangement is never to be realized. See ibid., 227–31.

63. "Today only the reality of the world, in all its immediacy and immanence, provides man with a context for possible self-understanding" (ibid., 147).

estrangement. Indeed, in the death of God, the absurdity of the world and of our existence in it emerges with even greater force and power. The death of God leaves us alone, estranged, cast adrift. Once God is dead, we are left to be God for ourselves.[64] Once God has died, the tragedy and finality of our existence threaten to overpower and consume us. Once God is dead, there is no one upon whom we might avenge ourselves. There is no one to whom we might turn, no one to whom we can protest our fate in anger or in sorrow. There is no God to hold the absurdity of our existence at arm's length. There is no one to whom we can pray, except ourselves.[65] Herein lies our tragedy. As long as we die, as long as the dissonance between the promise of immanence and the reality of separateness remains, we cannot be God for ourselves.

The God that lives in the distance needs neither the world nor human beings. A living God is innocent of our death. A distant God that lives outside our world can let us be, can let us be human. A living, distant God knows no rage, jealousy, or oppression. The God that transcends the world transcends our humanity. For Vahanian, this distance between the human and the divine is not the end of faith. Rather, this distance makes faith possible. Here God has no final or ultimate responsibility for the world or for human being,[66] and faith ultimately has no purpose. The world and human existence stand and fall alone. In one respect, the protest atheist,[67] or the antitheist, is correct: If God has everything to do with the way in which we live and die, then, one way or another, either because God is impotent or because God is guilty of our murder, faith cannot be maintained.

Belief in a God that is unable or unwilling to change our fate seems unwarranted. Love for a God that has a hand in our death is untenable. Clearly, if such a God existed, it would be necessary to kill it. In effect, from the perspective of the antitheist, this is precisely what has happened. The God that has everything to do with our life and our death is dead. That God died so that we might live. Its place has been taken by a God that is freed from the encumbrances placed upon it by the

64. Here the conclusion of Ivan Karamazov is quite clear: Since there is no God, everything is permitted and it remains for human beings to become God.

65. Ibid., 230–31.

66. For Altizer, Cox, Vahanian, and others, God is still seen as the creator of the universe—a creator who created but who then withdrew into the darkness.

67. Ibid., xxi; Ramsey refers to this position as "practical" atheism. Practical atheism does not seem to rule out the possibility that there is a God. Rather, the practical atheist is one who exists as though there were no God.

world and its immanence. Its place has been taken by a God that has nothing to do with the way in which we live and die. Openness to God is openness to a "Wholly Other"[68]—to a dark and distant stranger whom we might encounter at some mysterious moment in the distant and indifferent future. If God exists, if faith is possible, both that faith and that love lie well beyond the limits of the phenomenal world. What lies beyond the horizon of our world must be passed over in silence. Given the silence and the distance, human beings are left to live as though God is dead and we are alone. "Atheism," Ramsey wrote, "is not only a theoretical claim made by exceptional rebels; it is now also a *practical* possibility for countless men. . . . Find yourself and you will not need God; accomplish something in culture and evidently God is superfluous."[69]

Indeed, the death of God frees us both to be in the world and to be a part of it. To be in the world and to be a part of it is to share the immanence of the world, to be present in, to, and for the world. Once we are free to be in the world, we become aware of the world as the limit within which our existence is lived. Once we come to be present in, to, and for the world, we are bound to the world, and the world in turn is bound to us. The horizon of the world becomes the horizon of our existence.[70] Once bound to the world, we are no longer free to look over the horizon of the world for God. What lies beyond the world lies beyond our vision and thus lies beyond our humanity. To search for what lies over the horizon of the world is to lose sight of one's humanity. If we are to live as though we are alone, as though the death of God is a fact of our existence, then it would seem that by necessity faith in God can have no meaning. Faith makes no sense. Thus, Vahanian notes, we can believe in God or we can be human. But we cannot both believe in God and be human.

---

68. Ibid., 231.
69. Ibid., xxi.
70. The horizon that makes human existence possible also constrains and limits that existence. That is, to be human is to be in the world. The being that is there in the world (*Dasein*) is there only because the contours of the world are given shape by its horizon (Martin Heidegger, *The Basic Problems of Phenomenology* [Bloomington: Indiana University Press, 1982], 158–70). We can and should, as Heidegger notes, be open to that horizon—and this openness characterizes authentic human existence. Attentiveness to the horizon, however, precludes openness to any being that lies beyond or behind that horizon. We cannot see what lies beyond the horizon. Thus, if God is there over the horizon, God has no relationship to the world or to human existence. What is without relationship to the world and to existence has no meaning.

WITCHES AND UNICORNS

But in the last analysis, whether we say everything or nothing, faith in God is eclipsed by human suffering and death. First, if, following antitheism, we say that God is hidden in the darkness, we cannot see God. If God cannot be seen, faith in God and love of God are called into question. If God cannot be seen and loved, if God lies beyond the touch of a human hand, then it would make no sense to speak of a God that lies behind or beyond the horizon of our world. It makes no sense to talk about a distant God. Hiddenness implies absence, and absence implies either that belief in God is belief in an illusion or that the God that was once there is now dead.

Second, if God remains in the distance and is unmoved by our suffering, if God chooses not to hear our supplications, then once again the issue of God's complicity in our suffering and death must be raised. Human innocence implies divine guilt. Yet if we argue that God's presence in the darkness need not imply that it is by the hand of God that we die, the issue of God's complicity in our death is not brought to an end. For if God is there in the darkness and God is unable to enter into the world, if the horizon that binds us to the world cannot be overcome by God, then once again it would seem that God is impotent. Or, if God is free only in separation from the world, in isolation from the way in which human beings live and die,[71] then the limitations of God's being would make it difficult if not impossible for God to overcome our fate. Again, God's impotence lies close to the heart of our suffering and death. To be human is to suffer divine impotence.

The history of the faith of Israel can be seen as the history of human suffering in the presence of an impotent God. Israel suffers YHWH's impotence. In the presence of death, YHWH seems to be powerless, unable to overcome the limitations that bind our existence and our love. Human love, like human being in this world, remains bound by death. As long as our world and our love remain bound by death, the possibility stands that death has overpowered God as well. As long as God stands in the shadow of death, God cannot be loved with a love that knows no limits. Love of God is possible within the limits of our being and of our world—no more and no less.

But love unto death is not enough. The lustful, jealous, impotent God wants more. YHWH wants our hearts. Though we might desire

71. Both of these conditions are implied by Vahanian.

to give our heart to God, our heart is not ours to give. As long as we die, as long as we are given over to death from the moment of our birth, our hearts have already been spoken for. Death has already won our hearts. The only way God can win the human heart is by freeing human beings from death. For only when the human heart is freed from death are humans free to love God. YHWH's rage and bitter fury are a mark of its failure to free human beings from death. The exile, suffering, and abandonment that Israel experiences are all testament to the rage of an impotent God that consumes in lust and rage the heart it cannot possess. Such a God can be the object of human fear and anger, of human bitterness, and even of human pity, but such a God cannot be the object of our love. If human beings suffer because of God's impotence, faith cannot stand.

Third, the same silence that speaks of the impotence of God also discloses another possibility: All that we are we take from the hand of God. The God of life is the God of death. The omnipotent God holds dominion over our life and sentences us to death. A God that is guilty of our murder cannot be loved any more than love can stand in the presence of an impotent God. Belief in a God that takes our lives is unwarranted. Like an impotent, lustful, or pitiful God, such a God can be the object of resentment, anger, or fear. But that God cannot be loved. And if, for a moment, faith could be sustained, if we could bring ourselves to believe in such a God, it would be necessary to kill God that our own lives be sustained.[72]

Fourth, even if God could enter into the world and be present within the horizon that binds human existence, human suffering and death would remain unchanged. For God to enter into the world, God would have to cease being God. God would be bound by the same limits that bind and constrain us. Like us, God would be given over to death. God can either be God or enter into the world. If God enters into the world in order to save us from our humanity, then, like all that is human and all that exists in the world, God would be dead. A God that is itself subject to death, or to the limits that death imposes upon human being, ceases to be a God. In this sense, contra Moltmann, the death of God can have no effect upon human existence. The death of God is the death of God and nothing more. Human beings still die.

---

72. This is the thrust of Camus's call for the death of God. See Camus, *The Myth of Sisyphus* (New York: Random House/Knopf, 1955), 31, 49–51, 78–91, and *The Rebel* (New York: Random House/Vintage, 1956), 57, 252–54.

The facticity of death remains unaltered. The immanent God is either an illusion or just another being. If God is just another being, then God is dead. If God is an illusion, then in time, faith in God, like faith in witches and unicorns, will pass away. In any event, belief in a God that can do nothing to change our fate or that has itself suffered and died seems unwarranted. This God is no less impotent than a God that cannot enter into the limits of our world. An impotent God is no less culpable than a God that condemns human beings to death. With the awareness of God's impotence, faith passes away.

Neither God's immanence nor God's distance alters our death or secures our life. Neither makes death any easier to bear. God is no less guilty or impotent. The guilt, culpability, and impotence all stand in the way of faith and love. In the end, a God that is distant and detached is no more believable than a God that is dead or that takes our lives. A God that cannot touch or comfort us, a God that cannot pray Kaddish for us, is just as impotent as a God whose death upon the cross of our humanity has left our fate unchanged. A God that stands in the distance while we suffer and die and that turns a deaf ear to our cries of deliverance is no less responsible for our death than a God whose hands run red with our blood. Whether God is apathetic or pathetic, we suffer no less, we die no differently.

Thus we find ourselves caught in a contradiction from which escape seems impossible. A God that has chosen to remain distant from us, "a God who does not trouble himself about us, who does not hear our prayers, who does not see us and love us, is no God; thus humanity is made an essential predicate of God—but at the same time it is said: A God who does not exist in and by himself, out of men, above men, as another being, is a phantom; and thus it is made an essential predicate of God that he is non-human and extra human, a God who is not as we are, who has not consciousness, not intelligence . . . a personal consciousness . . . is no God."[73] Either way, faith in God may be unwarranted; God seems to be just another way to hold the world together as we are pressed against our death. Either way, we are alone and uncomforted; as such, the question of the reality and existence of

---

73. Feuerbach, *Essence of Christianity,* 207; Nietzsche, *The Antichrist,* sec. 113. "They have called 'God' what was contrary to them and gave them pain; and certainly, there was much that was heroic in their adoration. And they did not know any other way to love their God except by crucifying the man" (Friedrich Nietzsche, "Thus Spake Zarathustra," pt. 2, "On the Priests" [Walter Kaufmann, *The Portable Nietzsche* (New York: Viking, 1970), 203–4]; cf., *Sämtliche Werke,* 4:118). In essence, divine innocence demands human guilt.

God stands open on the cross of our humanity. The desolation of our isolation and abandonment is offered to a God whose presence we can neither verify nor ascertain. For all intents and purposes, like the immanent God before it, the distant God is dead. When God is dead, only the world and our humanity remain. The death of God marks the death of faith. Thus, whether we say everything or nothing, our life and our death remain, faith seems untenable, and the issue of God's innocence and guilt stands. Thus, antitheism and orthodoxy cannot sustain faith.

PROTEST THEISM

How, then, are we to answer the death question? How are we to settle the issue of God's involvement in our death, the issue of God's culpability? What has God got to do with the way in which we live and die? Where is God while we suffer and die? Is God silent because it is by the hand of God that we die? Is God silent because there is no God in the darkness? Is God silent because God is unable to change our fate? Do we die because we are human, or because we are guilty? Can we love a God that is responsible for our death? Can we love a God that is impotent? Can we love a God whose face is blackened by our death? Yet, if we press God into the distance, if we remove God from the world in which we live and die in order to preserve God's innocence and our faith, of what consequence is God's innocence and our faith? Of what use is a God that cannot comfort us, or pray for us as we go to our death?[74] Why in the presence of God is there death? Indeed, this is the dilemma. For it seems that between everything and nothing there is no middle ground. There is no partial responsibility. Either God has everything to do with our life and our death, or God has nothing to do with the way in which we live and die. Either God is innocent, or God is guilty. Either human beings suffer because God is impotent, or human beings suffer because God has condemned all that is human to death.

74. Elie Wiesel, *Night* (New York: Avon, 1969), 55–56. The question of the reality of God, which has dominated Jewish theology since the Holocaust, has often been the focus of Wiesel's work. He said, for example, "Some talked of God, of his mysterious ways, of the sins of the Jewish people, and of their future deliverance. But I had ceased to pray. How I sympathized with Job! I did not deny God's existence, but I doubted his absolute justice" (55–56). The death question calls the "absolute justice" of God into question.

The issue of God's innocence and guilt is inseparably bound to the death question. Insofar as the death question is the most human of questions, the issue of God's innocence and guilt is bound to the question of what it means to be human. In the death question, the questions of the reality of God and of God's innocence and guilt are finally human questions. As long as the question of God remains a human and humane question, the death question cannot be answered apart from our existence and apart from our being unto death. As long as human beings are given over to death, bound to a fate that can neither be altered nor changed, the death question stands open and unanswered. Moreover, as long as human beings are given over to death, the question remains unanswered and unanswerable. Thus, we cannot say that God has everything to do with our life and our death, nor can we say that God has nothing to do with our life and our death. If neither everything nor nothing, then what? For the descendents of Job, Qoheleth, Ezra, and Enoch, for those who stand beneath the cross of Jesus, for Nietzsche and Kierkegaard, for Heidegger and Camus, God has everything to do with the way in which we live but nothing to do with the way we die. This is protest theism.

Like antitheism, protest theism begins with the death of God. Nietzsche wrote:

> The madman jumped into their midst and pierced them with his eyes. "Whither is God?" he cried. "I will tell you. We have killed God—you and I. We are all his murderers. But how did we do this? How could we drink up the sea? Who gave us the sponge to wipe away the entire horizon? What were we doing when we unchained this earth from its sun? Whither is it moving now? . . . Do we not feel the breath of empty space? Has it not become colder? Is not night continually closing in on us? . . . Do we hear nothing as yet of divine decomposition? Gods too decompose. God is dead. God remains dead. And we have killed God."[75]

God was there, but God is now dead and we are alone. "You know how he died? Is it true what they say, that pity strangled him, that he saw how the *man* hung on the cross and that he could not bear it, that love for humans became his hell, and in the end his death?"[76] " 'God

---

75. Nietzsche, *The Gay Science,* Aphorism 125; cf. *Sämtliche Werke,* 3:480–81.
76. Nietzsche, "Thus Spake Zarathustra," pt. 4, "Retired" (Kaufmann, 372); cf. *Sämtliche Werke,* 4:323.

on the cross,' that mystery of unimaginable ultimate cruelty and self-crucifixion of God for the salvation of human beings."[77] The God that offered human beings its pity died because of that pity. God died on the cross, and given the facticity of death, God is dead and remains dead. At any point, given any option open to us, the presence of death in the apparent absence of God seems to stretch its bony hands over the possibility of faith.[78]

The issue for Nietzsche is not God's immanence and transcendence.[79] The question for Nietzsche is, What has God got to do with human being? What has God got to do with the way in which human beings live and die? It is not the God that is immanent in the world whose death is proclaimed by Nietzsche. The God that is dead is the God that has everything to do with the way in which human beings live and die,[80] that is finally and ultimately responsible for our death. Thus, to live, we must kill that God.[81]

This does not mean that a God that has nothing to do with our life and our death is any more acceptable. By default, a God that has nothing to do with the way in which human beings live and die is just as dead as a God that takes our lives. A God that is uninvolved, as we have seen, is no less impotent or responsible. Again, to save our lives, such a God must be killed. Furthermore, the focus of concern for Nietzsche is deeper than the relationship between God and the world. The focus of his concern is the relationship between the human and the divine. The point of concern is the question of God's responsibility for our death. For Nietzsche, faith in God is not possible if

77. Nietzsche, *Genealogy of Morals* (Garden City, N.Y.: Anchor/Doubleday, 1956), 1:8, cf. *Sämtliche Werke*, 5:269. This is Nietzsche's response to the argument that Jesus was the Christ and as such was one with the "Father."

78. The reason for that absence does not change the experience of God's distance.

79. See Lev Shestov, "Dostoevsky and Nietzsche: The Philosophy of Tragedy," in *Dostoevsky, Tolstoy, and Nietzsche*, ed. B. Martin and S. E. Roberts (Columbus: Ohio University Press, 1978); Shestov offers this analysis of Nietzsche: "There was just one question for Nietzsche: 'Lord, Why hath Thou forsaken me?' Do you know those simple words which are filled with such infinite grief and bitterness?" (p. 282). See Nietzsche's *Daybreak*, in *Sämtliche Werke*, 3, sec. 114, 104–7.

80. From a Nietzschean perspective, even though God is dead it is still possible to refer to that God in the present tense as long as the illusion of that God's existence continues.

81. Nietzsche, "Thus Spake Zarathustra," pt. 4, "The Ugliest Man": "But [God] had to die . . ." (Kaufmann, 378–79); cf. *Sämtliche Werke*, 4:328–30. An interesting but not totally convincing analysis of Nietzsche's critique of orthodox Christianity can be found in Richard Schacht, *Nietzsche* (London: Routledge and Kegan Paul, 1983), 119–30.

God is responsible for our death. The God that sends us to our death because we cannot fulfill an inhuman and inhumane law is as unacceptable as a God that can do nothing to stop our death. So that faith might be maintained, we have too often attempted to resolve the death question by proclaiming God's innocence and our guilt. The God of good and evil, the God of life and death, the just and punishing God, has served to mitigate divine guilt. Human beings die because human beings are guilty, not because we are human. We go to our death because we "deserve" to die, because death is the wage paid our sin.

For Nietzsche, this conclusion is unacceptable.[82] Faith is possible only insofar as God has everything to do with our life and nothing to do with our death. Any other alternative leads by necessity to the death of God. If God has nothing to do with the way in which human beings die, then death is our concern.[83] It is our responsibility.[84] Death is that which defines and limits our humanity. Death is the horizon within which we are free to be human. If God has nothing to do with the way in which we die, then death does not imply guilt—whether human or divine. If God has nothing to do with the way in which we die, then insofar as God has everything to do with the way in which we live, we are free to love God. We can give our hearts to God, not because God demands it or because we fear God or because we desire life after death, but because our heart is ours to give unto death. Always, that love, that being, that humanity which we bring to and before God, we bring unto death. Death remains the one fact, the one unalterable given, that we cannot overcome. As long as we are free to love and to be unto death, we are free to believe in God. Faith emerges as a possibility insofar as we are free to be human. To be free to be human, we must be free to live and die. We must be free to embrace our death as our own.

82. Because this "logic" is unacceptable, Nietzsche is moved first toward the denial of the categories good and evil in favor of the beautiful and the ugly and even love and despair (see his *Beyond Good and Evil* [New York: Random House/Vintage, 1966], Aphorism 153: "Whatever is done from love always occurs beyond good and evil") and second toward the "transvaluation," or "re-valuation," of all values (see his "Thus Spake Zarathustra," pt. 2, "On Immaculate Perception": "The will to love, that is the will also to die"). See also Schacht, *Nietzsche,* 342–67.

83. Camus wrote, "A God who does not reward or punish, a God who turns a deaf ear, is the rebel's only religious conception" (*Rebel,* 29).

84. The world in which we live is also our responsibility, a sense that figures prominently in Camus's works. "From the moment that man believes neither in God nor in immortal life he becomes 'responsible for everything alive, for everything that, born of suffering, is condemned to suffer from life'" (*Rebel,* 31–32; see also 67–68, 70–74).

Moreover, faith emerges with all of its force and power at the point where we are most human, at the point where we are pressed against the limits of our existence. Again, we are caught in a paradox. Death is both the end of our humanity and also its fulfillment. Insofar as death is that which defines our being as human, at the moment of death we are most human. In dying we realize our humanity. Faith emerges within the context of an existence that is lived before and unto death. The death question, then, is bound to the juxtaposition of love and death. The death question places the love and faith that are most human before God in the presence of our death. The death question places before God the end of our humanity, the end of our love, the end of our faith.

The death question, therefore, embodies the paradox of our humanity: The promise of love is presence, eternity, endurance, intimacy, humanity. But the same death that fulfills our humanity and is the telos of our being is the end of our love. The same death that fulfills our being empties our humanity and steals from us our heart. The promise of faith is that a love given unto death, a love given with all that we are, can and will bring God out of the darkness. But the same death that embodies the very possibility of love and faith and that holds open our hearts and the world is the end of love and faith. That same death, however, hides the face of God. As long as that face remains hidden, as long as death is the occasion of God's silence, and as long as we do not know why in the presence of God there is death, the question of God remains inseparably bound to the question of what it means to be human.

Insofar as it is both human and humane, the death of Jesus embodies the death question. The question long pressed against the heart of the sage, long the lament of the psalmist,[85] long suffered by the seer,[86] is broken open and placed before God. In the cry of despair upon the cross, Jesus puts the death question to God. Since the death question is put to God, it is God's to answer. We cannot answer the question for God.[87] But God has not come out of the darkness and answered the question. God has not broken its silence and uncovered its face. God has chosen to let the question stand. Insofar as the question stands,

85. See chapter 4.
86. See chapter 3.
87. In effect, this is what orthodox Christianity has attempted to do by arguing that God has everything to do with our life and our death, while at the same time placing responsibility for death upon human shoulders.

we do not know if we suffer and die because God is impotent, because God chooses to take our lives, or because there is no God in the darkness.

Here it seems that there are three options open to us. First, we can assume responsibility for death ourselves. We can say that we suffer and die because we are guilty.[88] We can accept responsibility for our death in order to establish God's innocence. As we have seen, this is the path orthodox Christianity has chosen. Second, we can kill God and be done with it. That is, we can proclaim our innocence and thus establish the guilt of God. We can argue that if God is there, God has nothing to do with the way in which we live and die. This is the path of protest atheism. Either God is innocent, or we are. Between these two options there seems to be no middle ground.

But for the protest theist, for the descendent of Job, for those who are moved by the faith of Qoheleth, for the children of Nietzsche and Camus, the issue is not innocence or guilt. The issue is love and death, presence and absence, the cry of despair and the silence. The issue is the absurd, which is born in the confrontation between human need and the unreasonable silence of God.[89] The issue is the cross itself, upon which both the human and the divine are called into question. The end of our humanity is the end of our faith, love, and being. The cross is the issue because the cross is the sign of our love for God, the sign of our willingness to die in love for God. For with love of God upon our hearts we go to our death. Because we love God, the cross becomes the sign of our despair over the end of that love. For we can love God unto death and then no more.[90] The cross is the sign of our refusal to let God be in the distance and in the silence. For in death all that is human—our love, our faith, our passion for the presence of God—decays. Insofar as the cross stands in the silence of God and that

---

88. Albert Camus, "Jean Rictus, the Poet of Poverty," in *Camus: Youthful Writings* (New York: Knopf, 1973), 100–101. In quoting Rictus, Camus argues that those who pray to God but who suffer only learn to scorn God. Also see his description of "the man who was born in order to die" and the emergence of suffering in human existence ("Voices from the Poor Quarter," in *Youthful Writings*, 108ff.).

89. Camus wrote, "The absurd is born of [the] confrontation between the human need and the unreasonable silence of the world" (*Myth of Sisyphus*, 21).

90. According to Nietzsche, this confrontation with one's death in the absence of God marks the movement toward a "death freely chosen, a death at the right time." This stance stands in sharp contrast to the "wretched and revolting comedy which Christianity has made of the hour of our death" ("Twilight of the Idols," sec. 36; cf. *Sämtliche Werke*, 6:134–35).

silence transcends our death and overpowers our humanity, insofar as all that is human decays, the death question stands open.[91]

Jesus' cry of despair is ours. But Jesus' cry is also a call to God to come out of the darkness. Jesus' cry is a refusal to let the question stand without answer. It is a refusal to let God be in the distance. It is a protest against death, hiddenness, and silence. It is a protest against our fate. But this protest, this refusal, is not born in the absence of faith. On the contrary, only because there is love and faith can there be a protest against a fate that, however human, is most inhumane. Only because there is faith and love can there be a protest against the silence and hiddenness of God. In this way the death question embodies both the protest and the silence.[92]

So the cross stands. And with it stands the silence of God. It is a silence that unnerves and overpowers, that speaks of the futility of all that is human, that speaks of the decay of all that we love, all that we touch, all that we hold near to our hearts. It is a silence from which there is no escape. It is a silence that leaves open the last prophetic sign—the sign of Jesus upon the cross of our humanity. Insofar as that sign stands open in the silence, there is no more for us to say. Nothing can be said, no word can be spoken by human lips, until God comes out of the darkness and speaks. Until then, we are left to wait in the silence beneath the shadow of the cross.

So the cross stands. And with it stands the silence of God. It is a silence that marks the beginning and the end of Christian theology. For about the cross, nothing can be said. About the man, there is nothing to say, except that his protest against death, against the silence of God, stands as a mark of all that is human. About the God, no word can be spoken. For until God has spoken, until God has emerged from the darkness, only our death and our protest, only the cross and our humanity, only the hiddenness and the absence, remain. And though God may slay us, yet shall we love God unto death.

---

91. Camus, *Myth of Sisyphus*, 23. Camus argues that the absurd ends with death. Yet in another sense the absurd is held open by death. That is, the experience of the death of another intensifies our experience of the absurd. The same is true of the death question: On the one hand, the question comes to an end with our death. On the other hand, the death question is intensified by the experience of another's death.

92. Camus, *Rebel*, 65ff., esp. 70.

INDEX OF ANCIENT SOURCES

CANONICAL HEBREW SCRIPTURE

Genesis
2:7—109 n.16
3:8-13—37 n.26
25:8—118 n.48
35:29—118 n.48

Exodus
3:8-9—112 n.29
4:12—56 n.3
5:22—42 n.52
6:6—86 n.87
20:1-21—114 n.36
20:18-21—56 n.3
20:19—38 n.34, 130 n.81, 131 n.86
23:23—34 n.15
32:11—42 n.52
33:12-17—131 n.86
33:12-23—130 n.81
33:18—113 n.35
33:18-22—37 n.27
33:18-23—41 n.47, 86 n.88
33:19-21—38 n.34

Leviticus
11:44-45—112 n.32
19:2—112 n.32
20:26—112 n.32

Deuteronomy
4:29—143 n.18
4:37—50 n.71, 56 n.5
5:6—50 n.71, 56 n.5
5:8-10—57 n.5
6:4—143 n.18
6:4ff—109 n.18
6:7—47 n.59

6:10-13—111 n.22
6:12-13—50 n.71, 56 n.5
6:20-22—50 n.71, 56 n.5
7:6-7—112 n.29
8:1-6—111 n.22
9:10-11—57 n.5
10:12—143 n.18
10:12-13—109 n.18
10:12-22—114 n.36
11:13—143 n.18
11:13-15—114 n.36
11:13-17—111 n.22
11:26—112 n.32, 142 n.17
13:3ff—142 n.17
18:13-22—56 nn. 3, 5
26:17-18—86 n.87
26:19—112 n.32
27:9ff—114 n.36
28:8-14—142 n.17
28:9—112 n.32
29:6-13—112 n.32
29:8-28—142 n.17
29:13—86 n.87
30:1-10—142 n.17
30:6—143 n.18
30:6-10—111 n.22
30:6-20—38 n.32
30:8ff—109 n.18
30:14-15—109 n.18
30:14-20—112 n.32
30:15-20—111 n.22, 142 n.17
30:15-28—140 n.9
31:17-18—34 n.34, 35 n.22, 38 n.33, 86 n.88, 109 n.16
32:15-43—38 n.32
32:20—34 n.34, 35 n.22, 86 n.88, 109 n.16

Numbers
11:11—42 n.52
11:16—42 n.52
12:6-7—56 n.3
20:14-29—50 n.71, 56 n.5
23:12-18—50 n.71
23:21-22—57 n.5

Joshua
24:2-13—50 n.71, 56 n.5
24:19—45 n.55
24:19-20—47 n.62
24:31—126 n.67

Judges
2:7-10—126 n.67
11:12-18—50 n.71, 56 n.5

1 Samuel
1:11—40 n.44
1:17—78 n.67
12:6-8—50 n.71, 56 n.5

2 Samuel
7:24—86 n.87
14:14—105, 138
24:1f—109 n.17
24:10-11—112 n.30
24:10-17—47 n.63, 50 n.69

1 Kings
18-19—65

2 Kings
4:27—34 n.16

1 Chronicles
12:5—40 n.40

169

NON-CANONICAL TEXTS

CHRISTIAN SCRIPTURE

INDEX OF MODERN AUTHORS

INDEX OF SUBJECTS